THE MAKING OF THE ENGLISH COUNTRY HOUSE 1500–1640

The Making of the English Country House
1500–1640

MALCOLM AIRS

The Architectural Press Ltd
LONDON

TO ALL MY FRIENDS

ISBN 0 85139 378 0

First published 1975

© Malcolm Airs 1975

Photoset, printed and bound in Great Britain by
R. J. Acford Ltd, Industrial Estate, Chichester, Sussex

Contents

Preface

Even though the age of gracious country house living is almost over, the buildings themselves still stand and are more accessible than ever before. By their sheer size as well as by their splendour they dominate the rural landscape in a way that is only sometimes rivalled by the parish church. From the day that they were built they have exercised a fascination for the spectator, and long before the financial plight of the aristocracy caused them to be thrown open to the general public, they were accustomed to receive a steady stream of privileged and critical visitors, whenever the family were not in residence. Their leading part in the development of the English architectural tradition has been readily appreciated and they are rightly seen as a most treasured part of our national heritage. Country house visiting is now so much a part of our way of life that most people have sufficient knowledge of architectural style to be able to differentiate between, say, a Tudor and a Georgian building.

But the history of the country house cannot be written solely in terms of its architecture. Individual houses are not simply examples of prevailing architectural fashion. They were built at particular times for particular reasons. Their exact position had to be chosen with some care. They had to be designed and they had to be paid for. The materials to build them had to be selected and brought to the site. Craftsmen and labourers, supervisors and clerks, had to be found to work on them and many crises of labour, materials and finance had to be overcome before the buildings could be successfully completed.

This book considers the practical aspects and daily problems of building a country house. It takes as its period the first great age of country house building, when the establishment of the Tudor State following the Wars of the Roses meant that for the first time men were free to build as they pleased, unfettered by considerations of defence or feudal obligation. In the 140 years before the Civil War more country houses were built than at any comparable period before or since. The immediate objects of the book have been to explain why so many houses were built, how they were built, and to examine in some detail the lives of the men who were involved. Due consideration, of course, has been paid to the men for whom the houses were built. Without their hopes and aspirations, their piety and their arrogance, their generosity and their meanness, the houses would never have existed. But their workmen were equally important in creating these monuments to their masters, and by careful research it has been possible to reconstruct something of their lives too. The insecurity of their employment, the homes that they lived in and the food that they ate have been examined as well as their hours of work, their weekly wage, and even their sickness benefits.

Technical matters have been considered only in so far as they relate to the practical problems of design. The main concern is with the men who commissioned the houses, the ways in which they organised and executed their building, the materials that they used, and the labour force they employed to carry out the work. The principal sources have been the building accounts of the houses themselves, and the correspondence of their builders. In the interests of historical accuracy, quotations have been given in their original spelling and sums of money have been expressed as £ s d. Because the book includes new and occasionally controversial interpretations of various aspects of the social and economic history of the period, it has been provided with a full scholarly apparatus, which it is hoped will also be valued as a comprehensive bibliography of the subject. Nevertheless, the book is intended to appeal to the general reader as much as to the specialist in the field and it would be gratifying to think that it might answer some of the questions which inevitably occur to him when he should chance upon a Tudor or Stuart country house. In the final analysis, these splendid buildings are just as much a testimony to the labours of the common people as they are a monument to a vanished way of life, and if their contribution has been rescued from the shadows cast by the art-historical approach to the study of architecture then the aims of the book will have been realised.

I must acknowledge the help and kindness that I have received at all the country houses I have visited. Without the unfailing generosity and efficiency of archivists throughout the country, the research would have been immeasurably more difficult: in particular Miss N. Briggs of the Essex Record Office patiently answered repeated queries over the years and Anne Crawford and Susan Avery at the Middlesex Record Office dispensed tea and encouragement with the documents in their charge. Working at the Bodleian Library was always a pleasure, and the friendliness of Mike Bull, Colin Harris, Patricia Maddison and Mr W. G. Harris provided an additional bonus. Mrs E. A. Cooke, the Librarian at Longleat, was most helpful and gave me every assistance. My debt to other people is immense. Information and encouragement was freely given by John Newman, O. J. Weaver, Sir John Summerson, David N. Durant, Dr Derek Keene, Dr John Broad, Dr Mark Girouard, John Walford and many others. Martin Weaver and Bob Weston kindly drew the figures on wages. Susan Beattie, Anne Riches, Frank Kelsall and Anthony Quiney, my colleagues in the Historic Buildings Division of the Greater London Council, were a constant support during the long years of research, as was the late W. A. Eden, our Master, whose belief in the importance of scholarship provided an ideal atmosphere in which to work. Much of the research was undertaken when I was living at The Great House, Great Milton, and I am grateful to Peter and Helena Lawrence for such idyllic surroundings.

My interest in history, first nurtured by F. A. Bareham, was like that of so many of my generation, profoundly influenced by the teachings of Professor W. G. Hoskins. I owe to him much more than my historical training and approach, for he first suggested to me the subject of this book and he kindly supervised the thesis on which it is based. If it is not quite the general survey of building in the period that he envisaged, I hope that he will find it an acceptable tribute to his methods and inspiration. At a personal level, three people above all others have made this book possible. Sissel Unger gave me the confidence to embark upon the research in the first place. A. G. Halliday provided me with the stability and friendship without which I would never have completed it. The spiritual and practical support supplied by Megan Parry during the last few years have been more important than I think she realises. Not only did she undertake the heroic task of typing the manuscript twice, but she also made many personal sacrifices so that I could have the time and encouragement to write it. Her infectious enthusiasm for the subject, too, has been a continual source of inspiration. To her, and to all the others included in the dedication, I would like to express my gratitude.

The Toll House
Stadhampton
Oxford

Illustration Acknowledgements

Figures refer to pages in which illustrations occur

Sir John Soane's Museum, London: 4, 5 top left, 7, 25 bottom, 78 bottom, 87 top; *Smythson Collection/Royal Institute of British Architects, London:* 5 top right, 31, 33 left, 41 left, 78 top; *Cecil Collection/Hatfield House:* 5 bottom; *Hampshire Field Club/National Monuments Record, London:* 10 top; *F. C. Hedger/National Monuments Record, London:* 10 bottom; *B. T. Batsford/National Monuments Record, London:* 11 top; *Malcolm Airs:* 11 bottom, 33 right, 97; *Reproduced by courtesy of the Master and Fellows of Emmanuel College, Cambridge:* 23; *The British Library Board, London:* 27 bottom; *National Monuments Record, London:* 40, 50, 85 top, 87 bottom, 91 top, 177; *Bodleian Library, Oxford:* 41 right; *Sussex Archaeological Society:* 76; *A. F. Kersting:* 85 bottom; *Peter Rogers (Photographic) Ltd./County Record Office, Stafford:* 91 bottom.

Part I: The Builders

1 Some Motives for Building

'Everie man almost is a builder and he that hath bought any small parcell of ground, be it never so little, will not be quiet till he have pulled downe the old house (if anie were there standing), and set up a new after his own devise'.

These words were written by William Harrison in 1577, during the reign of Elizabeth I.[1] Writing of the reign of James I, her successor, Bishop Goodman commented, 'no kingdom in this world spent so much in building as we did in his time'.[2] An examination of those buildings which still remain confirms these contemporary impressions of exceptional architectural activity.

In the county of Essex alone there are well over one hundred country houses still standing which can be dated to the 16th century. When the amount of materials and labour involved in building these houses are considered, the powerful effects that their construction had on the local community can be readily appreciated. And yet, these are only the survivors. In 1594 John Norden counted no less than three hundred and fifty-four houses belonging to the nobility and gentry in Essex, the majority of which must have been built or substantially altered during the preceding century.[3] The number of country houses built in the early decades of the 17th century was equally noteworthy. If only the firmly dated examples are included, seven major country houses were built in Warwickshire between 1500 and 1560, whereas twenty were erected in the period from 1560 to 1630,[4] and Professor Stone has estimated that the amount of country house building between 1570 and 1620 far exceeded that of any subsequent half-century.[5]

This remarkable building boom was not confined to the builders of large country houses. It was partly initiated by a continuous period of rising food prices which enabled all primary producers with security of tenure to accumulate the necessary capital to rebuild, and it went hand-in-hand with a general change in living standards discernible at all levels of society. The yeoman and the husbandman was remodelling the family home or building themselves a new house at the same time as their lord in the manor house was recruiting his labour force and contemplating his own more grandiose building schemes. The tangible evidence is all there in the buildings themselves, and it is easy in the mind's eye to draw up a picture of much of England resounding to the noise of the carpenter's hammer and the mason's axe.

Although the impetus for what W. G. Hoskins has described as the Great Rebuilding was felt throughout society, this study is only concerned with the houses of the gentry and their social superiors. At this level there were a number of additional influences at work which emphasised the obsolescence of the mediaeval house and inspired many men to become builders.[6]

The establishment of the Tudor state, and the change in social relationships that it implied, had a profound influence on the way that they built. The end of civil discord after the Wars of the Roses meant that it was no longer necessary, or indeed politic, to build houses that were primarily defensive in character. Even castles, such as Thornbury Castle, Gloucestershire, begun in about 1511 by the Duke of Buckingham, were fortified in name alone and could never have been designed to withstand a serious attack. Increasingly throughout the 16th century the great feudal magnates were becoming courtiers and office-holders, tied to the Crown by a mutual self-interest which effectively eliminated armed conflict. There were, of course, still personal and family feuds which sporadically erupted into bloody clashes, but they were never on a scale sufficient to justify a return to private castle building.

Parallel with this development was a change in the relationship between the great land-owners and the men on their estates. Direct farming of the demesne was becoming less significant for many of them, as increasingly the bulk of their wealth came mainly from rent. The less personal landlord-tenant relationship meant that the planning of their houses was no longer conditioned by their possible function as a centre of economic activity, and the gradual decline in the importance of a communal life centred on the great hall allowed a greater concentration of architectural effect on more private apartments such as the great chamber and the long gallery.[7]

The abolition of such restrictive factors as the need for defence and the community role of the great house, made many men discontented with the accommodation that had served their fathers. There was a growing emphasis on domestic comfort that could only be satisfied by a new house, or the extensive remodelling of an older house, to provide better sanitation and heating arrangements, more light, and suites of rooms that could be adapted to a more private way of life. As soon as men began to translate these ideals into bricks and mortar, houses inevitably became symbols of status. New features, such as a deliberately contrived symmetry or a vast expanse of window, drew attention to the builder's modernity and the prosperity of his estate. Architecture became a fashionable talking-point and the subject of much fulsome prose in the correspondence of the day. Sir Thomas Heneage, for example wrote to Sir Christopher Hatton in 1583,

'For my own opinion Holdenby is altogether even the best house that hath been built in this age; and it more showeth the good judgement and honour of the builder than all the charge that hath been bestowed upon stones by the greatest persons and the best purses that hath been in my time'.   [8]

They were not always so complimentary in their comments. In 1560 Sir Nicholas Bacon felt free to offer Cecil the practical advice that in his newly-built London house,

'Mary me thynkes ye prvye in ye west end ys wt ye lest and to nere ye logyng, to nere an hoven and to nere a lytle lardre. I thynk you had been better to have offendyd yor yey [eye] owtward then yor nose inward'.   [9]

2

But no matter what tone their observations took, they were intensely interested in each other's buildings, and this reflected esteem and social rivalry were powerful motives for many to build themselves.

Building could be inspired by a competitive determination to give visible proof of the builder's prosperity and social standing to all who cared to look, but it could no less be used to demonstrate his wit and intelligence to those who were capable of understanding. The cultured mind of the 16th century delighted in anything that could be called 'curious' or 'ingenious'; anything whose true meaning was obscure enough to require some thought before intellectual satisfaction could be achieved by arriving at its correct interpretation. This fascination can be seen in the preoccupation with allegory and metaphor which characterises much of the literature and painting of the period. It is reflected in the pleasure that the 16th century derived from emblems and devices, in which a philosophical truth or a line of conduct was reduced to an allegorical picture supported by a cryptic motto or some lines of verse. Geoffrey Whitney in his book *A Choice of Emblems*, published in 1586, defined an emblem as,

> 'having some wittie devise expressed with cunning woorkemanship, somethinge obscure to be perceived at the first, whereby, when with further consideration it is understood, it maie the greater delighte the beholder',

and his definition can be extended to embrace the contemporary meaning behind such words as 'conceit' and 'device', and their concomitant adjectives, 'curious' and 'ingenious'.[10] When John Chamberlain referred to the Queen's House as 'some curious devise of Inigo Jones',[11] or the ninth Earl of Northumberland announced his intention, now that he was a builder, to 'borrow of my knowledge somewhat out of Tibballs, somewhat out of every place of mark where curiosities are used',[12] they were expressing just such an intellectual concept.

Both the major contemporary collections of architectural drawings contain examples that demonstrate this almost child-like concern with artful ingenuity in building. In the Thorpe collection there are designs based on circles, squares, triangles, and combinations of these geometrical forms, together with an amusing plan and elevation for a house formed from his own initials and inscribed,

> 'Thes 2 letters I and T
> ioyned together as you see
> Is mete for a dwelling howse for mee
> John Thorpe'. [13]

In the Smythson collection there is an ingenious unexecuted design for a house in the shape of a Greek Cross with an open central courtyard, and a number of other plans which were actually built such as that for Hardwick Hall, which are clearly based on the deliberate disposition of various geometrical elements.[14] Similarly, in the architectural drawings collected by William and Robert Cecil there is 'a plot how to mak a hows in form of a Cross', and another plan, apparently for a fortification, but which is endorsed 'for a place of pleasure'.[15] This latter is related to yet another manifestation of the curious and ingenious conceit, whereby gardens as well as buildings were used as an opportunity for cerebral fun. John

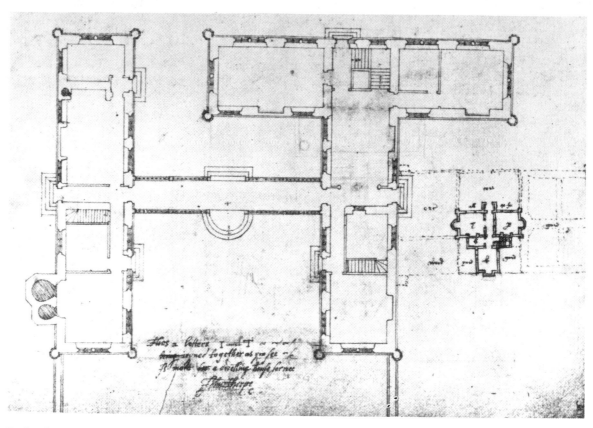

Design by John Thorpe for a house based on his own initials

Chamberlain graphically described such a garden when he visited Sir Henry Fanshawe at Ware Park, Hertfordshire, in October 1606 and found more than 40 workmen transforming the grounds of the house,

> 'And in the midst of it, instead of a knot, he is making a fort in perfect proportion, with his ramparts, bulwarks, counterscarps, and all other appurtenances, so that when it is finished it is like to prove an invincible piece of work'. [16]

Most of the executed buildings that were deliberately designed to display the builder's intellectual ingenuity date from the latter part of the 16th and the first half of the 17th century. They include the triangular Longford Castle in Wiltshire, begun in about 1580 for Sir Thomas Gorges, and a whole series of buildings which were characterised by three wings arranged in the form of the letter Y. One of these, Newhouse in Whitehouse, Wiltshire, is said to have been built for the same Sir Thomas Gorges shortly before 1619. Another, built

4

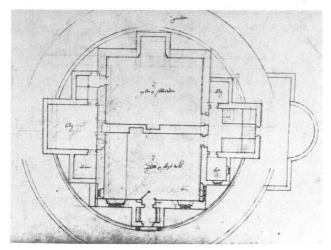

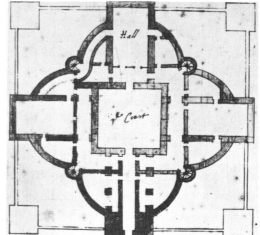

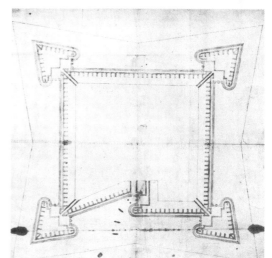

Ground plan by John Thorpe of Wothorpe, Northampton-shire, set in a circular garden. The house was built in the early 17th century for Thomas Cecil, Earl of Exeter and is now in ruins

Plan by Robert Smythson for a house in the shape of a Greek cross imposed on a quatrefoil

Plan in the Cecil Collection at Hatfield House for a fortified garden

as a parsonage at Goodrich, Herefordshire, for the Reverend Thomas Smith, in 1636, is similarly named Newhouse.[17] The triadic form of all these buildings was possibly inspired by the religious symbolism that John Thorpe assumed for Longford when he drew the house some years after its completion and added the sign of the Holy Trinity to one of his plans,[18] but of the deliberate spiritual motive for Sir Thomas Tresham's Triangular Lodge at Rushton, Northamptonshire, there can be no doubt. Tresham was brought up a Protestant, but was converted to Catholicism in 1580 and for the remaining years of his life he defiantly practised his new faith in the face of continual official persecution. Two of his buildings were undoubtedly little more than public proclamations of this faith. The Triangular Lodge, built

5

for his warrener between 1594 and 1597, is a most delightful allegory on the Trinity, which, in its consistent pursuit of the mystic properties of the figure three, can still provide the onlooker with immense intellectual satisfaction.[19] Each of its three sides is a third of a hundred feet long. It has three storeys with three trefoiled windows on each face, and is capped by nine gables and a triangular chimney-shaft. Even the inscription on the frieze above the upper storey is thirty-three letters long. The building is decorated with a wealth of religious emblems and inscriptions, and over the entrance doorway is the motto 'Tres Testimonium Dant', a characteristic pun on both the Trinity and Tresham's own name.[20] In 1604 he began another decorative lodge as part of an elaborate garden scheme on his estate at Lyveden. The New Build was designed on the plan of a Greek Cross, symbolising the Passion of Christ, and its polemical purpose was further underlined by the Catholic ciphers that adorn its external walls and proclaim the faith to all who pass.[21]

The religious belief that inspired the Triangular Lodge and Lyveden New Build can be clearly discerned from the buildings themselves, but there were other buildings of the period where a similar expression of faith would have been all but lost were it not for the chance survival of explicit documentary evidence. The E-shaped plan which was a commonplace of 16th and 17th-century architectural design, was specifically intended as a religious conceit at Chantmarle House, Dorset, built between 1612 and 1623 by John Strode, who noted that,

'Constructa est in forma, de Littera (E) sc. Emmanuel. id est, Deus nobiscum in Eternum'.   [22]

And the amateur poet and antiquary, Henry Oxinden, who had erected a circular lodge on his estate in Kent in 1631, only explained its significance in a doggerel verse composed during an illness some thirty-six years later:

'A Query why I made the house on the top of the Hill round?
Tell me how Henry in thy minde it came
Upon the Hill thy House so round to frame

Answere
I imitated the great Architector, Loe
Both Earth & Heaven, hee hath framed soe.'   [23]

In essence, the use of classical elements in English architecture in the 16th century was merely another aspect of this intellectual delight in the curious. With the exception of a few builders, such as the Duke of Somerset, Sir John Thynne, and Sir Thomas Smith, they were adopted as a novelty and for the intrinsic pleasure to be derived from their design, and not from any philosophical concept of ideal aesthetic perfection. John Shute referred to classical architecture as the 'new facion', and it was accepted as such by most of his contemporaries who simply absorbed its more striking motifs into their eclectic repertory of decorative elements. As a fashion it was liable to be superseded by other trends, such as the mannerism of Germany and the Low Countries, and the revival of interest in gothic forms in the later 16th century, and consequently to provide a motive for further alteration and rebuilding. At Burghley House, for example, the unmistakeably gothic inspired west front, and possibly

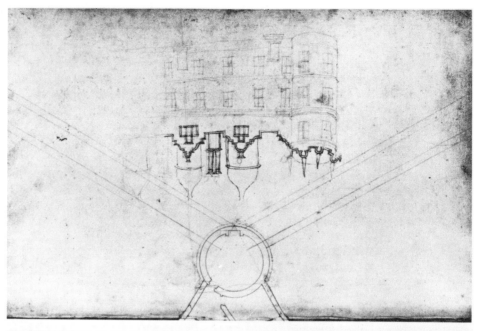

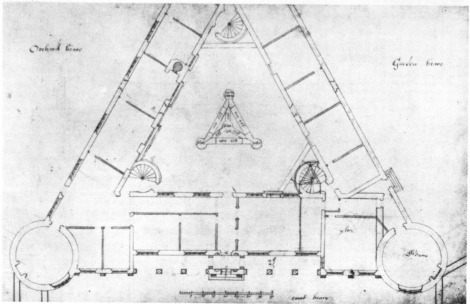

John Thorpe's plan of Longford Castle, Wiltshire, built in the late 16th century for Sir Thomas Gorges

the hammer-beamed great hall, seem to have succeeded the chastely classical courtyard in Burghley's complicated scheme of building which extended from the 1550s into the 1580s.[24]

The underlying theme behind this pre-occupation with ingenuity and passing fashion was a determination to draw attention to a builder's architectural achievement. It was not simply a matter of intense social rivalry, although elements of this were undoubtedly present. It was more a reflection of a contemporary concern with mortality, and of ways to outwit its effect which can be seen in such literary expressions as the 'time' sonnets of Shakespeare. Sonnet *lxv*, with its belief in the immortal qualities of artistic creation, provides a good example of the effect that many builders seem to have been striving to achieve,

'Since brass, nor stone, nor earth, nor boundless sea,
But sad mortality o'ersways their power,
How with this rage shall beauty hold a plea,
Whose action is no stronger than a flower?
O, how shall summer's honey breath hold out
Against the wreckful siege of battering days,
When rocks impregnable are not so stout,
Nor gates of steel so strong, but time decays?
O fearful meditation! Where, alack!
Shall Time's best jewel from Time's chest lie hid?
Or what strong hand can hold his swift foot back?
Or who his spoil of beauty can forbid?
O none, unless this miracle have might,
That in black ink my love may still shine bright.'

The need to believe that when a man died, his name and something of his deeds would continue to live, could be satisfied before the Reformation by the conspicuous adornment of the parish church, but after the break with Rome some more secular monument was required. The wealth of initials, dates, heraldic devices and mottoes to be found emblazoned on buildings of Elizabethan and Jacobean date are sufficient testimony to their builders' desire for immortality.

However, despite the intellectual impetus of the age, most builders had a more personal motive before they engaged in large-scale expenditure on building. It might be enforced retirement from public life caused by exclusion from Court, as in the examples of Sir Thomas Smith, and, in the following century, the Earl of Holland. Smith had been one of Somerset's proteges during the reign of Edward VI. With the eclipse of his patron he retired to Eton and built himself a house in the nearby manor of Ankerwicke. He returned to political life with the accession of Elizabeth and sat in her first parliament. However, disappointed in his hopes of office, he concentrated much of his energies on rebuilding Mounthall on his Essex estates. Building work came to a halt in 1562 when he was appointed ambassador to France. On his return in 1566, he continued to add to Mounthall and started work on the adjacent house of Hill Hall with a design incorporating some of the startling new architectural motifs he had seen in France. Progress on the new house was temporarily suspended by his return to Court in 1571 where he was appointed to the Privy Council, and in the following year succeeded Burghley as Secretary. In 1576, a serious illness led to his retirement, and he spent the remaining months of his life in a vain attempt to complete his advanced schemes for Hill Hall.[25]

Henry Rich, first Earl of Holland, was 'a handsome man of lovely and winning presence'. He had enjoyed a successful career at Court, being appointed Gentleman of the Bedchamber to Prince Charles and conducting the negotiations for his marriage to Henrietta Maria. On the accession of Charles to the throne he remained in high favour with the Queen, but in 1637 he was openly frustrated in his ambitions when the post of Lord High Admiral was granted to the Earl of Northumberland. According to his biographer, he 'retired to his house at Kensington in disgust', where he consoled himself by embarking upon an extensive building programme. Between 1638 and 1640 he spent more than £6,500 on a magnificent new stable block and an extra wing to the house that his father-in-law had built less than thirty years earlier.[26]

Social aspirations provided another powerful motive for building, especially for those whose wealth derived from trade or business. It was a common pattern for younger sons of the landed gentry to enter commerce, make sufficient money to invest in land, and then return to the ranks of the landed gentry themselves. Clement Sysley, for example, was the younger son of Richard Sysley of Sevenoaks, Kent. In 1557 he bought a farm called Eastbury, near Barking, Essex, from another London merchant, Sir William Denham. By 1560 he had taken up residence in the parish and begun to build. Soon after its completion in 1572, Sysley began to refer to it by the socially impressive title of Eastbury Hall, a name that it retained until it declined once more into a farm house in the 18th century.[27]

Successful lawyers were another class of builder desirous of the social esteem provided by landed estates and an impressive country house. Such a man was John Strode, Reader at the Middle Temple, member of parliament, and knighted in 1623. In 1606 he bought the Dorset estates of the Cheverells, a local gentry family in financial difficulties, and at Chantmarle he remodelled and enlarged the existing house on a grand scale.

The building career of another lawyer illustrates the influence exerted by political success. Educated at Cambridge, Nicholas Bacon was admitted to Gray's Inn in 1532. In 1537 he was appointed to the position of Solicitor with the Court of Augmentations, and ten years later he was made an attorney in the Court of Wards. Both these positions provided ample opportunity for considerable financial gain. In 1545 he began to build a modest country house at Redgrave in Suffolk. It was finished by 1554 at a cost of less than £1,500. Four years later Bacon was created Lord Keeper of the Great Seal and was assigned York House as his London residence. Redgrave, as originally conceived, was clearly inadequate for his new status, and between 1560 and 1562 he spent over £400 on building two additional wings. Still dissatisfied, the following year he began a completely new house at Gorhambury, near St. Albans, leaving Redgrave as a residence for his recently married son. The cost of Gorhambury was more than double the amount that he had spent on his first house. Completed in 1568, it was visited by the Queen on one of her progresses in 1572, when she is reputed to have told her host, 'My Lord, what a little house have you gotten'. Bacon, so legend would have it, made the telling

Newhouse, Whitehouse, Wiltshire, built *circa* 1619 possibly for Sir Thomas Gorges

Newhouse, Goodrich, Herefordshire,
1636

The Triangular Lodge, Rushton, Northamptonshire, built
between 1594—97 for Sir Thomas Tresham

reply, 'Madam, my house is well, but it is you that have made me too great for my house'.[29] Whether this story is apocryphal or not, shortly after 1572 considerable additions were made to the house, including a loggia with a gallery above it.[30]

The anecdote of the Queen's visit to Gorhambury shows Bacon to have been one of that small class of builders motivated by a more expensive reason than their own personal or social needs. Close to the Court were a small group of men dependent on the Crown for their jobs, or looking to it for the rewards of patronage. The summer progresses, when the monarch toured a part of the country living off the hospitality of the nobility and showing herself to her loyal subjects, provided an opportunity—or, more correctly, a necessity—for those anxious to preserve or increase their favour at Court, to entertain her lavishly. But, in order to accommodate the Queen and her retinue of Privy Councillors, courtiers and retainers, it was in the interests of those likely to be visited frequently to build on a scale far exceeding their normal requirements. The result was that group of what Sir John Summerson has so aptly called 'Prodigy Houses': houses such as Burghley, Theobalds, and Holdenby of Elizabeth's reign, and Hatfield and Audley End in the following reign. Houses which were envisaged more as occasional palaces for the monarch than as dwellings for her noble subjects. William Cecil, Lord Burghley, made explicit their inspiration when he stated in 1585 that Theobalds 'was begun by me with a mean measure but encrease by occasion of her majesty's often coming'.[31] His anonymous contemporary biographer confirms that,

'He buylt three houses, One in London for necessity. Another at Burghley of computency, for the mansion of his barony. And another at Waltham for his yonger sonne. Which at the first, he ment but for a little pile, as I hard him saie. But, after he came to entertayne the quene so often there, he was inforced to enlarge it, rather for the quene and her greate traine, and to sett poore on worke, than for pomp or glory. For he ever said "it would be to big for the small living he cold leave his sonne." '.   [32]

Even under Charles I, when the custom of royal progresses had declined in the face of the growing isolation of the Crown, there were still those who sought to ingratiate themselves with the monarch by building on a grand scale. Thomas Wentworth, Earl of Strafford, appointed Lord Deputy of Ireland in 1632, wrote to Archbishop Laud in 1637 about the house that he was building there.

'they say I build unto the sky. I acknowledge that were myself only considered in what I build it were not only to excess but even to folly . . . but his Majesty will justify me that, at my last being in England, I acquainted him with a purpose I had to build him a house at the Naas, it being uncomely that his Majesty should not have one there of his own, capable to lodge him with moderated conveniency (which in truth he has not) in case he might be pleased sometime hereafter to look upon this kingdom'.   [33]

It should be emphasised, however, that the royal influence exerted its hold over a comparatively small circle. There were others who did not look to the Court for aggrandizement, for whom the expense of playing host to a royal progress was a somewhat doubtful honour. Sir

William More, a man of limited political ambition, was threatened with a visit from the Queen in 1567 when his house near Guildford was still only half finished. With the aid of friends at Court he was able on this occasion to dissuade her by reason of 'what fewe smal romes and howe unmete' his house was; but even so, Loseley House was visited by the Queen on three subsequent progresses.[34] Sir Thomas Arundell is said to have been reluctant to have the name of Wardour Castle even mentioned at Court during progress time for fear of being visited by the Queen, and Lord Spencer went to the length of feigning illness to avoid entertaining Queen Henrietta Maria in 1626.[35]

Apart from some highly individual reasons for building such as that attributed to Thomas Cecil, Lord Exeter, who, according to Thomas Fuller, built Wothorpe Lodge, Northamptonshire 'to retire to out of the dust while his great house of Burghley was a-sweeping,' there remains to be considered those men who can only be described as compulsive builders. Men whose passion for building pursued them all through their adult life; men who continued to build, to alter and to remodel, long after their basic housing requirements had been satisfied. Some of them have already been mentioned in other connections. Sir Nicholas Bacon who, in addition, to his houses at Redgrave and Gorhambury, built Stiffkey Hall in Norfolk for his son Nathaniel, a London house for his son, Edward, and a chapel for Corpus Christi College, Cambridge. From 1545, when he began his first house at Redgrave, he was engaged in building in at least twenty-seven of the remaining thirty-four years of his life. Sir John Thynne devoted an even longer period of time to just one building. He began to build at Longleat in about 1546, and at his death in 1580 the house was still unfinished. During that time he had been building almost continuously and the design of the house had been developed through three distinct phases before the final architectural masterpiece was begun.

Other public figures were driven by a similar restless compulsion. Burghley, who had built Theobalds, Burghley, and Cecil House in the Strand, was succeeded in office by his son Robert Cecil, whose buildings included two London houses, a new exchange to rival that of Gresham in the City, Cranborne House in Dorset, and Hatfield House in Hertfordshire on which he spent nearly £40,000 and in the event only lived long enough to spend a few nights in the completed building.[36] The list of houses owned and built by the Earl of Shrewsbury and his wife, Bess of Hardwick, ran well into double figures.[37] After Bess was estranged from her husband she retired to her father's house at Hardwick. Between 1587 and 1589 she devoted herself to a major remodelling of the house and then in 1590, with the death of her husband, she abruptly stopped, leaving it unfinished, and began the new and even more magnificent Hardwick Hall only a few yards away.[38] The partly-built Kirby Hall in Northamptonshire was bought in 1575 by Sir Christopher Hatton even though he was already engaged on building Holdenby in the same county. The building of these two great houses, less than twenty-five miles apart, continued simultaneously throughout the decade. Despite the massive expenditure involved, Hatton wrote to Sir Thomas Heneage in 1580 that he was going to see his new house at Kirby for the first time 'leaving my other shrine, I mean Holdenby, still unseen until that holy saint may sit in it to whom it is dedicated'.[39] That holy saint, the inspiration for so much conspicuous expenditure on building, was, needless to say, Queen Elizabeth herself. It is sufficient to add that these are no more than the outstanding examples of men of high social or political rank who built with a compulsion that seems to spring from deeper reasons than mere ostentation or competitiveness.

The same sort of passion for building can be seen in a more limited form amongst less prominent men. Men such as Edward Pytts, who was almost fifty when he purchased the ruined castle at Kyre, Worcestershire, in 1586. By 1595 he had completely transformed the building. He then built himself a house in London, and in 1611 at the age of seventy-five he turned his attention once again to his country house. The second phase of building at Kyre was undertaken with the advice of some of the most sought-after craftsmen of the day, including John Bentley of Yorkshire and Oxford, and was still in progress when Pytts died in 1618.[40] Sir Thomas Tresham was another man with an apparently never satisfied urge to build which he pursued in the face of the most daunting personal circumstances. Most of his building activity was concentrated in the decade after 1593 when he was released from imprisonment for his recusancy. Despite further spells of imprisonment from 1596 to 1597 and 1599 to 1603, the payment of substantial marriage portions for his six daughters, and the imposition of irregular and hefty fines for his continued recusancy, he made important additions to his country seat at Rushton, built the Triangular Lodge, the Hawkfield Lodge and Lyveden New Build, altered the old house at Lyveden, improved the church at Rushton, and undertook a number of other minor works on his estate, including new bridges at Rothwell and Rushton, and a dam at Pipewell.[41] The frenzy with which he built is almost frightening in its intensity, and yet, in the final analysis, it is little more than an extreme form of an enthusiasm for building which was highly characteristic of the age in which he lived.

1 Notes

1 *Harrison's Description of England in Shakespeare's Youth* ed. F. J. Furnivall (New Shakspere Society, vi, 1877) p. 341

2 G. Goodman, *The Court of James I* ed. J. Brewer (London 1839) i, 199

3 *Camden Society* ix (1840), p. 42

4 G. C. Tyack, *Country House Building in Warwickshire, 1500–1914* (Oxford University B. Litt. thesis 1970) p. 5

5 L. Stone, *The Crisis of the Aristocracy, 1558–1641* (Oxford 1965) p. 551

6 The term 'Builder' has been used throughout to refer to the men for whom the houses were built

7 For an elaboration of this theme, see E. Mercer, 'The Houses of the Gentry' *Past and Present* 5 (1954), 11–32; *idem, English Art. 1553–1625* (Oxford 1962) pp. 12–59

8 E. S. Hartshorne, *Memorials of Holdenby* (Newcastle 1868) p. 16

9 E. R. Sandeen, *The Building Activities of Sir Nicholas Bacon* (Chicago University Ph.D. thesis 1959) p. 142. Hereafter cited as Sandeen

10 For a full discussion of this intellectual aspect of the period, see M. Girouard, *Robert Smythson and the Architecture of the Elizabethan Era* (London 1966) pp. 35–92. Hereafter cited as Girouard, *Smythson*

11 *The Letters of John Chamberlain* ed. N. E. McLure (Philadelphia 1939) i, 83

12 Historical Manuscripts Commission, *Cecil* xv, p. 383

13 Sir John Soane's Museum, The Book of Architecture of John Thorpe, T56, T28, T145–6, T151, T30 & 50

14 R.I.B.A. Library: Drawings Collection, Smythson Collection, II/10, I/8

15 British Museum: MSS Facs. 372 (i). I am indebted to Sir John Summerson for discussions on the problems of this plan

16 *The Chamberlain Letters* ed. E. N. Thomson (London 1966) p. 61

17 See also Warmwell House, Dorset, of *circa* 1618

18 Sir John Soane's Museum: *op cit* T156

19 British Museum: Additional MSS 39832

20 J. A. Gotch, *A Complete Account . . . of the Buildings Erected in Northamptonshire by Sir T. Tresham, 1575–1605* (Northampton 1883) pp. 24–6 gives the most complete reading of these sometimes obscure emblems and inscriptions

21 *Ibid* pp. 31–44

22 Dorset County Record Office: MW /M4, f. 24

23 British Museum: Additional MSS 54332

24 M. Girouard, 'Elizabethan Architecture and the Gothic Tradition', *Architectural History* 6 (1963) 23–40

25 This paragraph is based on the interpretation of Smith's building activities given in M. Dewar, *Sir Thomas Smith, a Tudor Intellectual in Office* (London, 1964). This differs in certain details from that of N. Pevsner, 'Hill Hall, Essex' *The Architectural Review* cxvii (1955) 307–9

26 The Earl of Ilchester, *The House of the Hollands, 1605–1820* (London 1937); Leeds City Library: TN /EA /13 /74

27 Unpublished account by the author prepared for the Historic Buildings Board of the Greater London Council

28 A. Oswald, 'Chantmarle, Dorset' *Country Life* cvii (1950) pp. 1966–71. Dorset County Record Office: MW /M4 f. 22v

29 J. Spedding, *The Letters and the Life of Francis Bacon* (London 1872) vii, 114

30 The most detailed account of Bacon's buildings is E. R. Sandeen, *The Building Activities of Sir Nicholas Bacon* (Chicago University Ph.D. thesis 1959). A microfilm copy is deposited in the Bodleian Library, Oxford, 1959 Chicago 9

31 J. Nichols, *The Progresses and Public Processions of Queen Elizabeth* (London 1823) i, 205n

32 F. Peck, *Desiderata Curiosa* (2nd edition, London 1779) p. 25

33 H. G. Leask, 'Early Seventeenth-Century Houses in Ireland' in *Studies in Building History* ed. E. M. Jope (London 1961) p. 244

34 *The Loseley Manuscripts* ed. A. J. Kempe (London 1836) pp. 265–6

35 L. Stone, *The Crisis of the Aristocracy, 1558–1641* (Oxford 1965) p. 454

36 L. Stone, 'The Building of Hatfield House' *Archaeological Journal* cxii (1955), pp. 100–28

37 Girouard, *Smythson* p. 98

38 *Ibid* p. 118

39 E. S. Hartshorne, *Memorials of Holdenby* (Newcastle 1868) p. 16

40 Mrs Baldwyn-Childe, 'The Building of the Manor-House of Kyre Park, Worcestershire, 1588—1618' *The Antiquary* xxi–ii (1890)

41 British Museum: Additional MSS 39830–6

Part II: The Building Process

2 Sites

Even before a prospective builder had decided what his house would look like, he had usually considered where to place it. This was clearly a matter of considerable importance. Andrew Boorde devoted several chapters to the requirements necessary for selecting the ideal location in his book *A Compendyous Regyment or a Dyetary of Helth*, first published in 1549. The provision of an adequate water supply and sufficient wood for fuel and repairs were considered essential, as was the correct orientation of the house 'so that the pryncypall and chefe prospects may be Eest and Weest . . . for the South wynde doth corrupt and doth make evyl vapours'. As Francis Bacon drily commented in his essay 'Of Building' 'He that builds a fair house upon an ill seat, committeth himself to prison'.

The chosen site could be somewhere on the builder's existing demesne, but often it seems that the final impetus to build was provided by the acquisition of a new estate. In either case it frequently happened that the best position for the new house was already occupied by an earlier building. Thus when Sir William Petre bought the manor of Ingatestone in 1539 he had to pull down 'an old house scant meet for a farmer to dwell upon' before he could begin to build the following year,[1] and at Blickling in Norfolk, Sir Henry Hobart, the Lord Chief Justice, demolished the medieval moated mansion when he purchased the manor in 1616, shortly before he commenced work on a new house in its place.[2] Sometimes the new owner would simply remodel the existing house, although this could be on such an extensive scale that the resulting house bore few traces of its origin. When in 1573 Sir William Petre's son, John, purchased the seat of the Mordaunt family at West Horndon in Essex, he began almost immediately to remodel it in a leisurely fashion working from room to room. It was over twenty years before he was finished but, in external appearances, his house now showed no signs of its 15th-century core.[3] After acquiring the manor of Kyre Wyard in Worcestershire from Lord Crompton in 1586, Edward Pytts began in 1588 'the newe buildinge the house of Kyer Court now ruyned'.[4] Work was still in progress at his death in 1618, and when his son, James, had completed it, only a single wing of the 14th-century house remained. John Strode's new work at Chantmarle in Dorset in the early 17th century was,

'so fitly adjoyned to the old buildings by the care & direcion of old Gabriell Moore (a skilfull architect) as that they have good use of, and passages to the chambers over the old chapell & the Dairy houses, and likewise to ye Chambers over the old cellar & Brewhouses as if they had been built together with them'. [5]

Occasionally the main structure of the old house was demolished but the foundations were retained and partly incorporated in the new building, presumably for reasons of economy. Stiffkey Hall, Norfolk, begun in August 1576, contains the cellars of the house that existed on the site when Sir Nicholas Bacon bought the manor in 1571, and Hadham Hall in Hertford-shire was built about 1572 by Henry Capell using part of the foundations of the house erected by Thomas Baud in the mid-15th century.[6]

Sometimes the new house was built at a distance from the existing house, as at Gorham-bury where Sir Nicholas Bacon used materials from the house on the site that he had bought in 1561 for his new building begun in 1563,[7] and at Wollaton where Sir Francis Willoughby deserted the valley site of his ancestral home to build his new house on the top of hill where Camden saw it 'standing bleakly but offering a very goodly prospect to the beholders far and near'.[8] In these examples both the builders demolished the existing house before commencing to build the new house, but this was not always common practice. Besides acting as an easy source of material, a habitable building on the site could fulfil a number of useful functions while the actual building operation was going on and could even in certain circumstances prove a permanent asset after the completion of the work. As Sir Edward Hext wrote to John, Lord Petre, in March 1610, describing the site of the proposed Wadham College at Oxford,

> there is 'a fyne newe house which cost cc *li*, a backesyde cont. half an acre, which ys most necessary to lay yn our tymber & stone, & about yt many hangyng houses which will serve to hewe our stones in or work in tymber in all weathers, & the house necessary for our workman and his wyef to be yn, that he may contynually attend the worke, & after will serve for a landry or many other uses for the Colledge, or lett out for a rent'.   [9]

Sir William Cecil used the moated manor house already existing on the site for occasional residence while his new house at Theobalds was being built,[10] and his son, Robert, although he pulled down much of the Bishop's Palace at Hatfield, retained part of the hall range which was converted into stables in 1628, a use in which it continued until early in the present century.[11] At Denton Court in Kent, Captain Percivall, in 1640 'builded the new farme house against the Mansion house & converted that which was the farme house before into stables etc.'[12] When Francis Bacon began to build Verulam House in about 1617 in the grounds of Gorhambury, he wisely left his father's house still standing. Verulam House was demolished within fifty years, while Gorhambury remained in use as a residence until the latter part of the 18th century.[13]

If the purchase of a new estate was often the stimulus for a man to become a builder, the dissolution of the monasteries released an enormous number of potential building sites onto the market. In addition to the actual monastery buildings themselves, there were also large numbers of monastic manors and other dependent buildings which passed into lay hands. Professor Stone has traced the way in which they were exploited by the nobility,[14] and the pattern that he found can be extended to the gentry and other builders of country houses. In general it was the more powerful men, and those officials who played a leading part in the actual process of dissolution, who were the first to make use of the new opportunities for building provided by the alienated ecclesiastical property. Some were brazen enough to convert the monastic church itself to domestic use, as for example at the Augustinian priory of Mottisfont in Hampshire where Lord Sandys divided the nave horizontally and added brick wings shortly after he acquired the property at the dissolution. Also in Hampshire, Thomas Wriothesley, Earl of Southampton, had adapted and completed his work on the Premonstratensian abbey church of Titchfield as early as 1542, whilst in Wiltshire, Sir William Sharington began his alteration to Lacock Abbey shortly after 1540. Richard Rich, Chancellor of the Court of Augmentations, was granted the Augustinian priory of Little Leez in Essex as early as the spring of 1536 and he began to build on the site almost immediately, incorporating part of the nave in his great hall.

Many of the early builders with monastic sites, however, daunted by the sacrilegious implications of using the church for secular purposes, preferred to incorporate only the domestic buildings and offices. Somerset used part of the buildings of the Bridgettine convent at Syon, whilst Sir John Thynne incorporated a part of the house of the Austin canons at Longleat.

John Cheney, who was granted a lease of Harrold Priory in Bedfordshire, in 1537, the year after its surrender, seems to have done little beyond simply adapting the buildings to domestic use. Despite the erection of a new house in the early years of the 17th century, the monastic buildings were still standing in 1614, when they were described as 'the auncient mancion howse of the said Priory or Mannor of Harrold with the outhowses thereunto belonging'.[15]

Many of the owners of dissolved monastic land seem to have been reluctant to build on their new sites. Probably this was partly as a result of caution bred by an uncertainty about the future course of the religious settlement. It was only the most confident who were prepared to indulge in large capital expenditure on land which might eventually be restored to the church. The potency of a basic religious faith, and the fear of committing sacrilege, must also have played a significant part. In the early years after the dissolution, it was more common for monastic buildings to be used as a source of material for buildings being erected elsewhere. Sir Thomas Kytson, whose house at Hengrave in Suffolk was nearing completion by the time of the dissolution, was buying ex-monastic stone as early as July 1535, from Bromehill Abbey in Norfolk.[16] In 1536 and 1537 he bought further stone from monastic sources at Ixworth and Thetford in addition to lead and iron from Ixworth and, later, from Bury St. Edmunds. Nicholas Bacon, in addition to the monastic materials already existing on the site of the Abbey hunting lodge which he purchased at Redgrave, also used stone from Ixworth and Bury, and, after the act of Edward VI ordering the removal of altars from parish churches, he used the 'Altur-stones' from the four local churches of which he was patron.[17] John Hynde built the kitchen range of Madingley Hall, Cambridgeshire, in the 1540s of stone from Anglesey Abbey, which he had been granted at the dissolution.[18] But even the re-use of monastic materials elsewhere seems to have met with a certain amount of reluctance on the part of many of the new owners, and often a generation elapsed before they fully exploited the assets that they had acquired at the dissolution.

With the death of Mary and the accession of Elizabeth, the holders of monastic lands probably for the first time felt secure in their possessions. In addition, having paid off the purchase price of the land, they were now able to consider further capital expenditure in the form of building. It is only in the 1570s and 1580s that the full effects of the dissolution of the monastries on building activity is apparent. It is more than coincidence that it was in these same years that the strong incentives to build already noted were growing in intensity. It is possible to see the late exploitation of monastic property as just one of the effects of this powerful social trend, but this would be an incomplete reading of the situation. Some of the beneficiaries of the dissolution were indeed conserving their monastic resources against a time when they might wish to build. In 1574, Edward Paston of Binham Priory, Norfolk, for example, refused Nathaniel Bacon stone from the Priory to help in the building of the neighbouring Stiffkey Hall, on the grounds that he was possibly going to use it for a new house for himself.[19] But on the whole, the evidence that remains suggests that for many builders the impropriety of putting former ecclesiastical possessions to secular use, and the lingering uncertainty of their tenure, meant that they were prepared to wait for a period before beginning to realise on their potential. Often the property was sold or had passed to later generations before it was exploited, and it is not unreasonable to suggest that this further transaction helped to free it from the inhibitions arising from its religious associations. Buckland Abbey in Devon had been granted to Sir Richard Grenville in 1541, but it was his grandson, Sir Richard, who carried out the conversion of the church into a domestic dwelling in the 1570s.[20] Eastbury in Essex was a demesne tenement of Barking Abbey before the dissolution. In 1539 it was granted to Sir William Denham who continued the lease on the farm that Nicholas Stoddard had taken out with the Abbess of Barking in 1543, and it was only after 1557 when Clement Sysley had bought the property from Denham's son-in-law that a new house was built on the site.[21] When considering houses occupying former monastic sites, it is significant that many were not begun before the last quarter of the 16th century and some, such as Trentham Hall, Staffordshire, were not built until well into the 17th century.

2 Notes

1   F. G. Emmison, *Tudor Secretary, Sir William Petre at Court and Home* (London 1961) p. 27
2   C. Hussey, 'Blickling Hall, Norfolk', *Country Life* lxvii (1930) 817
3   Essex County Record Office: T /Z13 /27
4   Mrs Baldwyn-Childe, 'The Building of the Manor-House of Kyre Park, Worcestershire' *The Antiquary* xxvi (1890) 202
5   Dorset County Record Office: MW /M4 f. 24v
6   W. Minet, *Hadham Hall* (Colchester 1914)
7   J. C. Rogers 'The Manor and Houses of Gorhambury,' *St. Albans and Hertfordshire Architectural and Archaeological Society Transactions* new series iv (1933) 35—112
8   Quoted in Girouard, *Smythson* p. 79
9   Essex County Record Office: D /DP Q13 /3 /13
10   J. Summerson, 'The Building of Theobalds, 1564—85', *Archaeologia* xcvii (1959) 108
11   N. Pevsner, *The Buildings of England: Hertfordshire* (London 1953) p. 111.
12   British Museum: Additional MSS 54332
13   Rogers, *op cit*
14   L. Stone, *The Crisis of the Aristocracy, 1558—1641* (Oxford 1965) pp. 549—50

15   Bedfordshire County Record Office: TW 11 /110

16   Cambridge University Library: Hengrave Hall Deposit 80

17   A. Simpson, *The Wealth of the Gentry, 1540–1660* (Cambridge 1961) p. 53

18   S. D. Spittle, 'Madingley Hall' *Archaeological Journal*, cxxiv (1967) 225

19   Sandeen, p. 188

20   N. Pevsner, *The Buildings of England: South Devon* (London 1952) p. 70

21   British Museum: Egerton MSS 2599, ff. 159–60; Essex County Record Office: D /D ST T1; Public Record Office: C142 /86 /74

3 Design and Designers

Once a site had been settled upon the builder could turn his attention to the appearance and planning of his new house. Unfortunately the surviving evidence relating to the processes of design and the role of the designer in the 16th century is of a very fragmentary nature. Few of the building accounts even mention the subject, and in order to draw tentative conclusions it is necessary to refer to the more circumstancial evidence, such as contemporary correspondence and literary references and to the few facts that are known about the lives of the individual craftsmen themselves. What is clear is that the architect, in Sir Nikolaus Pevsner's definition,

> 'one who plans buildings as opposed to one who executes them, and furthermore one who plans with a view to aesthetically as well as functionally satisfactory results, as opposed to one who concerns himself only with the technical requirements of building—in short, the architect as opposed to both the mason and the builder' [1]

hardly existed in the 16th century.

In the latter part of the century the word 'architect' is encountered with increasing frequency, but it is used in a vague and imprecise way. James Baret in his *Alvearie or Quadruple Dictionarie* of Latin, Greek, French and English, published in 1580, translated the word as 'the maister mason, the maister carpenter, or the principall overseer and contriver of any work'. In its Latin form, the word 'Architector' is sometimes found in English medieval accounts, but with a meaning considerably removed from its later meaning. Salzman gives examples of it being used to mean thatcher or tiler,[2] and in the 15th-century accounts of St. John's Hospital at Winchester it was applied to ordinary carpenters.[3]

In England the intellectual basis of Renaissance architecture was not fully appreciated before Inigo Jones, and even then, as a result of the prevailing political climate, it was confined to a small group immediately surrounding the court. The 16th-century approach to Renaissance architecture was to treat it as a conceit, a new fashion, to be grafted on to the indigenous building tradition. For a brief period around the middle of the century a small number of public men, all connected in some way with the Duke of Somerset, showed indications of a deeper understanding of the architectural implications of the Renaissance, but their influence was small and of too short a duration to have any radical effect on the development of the English architectural tradition. Somerset's brother, the Duke of Northumberland, went so far as to send one of his household, John Shute, to Italy 'there to cofer wt the doiges of y skilful maisters in architectur, & also to view such auciet Monumentes herof as are yet extant' [4] but, as far as it is known, Shute was never given the opportunity to design any buildings on his return and the derivative treatise on architecture that he published in 1563, the year of his death, although significant as the first English architectural book, is noticeably reticent about contemporary Roman architects and architecture, and contains little that could not be gleaned from the existing continental architectural books. On the title page of his book, Shute styled himself 'Paynter and Archytecte', but this latter title was probably more a wishful reference towards his Italian experience than an exact statement of his accomplishments.

Another early use of the word 'architect' was by Sir Thomas Smith who, in his will of 1576, left £20 to Richard Kirby 'his chief architect'.[5] Smith, one of the men associated with Somerset, was a scholar of considerable reputation. His interest in classical architecture, stimulated by his foreign travels as ambassador to France and his service with Somerset, is reflected in the six separate editions of Vitruvius that he owned. Of all the men surrounding Somerset, Smith was the most intellectually able, and the one with the greatest first-hand knowledge of Renaissance ideas, but his use of the term 'architect' was probably intended more as a demonstration of pedantic scholarship than as an accurate description, for Richard Kirby was strictly an artisan who can be identified with the Richard Kyrbe employed by Sir Thomas Kytson as a mason and bricklayer at Hengrave Hall, Suffolk, in 1537.[6] The overall supervision of the work at Hill Hall was carried out by John Dighton, Smith's household steward.[7] It was in a similar academic fashion that another craftsman, Ralph Symons, was described in the inscription to his portrait which hangs in Emmanuel College, Cambridge as 'architecti sua aetate peretissimi'. Symons always called himself 'freemason'[8] and although he is known to have made drawings for King's College, and St. John's, and provided a model for the hall of Trinity College, his work on St. John's, which is the best documented of all his Cambridge work, was clearly undertaken in accordance with the detailed instructions of the College.[9] He also apparently took part as a working craftsman, for he was said to have lost the use of one of his hands as a result of an accident during the course of the building.

At the university of Oxford the title of 'architect' was used in an equally loose way when John Bentley was described as 'architectus peritissimus' of the Schools and Thomas Holt was also called 'scholarum publicarum architectus', whereas it seems that if any single person provided the design it was John Akroyd, who was merely described as 'chief builder'.[10] Akroyd, however, had previously been called 'the architect' of the new quadrangle at Merton College for which he had contracted to 'be the stone mason' in January 1609.[11]

The word 'architect', as used at Oxford and Cambridge and elsewhere, seems to have had the general meaning of supervisor of the works, rather than implying the designer of the building, and it was in this sense that Sir John Strode wrote that his new buildings at Chantmarle 'are so fitly adjoyned to the old buildings by the care & direcion of old Gabriell Moore (a skilfull architect)', who, he adds, was employed 'only to survey & direct the building to the forme I conceived & plotted it'.[12] A similar meaning was probably intended when Robert Liminge was buried at Blickling in Norfolk in 1628 and the parish register recorded that he was 'the architect and builder of Blickling Hall', and even the inscription on Robert Smythson's tomb in Wollaton Church that he was the 'Architect and surveyor unto the most worthy house of Wollaton' was probably originally of little greater significance.

Ralph Symons (*fl.* 1585–1605) a Hertfordshire freemason given the title of architect by his employers at Emmanuel College, Cambridge

However, even though the term 'architect' was loosely used in the 16th century, with a meaning that was not synonymous with that which it now has, many of the men to whom it was applied were clearly able to make designs. But most of them remained 'mechanics', employed as wage earners and servants of the builder. None of them had the social status that a few years later was to enable Nicholas Stone to write of 'my very nobell frind Ser David Cuningham',[13] or which allowed John Webb in the 1650s to sign his letters to Sir Justinian Isham, for whom he had designed Lamport Hall, Northamptonshire, 'Your assured ffreind'.[14] Almost without exception their background was that of a working craftsman, and although a few rose in the social hierarchy, there were none who were in a position to address their employers on anything approaching equal terms. This social inequality did not, of itself, mean that their role as designers was necessarily unimportant. But it did mean that their opinions, apart from those concerned with purely technical matters, were wholly subservient to those of the men who employed them. Even now, of course, architecture invariably represents a compromise between the opinions of the architect and the wishes of the client; but it is a compromise that recognises the architect's professional knowledge and skill in interpreting his client's desire. In the 16th century, however, the inferior social status of the craftsmen-designers meant that their influence was of importance only in so far as their patrons or employers allowed it to be so. In some cases they were given considerable freedom, but more frequently the personal interest taken by the builder strictly curtailed their independence in matters of design.

The influence of the craftsmen was further restricted by reasons related to the development of architectural design in England. Connected as they were with opportunities of education and patronage which were largely outside the craftsman's own control, they had a crucial influence on the shape in which the architectural profession eventually emerged in the latter half of the 17th century and the early part of the 18th century, and explain the reasons why it is necessary to consider at such length the processes by which designs were made in the 16th century. In the medieval period considerations of defence and safety acted as powerful limitations on the development of domestic planning and, generally speaking, it is only in architectural and constructional details that any clear sense of change can be discerned. Development in, for example, roof forms and window mouldings, took place within a continuing craft tradition, and innovations, perhaps initiated by a few master craftsmen, were quickly absorbed into that tradition and spread by example from their place of origin throughout the rest of the country.[15] Medieval architectural styles are primarily identified by their details of form which, as Mr John Harvey has written, were 'matters governed by the individual knowledge and creative imagination of the designer (the master craftsman), and not a part of the programme (plan, proportions, functional arrangements) largely or even wholly dictated by the needs of the client'.[16] It is on these ground that the same author has been able to describe many of the medieval master craftsmen as architects.[17]

The changed social circumstances of the 16th century already discussed had far-reaching effects on country house building. The greater freedom in planning that resulted and, more especially, the gradual infiltration of Renaissance ideas in decorative detail, radically altered the importance and position of the craftsmen-designers. The ultimate inspiration for the 'new

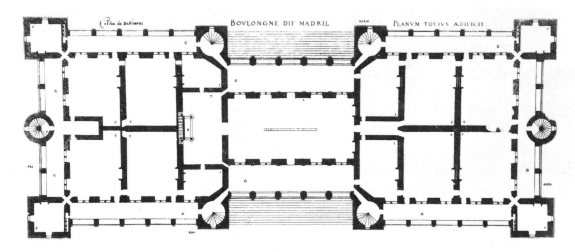

Plan of the Château de Madrid, Paris from J. Androuet du Cerceau's *Le Premier Volume des Plus Excellents Bastiments de France* published in 1576

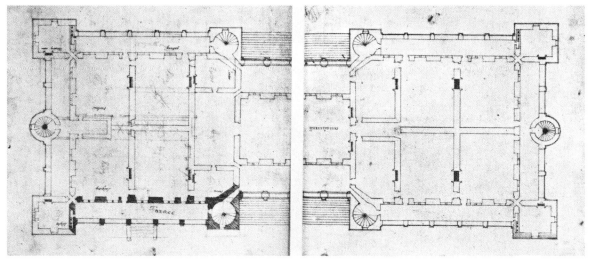

Copy by John Thorpe of the plan of the Château de Madrid taken from du Cerceau

fashion' in design was foreign. Originating in Italy and France it mainly reached England via the free interpretations of the Low Countries. Initially access to it was to be had in two ways. By travel into Europe where the buildings themselves could be seen, or by study of the growing number of illustrated treatises and books on architecture. With the sole exception of

John Shute's *The First and Chief Groundes of Architecture,* first published in 1563, the latter were exclusively foreign. A number of the more architecturally advanced buildings of the 16th century were built for men who had spent some time abroad. Sutton Place, Surrey, one of the earliest country houses to exhibit Renaissance forms of ornamentation, was built by Sir Richard Weston who had travelled in France and who had accompanied Henry VIII to the Field of the Cloth of Gold in 1520. Hill Hall, Essex, was built by Sir Thomas Smith who had been ambassador to France between 1562 and 1566. John Trevor, the builder of the symmetrical Trevalyn Hall in Denbighshire, had spent several periods abroad in the service of Sir Thomas Sackville who was on a grand tour in France and Italy from about 1563 to 1566, and who was again in France in 1568 and 1571.

Some of the men who had been on the Continent also took the opportunity to build up their own libraries of books on architecture. Smith possessed over twelve important architectural books including six editions of Vitruvius. Others, who had no first-hand experience of continental buildings themselves, were able to learn about Renaissance architecture from books imported from Italy and France, and Switzerland, Germany and Flanders. The first illustrated edition of Vitruvius had been published in 1511. The highly influential volumes of Serlo had come out in 1537, 1540, 1545, 1547, 1551, and, posthumously, in 1575. Hans Blume's book on the Orders was published in Zurich in 1550. Vredeman de Vries brought out his *Architecture* in Antwerp in 1563, and his *Compertimenta* in 1566. The number of other foreign books known and used by Englishmen, such as those of Philibert de l'Orme, du Cerceau, Palladio, Alberti, and Wendel Dietterlin, are far too numerous to mention in detail. At home the popularity of Shute's thin volume on architecture led to subsequent editions in 1579, 1580, 1584, and 1587. At least some knowledge of architecture must have formed part of the education of many gentlemen. William Harrison, for example, knew the names, if not the writings of 'old Vitruvius, Leo Baptista, and Serlo'.[18] The interest of some of these men in the theory of architecture was far from superficial. At least three builders of the period are known to have had extensive architectural libraries, and there were undoubtedly others. That of Sir Thomas Smith has already been mentioned. Although large for the period, it cannot compare with the remarkable collection made by Sir Thomas Tresham who owned well over twenty books on architecture, including three editions of Vitruvius, two editions of Serlo, one of which was the lavishly illustrated Frankfurt edition of 1575, Alberti, de l'Orme, de Vries, Shute, Palladio, and several other treatises, including those of du Cerceau, Labacco and Cataneo.[19] Henry Percy, ninth Earl of Northumberland, is known to have owned at least a dozen books on architecture,[20] and several of his contemporaries clearly possessed similar collections. Lord Burghley asked Sir Henry Norris to send him de l'Orme's *Nouvelles Inventions* from Paris, and almost certainly he owned other architectural books, for his interest in the subject, and that of his son Robert, led them to make a large collection of original plans and designs.[21] In the 17th century, Sir James Pytts, finishing the house that his father had begun at Kyre Park, Worcestershire, is known to have owned at least one 'booke of Architecture';[22] and in 1621, six unnamed books of Sir Roger Townshend were carried from London to Raynham where he was engaged on building.[23] It is almost certain that these were architectural books for the cost of their transportation was entered in the building accounts, and a later letter

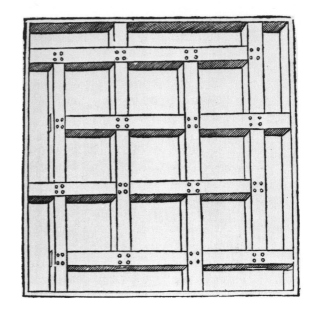

Timber framework for a floor from Book I of
Sebastiano Serlo's *Tutte l'Opere d'Architettura*

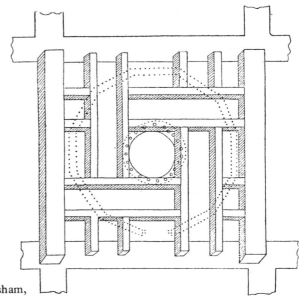

Designs by Robert Stickells for Sir Thomas Tresham,
including a method of floor-framing clearly based on Serlo

27

of Sir Roger Pratt testifies that Townshend owned 'many Italian and French books of Architecture'.[24]

For the majority of artisans the methods of access to Renaissance designs presupposed opportunities which were ordinarily denied them; the ability to travel abroad, and the formal education necessary to enable them to read and understand the essential source books. John Shute, of course, had been sent to Italy by Northumberland specifically to meet Italian architects and to study their buildings, but insufficient is known of his background to enable him to be confidently called an artisan. The only documented example of a craftsman being taken abroad by his master, presumably to study building, occurs well into the 17th century, when Sir Roger Townshend took his leading mason with him to the Low Countries for much of the summer of 1620 shortly after he had begun to build Raynham Hall, Norfolk.[25] Nicholas Stone, the son of a Devonshire quarryman, had lived and worked in Amsterdam between 1606 and 1613, but he initially went abroad simply to work for Henrik de Keyser, the Dutch mason and sculptor, and probably without any strong educational motives.[26]

The majority of building craftsmen were illiterate and thus unable to acquire a knowledge of the principles governing Renaissance design from literary sources. However, James Pytts lent his 'booke of Architecture' to his mason, presumably to enable him to make copies from the illustrations that it contained.[27] In a similar fashion, some of the plans in the Thorpe Collection were traced from Palladio's *Quattro Libri*[28] and others were based on du Cerceau,[29] whilst the drawings of Robert Smythson include copies of details from Vredeman de Vries which he used in his designs for Wollaton Hall, Nottinghamshire.[30] In addition, the sketch books compiled by the Abbott family of Devon plasterers show that relatively provincial craftsmen could be full conversant with current books of engravings.[31]

But the true basis of Renaissance architecture was intellectual, and an understanding of its rules necessarily implied book-learning. It was one thing to copy attractive motifs from the published wood-cuts, but it was something else entirely to make truly classical designs. Even men from craft backgrounds who managed to give themselves some sort of education such as John Thorpe, who certainly knew some Latin and possibly translated Hans Blume's book on the orders for the English edition of 1608,[32] showed little appreciation of the philosophy underlying the writings of the foreign architects. They looked to them for inspiration in forms, but they were ignorant of—or unsympathetic to—the spirit that they represented. In this respect it is unfortunate that insufficient details of the life of Robert Stickells have survived, for he seems to have been a craftsman with greater intellectual aspirations than the majority of those connected with the building industry at the time. The editors of the 1631 edition of Stow's *Chronicle* even called him, posthumously, 'the excellent Architect of our time'. Employed in a lowly administrative position in the Office of Works for much of his working life, he also had a reputation as an engineer, worked as a joiner, and called himself freemason in his will. He is known to have supplied designs to private builders on at least two occasions —in 1605 to Sir Thomas Tresham for Lyveden New Build and in 1613 to Sir Edward Pytts—and probably designed a lodge in Richmond Park for the Crown.[33] His knowledge of classical architecture was competent, as a letter to Tresham noting the importance of modular proportion in the Doric order, and a drawing by him also among the Tresham papers, illustrating a method of floor-framing based on Serlo, make clear.[34] What is more noteworthy, however, is that his approach to architecture was, at least in part, intellectual, and that he attempted to record some of his ideas on the subject in a literary form. The two obscure and confused papers that he left behind, although firmly in the Elizabethan architectural tradition in their conclusion that 'the bookes of Architecktur, Victriuces [Vitruvius] and all thoos Authers have taken the wrong sence; ther inwardes woorkes ar dead when theay shewe no lif in ther owtward doweinges',[35] are important as the only known commentary on architecture as a serious art by a working designer before the middle of the 17th century. But Stickells is, at best, a shadowy and elusive figure who, lacking the consistent private patronage accorded to men such as Smythson, never achieved social status, and his contemporary importance was probably slight.

With these few notable exceptions, it follows that the one social class that had the ability and the opportunity to study the sources was the country house builders themselves and consequently that their potential influence on the design of their own houses was of great importance. In practice their influence was limited by the amount of time they were prepared to devote personally to acquiring a knowledge of architecture, and by their technical ability to represent their ideas on paper in a form capable of being translated into a three-dimensional building. Even William Cecil, who was accustomed to making sketches to guide his workmen at Burghley, was capable of making only the most elementary drawings, as a letter that he wrote to Sir William More at Loseley in 1591 indicates:

'Sr, this other daie at my being at Guildford, when I vewed the Priorie theare, I made a rude trick thereof, in a manner of a platt wth mine own hand, at wch time a servant of yors or Mr Wolleis beinge present, and being a mason, as I remember, he offered him to mak the same more parfitlie'.   [36]

Only a minority of the builders, men such as Sir Thomas Smith and Sir John Thynne, were willing to subject themselves to the discipline necessary to achieve sufficient expertise in the new architecture. The majority of them as has already been suggested, thought of it as just another fashion, like the changing fashions in dress or the contemporary enchantment with the 'ingenious device', and in consequence never had more than a superficial understanding of the principles governing Renaissance design. As a result, they delegated much of their personal responsibility for their buildings to the men who were in charge of the day to day supervision of the works and to the leading craftsmen who carried out the actual works. They were, of course, subject to the will of the builder at every stage of the enterprise, but in many cases they seem to have been given considerable freedom of action within this framework, as when Nicholas Stone noted in his agreement for two chimneypieces with Sir Robert Pye in 1636; 'he hath left the forme to my decresion and allso the prices he referes himself unto me'.[37] In this way the design of many 16th-century buildings emerged as a combination of a number of influences ranging from the builder, through his supervisor or surveyor, to his more important artisans. Of these, the will of the builder was ultimately of sole importance, but the influence of the others in interpreting and arriving at his final will was far from negligible.

To understand how the buildings of the 16th century were designed it is therefore necessary to consider in closer detail these influences. As suggested above, that of the builder was potentially the most important. The surviving correspondence of Sir John Thynne gives some indication of the technical expertise and personal involvement that must have been characteristic of many of the builders. During the 1540s while work was going ahead on the first Longleat, Thynne was actively following his career as secretary to the Duke of Somerset. Yet, although he was rarely in Wiltshire to see his building at first-hand, he kept a tight control over all its aspects by means of a comprehensive correspondence with his steward, John Dodd, and by regular consultations with his leading craftsmen who were sent up to London for that purpose. No matter how busy his public life kept him, he always found time to write at length to Dodd, sometimes as often as five times a week, and occasionally two letters in one day. Thynne, as befitted a man who administered Somerset's extensive building works, was well aware of many of the practical aspects of building, and his correspondence contains many references to minutiae, such as the necessity for seasoning wainscot and even the method of doing it.[38] Thynne's close personal involvement in every stage of the building is clear enough, but his exact role as a designer is rather more obscure. For the first Longleat at least, there seems to have been little more than a vague overall conception of what the completed building would look like. Individual features were considered as they arose. In April 1547, when he wrote asking for Berryman, his chief mason, to be sent to London, it was 'to thentent I may show him my pleasur in suche things as I wolde have doon this year at my house'.[39] When he arrived, early in May, Thynne showed him his 'mynd for the two gats at the lane ends to be mad and for altering my ch[ambe]r over the p[ar]ler and for the paving of my haull chapell buttry pantry kchyn larder and other placs'.[40] The instructions that Thynne gave were probably only verbal, and it is likely that they were not very precise. It was Berryman's responsibility to use them as a basis for drawings which were then submitted back to Thynne. Thus in June 1547 Thynne wrote to Dodd, 'when Beryman may have tyme I wold be glad to have the plat of myn outhouses and the rest set forth as hertofore I did apoint & to be sent unto me'.[41]

The key to the whole problem of design is related to the question of just how much freedom the craftsmen were given in making such drawings. Thynne's instructions extended as far as writing that,

'I wol have my walles from the first floor upward to be but two briks length in thickness as hertofore I declaryd to Berryman',   [42]

but this was only a technical specification which, although important, still left open the matter of appearance. On occasion Dodd was forced to write to Thynne for more precise advice about decorative treatment,[43] and the craftsmen themselves were not afraid to suggest alterations to approved plans. In 1546 Dodd reported to Thynne that,

'The oppenion of William Love ys that the Chapell weyndow in the South syde wh you appointyd to stand will do very yll and much disvigure yor building wherfore he wold you shuld make an new weyndoo ther wh coold be but litle more cost to you'.   [44]

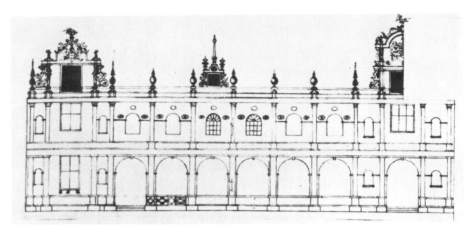

Elevation of the New Exchange in the Strand drawn
by Robert Smythson on his visit to London in 1609

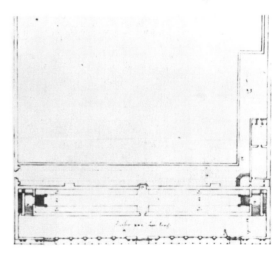

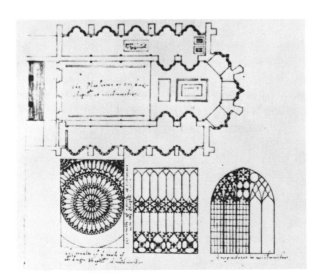

Drawings of Westminster Abbey made by
Robert Smythson on his visit to London in
1609

Love, who was the principal mason before the employment of Berryman went on to advise several other changes in the design and made drawings incorporating his suggestions. However, the conclusion of this part of the letter, 'that your pleasure may be knowen herin with sped or ells he must go in hand according as you last appointed', makes it clear that these were only suggestions, and that the initiative for any action remained solely with Thynne. Unfortunately it is no longer possible to see whether he followed Love's advice. It can only be assumed from the manner in which the advice was offered that it was not considered out of place for the leading craftsmen to prepare amendments to the schemes which were drawn up for the builders. Indeed, the initial schemes seem to have been so vague and lacking in essential detail that it would be surprising if they were not modified in the light of practical, and even aesthetic, conditions apparent only on the site.

Thus the design of the first Longleat emerges as the rather flexible result of a continuous dialogue between Thynne and his master mason, with the initial and dominant impetus coming from Thynne but with his ideas being rendered into practical form and to a certain extent modified by his principal executive.

The evidence from Thynne's later three remodellings of Longleat is not as informative on questions of design, for with the fall of Somerset in 1549 and his ultimate execution in 1552, Thynne retired from public life to live on his estates and consequently it was no longer necessary for him to correspond at length with his building officials. What evidence that remains, however, suggests that the basic methods of design differed little from those used in his earlier building, although his employment of more competent and sophisticated workmen led to a corresponding increase in their influence over his ideas. By the time that the design for the fourth and final Longleat had been evolved, the French sculptor Allen Maynard and the English mason Robert Smythson were able to claim that 'the ordenanse therof cam frome us'.[45] Maynard's known skill in the classical idiom and Smythson's genius for architectural composition, convincingly documented in his drawings and later buildings, are reason enough to accept the substance of their claim, but it is difficult to conceive of their achievement without the inspiration and drive of Thynne. There can be no doubt that he remained the dominating influence, in the words of William Darell, 'musing many a tyme with great care and now and then pulling downe this or that parte . . . to enlardge sometyme a foote, or some few inches, uppon a conceyt, or this or that man's speech, and by and by beat downe windows for this or that fault here or there'.[46] Longleat is a monument to his fanatical search for perfection, and its final form is as much a result of Thynne's own architectural development as it is a testimony to the skills of the exceptional artisans that he employed.

The evidence from Longleat, especially the correspondence of the early years, is the most important surviving source for the processes of architectural design in the sixteenth century. Other sources are more fragmentary, but the overall picture that they present differs only in detail from the situation at Longleat. In general the differences seem to result from the individual personalities and capabilities of the men involved, and in this context it is significant that some builders who were unable to make their own designs turned for help to friends of their own social class rather than to the building craftsmen. The lodge that Sir Richard Carew built in the fishpond at Antony in Cornwall was 'devised for me by that perfectly accomplished

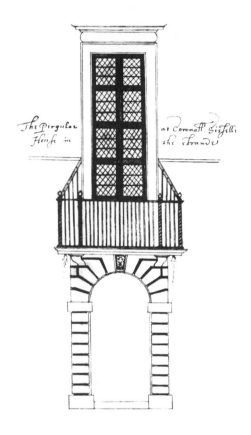

Detail of Edward Cecil's house in the Strand, drawn by John Smythson on his visit to London in 1618–19

Main entrance to The Keep, Bolsover Castle, Derbyshire, designed by John Smythson

33

gentleman, the late Sir Arthur Champernowne'.[47] In 1569 the Duke of Somerset's son, Lord Hertford, applied to Sir John Thynne for architectural advice, and was supplied with plans provided by Thynne with the help of his leading craftsmen.[48] Sir Nicholas Bacon sent his son, Nathaniel, plans for Stiffkey that he had drawn himself,[49] whilst another of his sons, Francis, made a note in his notebook on 28 July 1608 'To give directions of a plott to be made to turn ye pond yard into a place of pleasure and to speak of them to my L. of Salisbury'.[50] Salisbury's father, Lord Burghley, had been consulted in a similar manner by other builders. In August 1577, for example, the Earl of Shrewsbury wrote to him, 'I have sent Greves a plat of a front of a lodge that I am now building, which, if it were not for troubling your Lordship, I would wish your advice theron'.[51]

Many builders were forced by domestic reasons or by the demands of public life to spend long periods away from the sites of their new buildings, and as a result of these prolonged absences their administrative officers were given an opportunity to exercise an influence on the design of the building. In Cecil's absence, Peter Kemp, his steward at Burghley, played an important part in modifying the design for the house. Usually he sought Cecil's permission before he actually initiated any changes, as for example, in October 1561 when he wrote 'I thynck it good to lay the flore over the pantre somwhat hegher thàn the flore of my ladyes chamber', and added, 'I pray yo let me know yor plesur herin shortlye becawse it is in hande precelye'. But on occasion, he carried out alterations on his own initiative, and merely reported to Burghley 'I do not prosed after the tryck I sent yo'. Although in May 1562 Kemp was prepared to support his suggestion for lowering the ground table of the loggia with his own aesthetic judgement that it would be 'no fowle syght but rather a bewte', the alterations that he was concerned with were mainly restricted to those necessitated by practical considerations which became apparent as the building progressed, and his recommendations were taken in consultation with the leading craftsmen.[52] The influence of the steward seems to have been similarly restricted to practical matters in the realisation of the design on the other documented building projects of the period. Such considerations could have a profound effect on the final form of a building, but they were largely accidental, and in the majority of cases only resulted in minor modifications to the external design. The conscious designing role of the steward must have been considerably less important than that of the principal craftsmen.

Although the position of the builder as the predominant influence on architectural design has been strongly emphasised, it is equally clear that the working craftsmen's advice was crucial in the drawing up of a feasible scheme. In 1610 when the Earl of Salisbury was building at Cranborne, William Arnold, his master mason, was said to have spent 'every day a whole houre in private with' him discussing the work.[53] It has already been noted that the craftsmen at Longleat had regular consultations with Sir John Thynne and that the vagueness of his instructions must have transferred some of the responsibility for detailed designs to them.

Sometimes the advice was sought of craftsmen who were unconnected with the work. In a letter of May 1617 to the master of Jesus College, Cambridge, Fulke Greville wrote from London,

'Let me entreat you farther, that a Platt may be drawne to shewe the contrivinge of the lights, stayre-cases, chimneyes and studies, with the severall charges of them, to the intent, that by conference with some workmen here, I may see if anie thinge may be altered for the better'.   [54]

Although these independent craftsmen were called upon only to make revisions and comments to an existing scheme, the practice was only a short step away from commissioning them to initiate completely new schemes. From the end of the sixteenth century there are indications of the emergence of a class of professional designing craftsmen who, although still connected with the mechanical side of building, were of sufficient reputation as designers for their service to be occasionally used in that way. Many smaller country houses, outside those of the nobility, were probably partly designed by these working craftsmen. Men such as the mason Walter Hancock, of whom the parish register of Much Wenlock, Shropshire, stated when recording his burial in 1599 that he was skilful

'in the art of masonry, in setting of plottes for buildinges & performinge of the same, ingravinge in ale blaster and other stone or playster, and in divers other giftes that belonges to that art as dothe appeare by his workes which may be seene In divers parts of England & Walles, moste sompteouse buildinges, moste stately tombes, most curyouse pictures . . .'   [55]

It is clear from this that not only did Hancock have a local reputation as a designer in several allied fields, but that he was also a building contractor and working mason as well. He is known to have worked as a craftsman on Condover Hall, Shropshire, and to have been employed by Sir Francis Newport, the builder of High Ercall and Eyton-on-Severn. The latter thought highly of him, for he recommended him to the bailiffs of Shrewsbury in 1595 as a suitable mason for their new market house,[56] but it was for his expertise as a workman that he was praised and not his skill as a designer. His ability in the 'setting of plottes for buildinges' was, no doubt, considered to be an exceptional talent for what was a basic part of his craft.

This talent was recognised in other craftsmen, but the designs that were commissioned from them were subject at every stage to the ideas of the builder; and most builders were sufficiently conscious of architecture to impress their personalities on their own buildings. This is apparent from the various stages in the construction of Kyre Park, Worcestershire. In 1588, on one of his visits to London, Sir Edward Pytts employed John Symonds, one of the leading craftsmen of the Royal Works, to make a design for the house. Shortly afterwards Pytts changed his mind about the design and paid 'the same John Symons for drawing my latter platt according to my newe purpose'. Symonds never visited the site, and his only connection with the building was in providing designs, but it is clear that these designs were no more than an articulate expression of Pytts' requirements and ideas. Pytts, having completed the first stage of his building in 1595, again turned to a well known craftsman in 1611 when he decided to enlarge the house. In the early summer of that year he

'brought John Bentley, freemason, from Oxford (where he wrought the newe addition to Sir Thomas Bodleigh his famous library) with me as I came from London to Kyer',

35

but Bentley's contribution was strictly defined. He was

> 'to take instructions from me by veinge the place to draw me a new platte for I altered my first intent because I wold not encroche on the churchyard'.

At the same time Pytts brought another mason called Sergianson from Coventry to discuss the design, 'though he died nothing in that busynes'. Despite the comparatively large sums that Pytts spent on architectural advice, there can be little doubt that he exercised a very strong influence over the layout and appearance of his building. Symonds and Bentley were something more than draughtsmen, but they were certainly not the architects of the house in any modern sense of the word. His patronage of outstanding workmen and the regularity with which he altered his original schemes were not confined to his country house, for an entry in his accounts of December 1613 notes £3 'Paid to Stickles of London for drawing the platt of my house anewe'. This was almost certainly Robert Stickells, and probably refers to Pytts' London House for which he had previously paid £2 to 'Carter of St Giles Lane by Charing Crosse' for an elevation.[57]

Stickells is also known to have provided designs for Sir Thomas Tresham, and it is conceivable that he had other patrons amongst the gentry. Other prominent employees of the Works, such as Robert Adams, and Lawrence Bradshaw were certainly commissioned to make designs for private builders or for the private use of public figures.[58] However their relationship with their patrons probably differed little from that of Sir Edward Pytts and the various craftsmen that he consulted. It is possible that in time these superior craftsmen eventually would have achieved the function and status of architects. Nicholas Stone, although primarily a monumental mason, achieved this status through the patronage and friendship of his noble clients. But the majority of craftsmen-designers failed to rise above their artisan level. Instead, social and intellectual trends in the early part of the 17th century resulted in the emergence of a new type of architectural designer. Once the principles of Renaissance thought had been accepted it was possible to design a building based on the rules and proportions of the classical orders, without any previous experience of the practical aspects of building; and this divorce from the mechanical side gave the study of architecture the status of a 'liberal' art. As such it was a pursuit fit for a cultured gentleman, and it was even socially acceptable for the gentry to practice professionally, much as younger sons might have gone into the law or commerce. This social acceptance was a gradual achievement, and it was not won without a struggle. The well known dispute between Inigo Jones and Ben Jonson was partly a reflection of this battle for the status of the architect.[59]

The ability of Jones, and the opportunity provided by his royal patronage were influential factors in gaining respectability for the architect, but the notion also received indirect support from men of higher birth who were beginning to consider intellectual as well as aesthetic aspects of architecture. In 1570 Henry Billingsley's translation of *The Elements of Geometrie of Euclid* had been published with a long introduction by John Dee, in which Dee asserted the primacy of architecture over all the other mathematical arts and carefully explained the Renaissance idea of the architect. He supported his argument with long quotations from Vitruvius and Alberti, and lamented that few 'in our days' had attained to the excellence of a true architect.[60] Dee's remarkably advanced views seem to have met with little immediate response and it was only with the following generation that they began to gain acceptance. By 1607 James Cleland in *The Institution of a Young Noble Man* was able to refer to 'the principles of architecture: which I think necessary also for a gentleman to be known', and by 1660 John Webb confidently stated that 'most gentry have some knowledge of the theory of architecture'.[61] In terms of literary output, this certainly seems to be true. Sir Francis Bacon published his essay on architecture in 1623, and according to Aubrey was 'the chiefest architect' of his own house near St. Albans.[62] Sir Henry Wotton, who was ambassador in Venice and later become Provost of Eton, published an influential treatise on the *Elements of Architecture* in 1624. Sir Balthazar Gerbier, the courtier and diplomat, was designing buildings for the Duke of Buckingham in the 1620s, and in 1662 published *A Brief Discourse Concerning the Three Chief Principles of Magnificent Building*, following this with *Counsel and Advise to all Builders* . . . in 1663.

The discovery of the noble qualities inherent in the pursuit of architecture had its first practical flowering amongst the gentry in the person of Sir Roger Pratt. Although he did not design his first building until 1650, his career and his writings are important as an indication of the new influences on English architecture that were emerging during the 17th century. Born in 1620, he was educated in a way common to many of his social class. In 1637 he matriculated at Magdalen College, Oxford, and in 1639 entered the Middle Temple. Between 1643 and 1649 he travelled extensively in Europe, visiting Italy and France and building up a considerable library of architectural books. The year after his return to England, he designed and supervised the building of Coleshill House, Berkshire, for a relative, Sir George Pratt. This was his first architectural work, and he was assisted in his task by the advice of Inigo Jones. It established a reputation for Pratt as an architect, and in 1662 he was simultaneously engaged on Kingston Lacy, Dorset, for Sir Ralph Bankes, and Horseheath, Cambridgeshire, for Lord Allington. In 1664 he began work on Clarendon House in Piccadilly for Edward Hyde, the Lord Chancellor. In 1667 Pratt inherited the family estates at Ryston in Norfolk and, apart from serving as one of the commissioners for rebuilding the City of London, retired to live the life of a country gentleman. In 1669 he rebuilt his own house. As far as it is known, these five buildings represent his total output over a period covering almost twenty years. Their influence on domestic design was considerable, but they are equally important in showing that the actual practice of architecture was a suitable occupation for a gentleman by the time of the Restoration.

The attitude of Pratt's class to the process of architectural design is summarised in the unpublished advice to prospective builders that he wrote in 1660:

'First resolve with yourself what house will be answerable to your purse and estate, and after you have pitched upon the number of the rooms and the dimensions of each, and desire in some measure to make use of whatsoever you have either observed, or heard to be excellent elsewhere, then if you be not able to handsomely contrive it yourself, get some ingenious gentleman who has seen much of that kind abroad and been somewhat versed in the best authors of Architecture: viz. Palladio, Scamozzi, Serlo etc. to do it for you, and to give you a design of it in paper, though but roughly drawn, (which will generally fall out better than one which shall be given you by a home-bred Architect for want of his better experience, as is daily seen) . . .'   [63]

It is probable that Pratt originally intended to publish his writings as an architectural treatise, and in that context this passage is clearly an advertisement for his own services, but it is also revealing as a statement of architectural practice at the middle of the 17th century. The initiative was still necessarily with the builder, but the accomplishment of his requirements was, if not by himself, by one of his social equals. It was not simply a coincidence that many of the leading Restoration architects were of gentle birth. Hugh May was the seventh son of John May, Esq, and cousin of Baptist May, the Keeper of the Privy Purse to Charles II,[64] and Roger North was the sixth and youngest son of Dudley, fourth Lord North.[65] The craftsmen-designers remained, and continued to be patronised, but the gentleman-architect had taken his place alongside them, and it was his taste that was to be the predominating factor in English architecture during the following hundred years.

However, the importance of the gentleman-architects before the Restoration must not be over-emphasised. The seeds of their eventual predominance were certainly present in the years before 1640, but, considered on a quantative basis, the most influential men were still the craftsmen designers. It remains to explain how they gained their knowledge of architectural design, and how the styles that they helped create were disseminated throughout the country.

Masons are known to have made collections of drawings and plans, which they valued highly, and which they bequeathed with care to their sons or apprentices along with the tools of their trade.[64] Cornelius Brownstone, for example, a master mason of Westminster who died in 1562, left John Sparrowe, his apprentice, 'all my plats and platerns', as well as his tools, a gown, and a compass.[67] Sometimes the collections of drawings were divided up. William Cure bequeathed some of his 'paternes' to his son-in-law, and the remainder he gave to his son, Cornelius.[68] The Thorpe collection probably began in this way, for it contains a number of early plans and elevations that John Thorpe inherited from his mason father, Thomas Thorpe. The plans are all of upper floors, and only one of them has a corresponding elevation. The missing plans and elevations were presumably divided up amongst John's brothers.[69] The collections were not confined simply to buildings that the craftsman himself had worked on but included notable buildings, both ancient and modern, that he had seen and wished to remember. On a journey from the Midlands to London in 1609, Robert Smythson made a large number of drawings, including a plan of King's College chapel, Cambridge, and details of the window tracery in Henry VII's chapel in Westminster Abbey, as well as a plan and elevation of the New Exchange in the Strand which had only been opened in April of that year.[70] He recorded what was new and what was of interest to him amongst the old. What he saw had little influence on his own work for he was already an old man when he visited London and he was to die shortly afterwards. But when his son John made a similar trip ten years later and drew details of many of the newest buildings in London, including the incomplete Banqueting House; the 'Holborn gables', the 'pergulas', and the rustication that impressed him were incorporated in his subsequent work at Bolsover Castle. On his way to

London, John had also visited Theobalds and made a drawing of some of its panelling, which he later used as a model when he came to design the panelling of the Pillar parlour at Bolsover.[71]

The Smythson drawings are just such a collection as were mentioned in the wills of other masons. The presence of three late gothic drawings suggests that, as with Thorpe, Robert Smythson inherited the nucleus of the collection. They passed from Robert to his son, John and from him to his grandson. They were used by the family as a working tool, and they show the Smythsons' readiness to absorb and use new influences. They demonstrate in a particularly clear way how the novel architectural features in one part of the country rapidly spread to other areas. It is reasonable to assume that the collections by other craftsmen were used in a similar fashion as practical working aids, and were equally influential in the dissemination of new ideas.

The craftsmen's first hand architectural knowledge was also on occasion supplemented by information derived from books. A number of masons certainly possessed their own books, and bequeathed them along with their drawings and tools. The will of John Multon dated 1546 mentions 'all my portatures, plaates, books with all other my tooles and instruments',[72] and William Cure left all his 'books paternes toles and other necessaryes' to his son in 1579.[73] At his death in 1634, John Smythson had a room in his house at Bolsover which he called the library,[74] and examples have already been mentioned of drawings in both the Thorpe and the Smythson collections which were direct copies from architectural books, and of craftsmen being lent such books by their employers. Undoubtedly it was the illustrations rather than the text which were of most practical use to the craftsmen, and they used them simply as pattern books. The books of Serlo, de Vries, and Dietterlin were particularly influential on architectural decoration in the late 16th and early 17th centuries. The first recorded English pattern book was *A Booke of Sundry Draughtes principally serving for glasiers; and not impertinent for plasterers, and gardiners; besides sundry other professions*, by Walter Gedde. Published in 1615, it contained over a hundred different designs, and was specifically intended as an aid to the craftsmen, 'Knowing the expert maister is not unfurnished of these usuall draughts, though each workeman have not all of them'.

However, although printed books played a demonstrable part in the creation of a national architectural style, they were only rarely a direct influence. More frequently they provided a basic inspiration on which the craftsmen exercised his individual ingenuity, and the process of adaptation was further extended by the widespread practice of seeking inspiration from existing buildings. This has already been inferred from the drawings in the Smythson Collection, and can be supported by a large body of documentary evidence. Several surviving building contracts specify that certain features were to be modelled on those of other buildings, and there is evidence, other than the well-known letter of 1603 from Northumberland to Cecil already quoted,[75] of builders going to see comparable buildings before starting work themselves. Usually they were accompanied on these journeys by their principal craftsmen. Before commencing the design of the hall at Trinity College, Cambridge, in 1604, the supervisor of the works took his carpenter to London where they paid a total of 10s to 'Carpenters and keepers of dyvers Halles to viewe and measure them', and the hall that they built was of

Panelling in the Pillar Parlour, Bolsover Castle, Derbyshire, based on the panelling at Theobalds

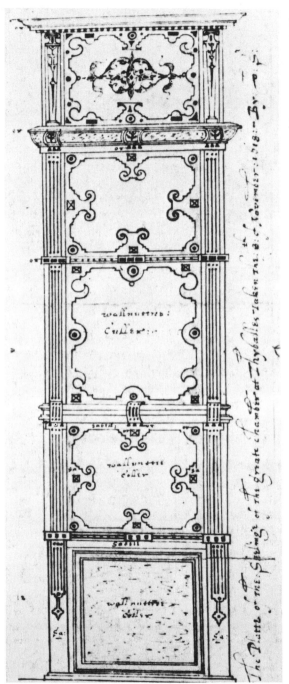

Typical geometrical design from Walter Gedde's *Booke of Sundry Draughtes....* published in 1615

Panelling in the Great Chamber, Theobalds, Hertfordshire, drawn by John Smythson in 1618

41

exactly the same dimensions as the hall of the Middle Temple.[76] In the early years of the 17th century Northumberland had his carpenter, John Dee, compile *A Booke of Computations for Buildings*, which included a collection of notes on the size of the main rooms of ten important contemporary buildings.[77] The principal carpenter working on Little Saxham Hall, Suffolk, in 1505 was instructed to copy the roof of Horham Hall, Essex, which had only recently been begun, and the same carpenter was also sent to look at the house in Tower Street, London, of the wealthy merchant, Angel Donne. In 1506, when the bricklayer was preparing to make a bridge across the moat, he had his expenses paid 'to se a bruge in Essex', and similarly in 1509 the glazier was sent to Horham before starting the chapel window.[78]

Another factor leading to the diffusion of general stylistic trends throughout the country was the itinerant nature of many of the craftsmen's jobs. The maximum length of time that they might be employed on one house was something like ten years. They would then have to move on elsewhere to find employment, and they would take with them their own particular skills and stylistic preferences. Sometimes they continued to find employment within the same locality, and in consequence it is possible to find particular architectural motifs confined to a relatively small area. In Essex, for example, the fireplaces in at least three houses built in the latter half of the 16th century showed a curious variation on what was basically a common type. They were all of freestone with moulded jambs and flat pointed arches, but their shoulders were cut obliquely in a straight line rather than the usual rounded form, and the decorative frieze of alternate circles and lozenges filled with roses and leaves, was substantially similar in each case. The houses for which they were made, Eastbury Hall, Little Belhus, and Albyns, were all within a few miles of each other, and it seems reasonable to postulate that the fireplaces were all executed by the same craftsmen.

Often, however, the craftsmen travelled a considerable distance to their next job, as when many of the Longleat craftsmen moved on to Wollaton in Nottinghamshire in 1580, and their influence was inevitably felt over a wide area. In combination with the practice of viewing other buildings as models, it meant a rapid diffusion of architectural innovations throughout the whole country.

With each successive job the craftsmen themselves were open to new influences from their fellow craftsmen, the majority of whom had invariably been employed on a number of different houses. The later work of Robert Smythson probably owes much to the experience that he gained from working with the gifted French mason and carver, Allen Maynard, and similarly Smythson must have inspired and influenced some of the craftsmen working for him at Wollaton, Worksop and Hardwick. They, in turn, eventually moved to other buildings sites where their accumulated experience was able to influence, and be influenced by, other craftsmen. In this way the peculiar conditions of English house design, whereby considerable freedom was given to the executive craftsmen, produced a distinct national architectural style which was freely eclectic and basically unsympathetic to the rigid rules of the Court architecture of Inigo Jones. By the end of the seventeenth century, however, the gentlemen architects had imposed their intellectual discipline on the mainstream of English architecture. The basis for this domination had been laid by the end of our period.

3 Notes

1 N. Pevsner, 'The Term "Architect" in the Middle Ages' *Speculum* xvii (1942) 549

2 L. F. Salzman, *Building in England Down to 1540* (2nd edn., Oxford 1967) pp. 228 & 420. Hereafter cited as Salzman

3 Winchester City Archives, St. John's Hospital Accounts, 69 & 70, (1462–3), *Ibid* 65 (1459–60). I owe both these references to the kindness of Dr D. J. Keene of the Winchester Research Unit

4 J. Shute, *The First and Chief Groundes of Architecture* (London 1563) preface

5 J. Strype, *The Life of the Learned Sir Thomas Smith* (Oxford 1820 edn.) p. 171

6 Cambridge University Library: Hengrave Hall Deposit 80

7 Strype, *op cit* p. 171

8 R. Willis & J. W. Clark, *The Architectural History of the University of Cambridge and of the Colleges of Cambridge and Eton* (Cambridge 1886) ii, 693n. Hereafter cited as Willis and Clark

9 *Ibid*, ii, 251 *et passim*

10 I. G. Philip, 'The Building of the Schools Quadrangle' *Oxoniensia* xii (1948) 42

11 T. W. Hanson, 'Halifax Builders in Oxford' *Transactions of the Halifax Antiquarian Society* (1928) 253–317

12 Dorset County Record Office: MW /M4 f. 24v

13 *The Account Book of Nicholas Stone* ed. W. L. Spiers (Walpole Society vii 1919), p. 65

14 N. Pevsner, *The Buildings of England: Northamptonshire* (London 1961) p. 274

15 As an illustration of the process, see J. H. Harvey, 'The Origin of the Perpendicular Style' in *Studies in Building History* ed. E. M. Jope (London 1961) pp. 134–65

16 *Ibid* p. 134

17 J. H. Harvey, *English Medieval Architects* (London 1954)

18 *Harrison's Description of England in Shakespere's Youth* ed. F. J. Furnivall (New Shakspere Society series vi 1877) p. 238. Only Vitruvius and Serlio were mentioned in the 1577 edition. The name of Alberti was added for the edition of 1587. It is revealing that Harrison only identifies him by his christian names, suggesting, perhaps, that he had not actually read him

19 British Museum: Additional MSS 39830, f. 191 v

20 Historical Manuscripts Commission, *Portland* ix, 152

21 The collection, which is kept at Hatfield, is available in facsimile at British Museum: MSS Facsimiles 372 (1 and 2)

22 Mrs Baldwyn-Childe, 'The Building of the Manor-House of Kyre Park, Worcestershire' *The Antiquary* xxii (1890) 53

23 H. L. Bradfer-Lawrence, 'The Building of Raynham Hall' *Norfolk Archaelogy* xxiii (1927) 126

24 Pratt was writing to Sir Horace Townshend who had inherited Raynham in 1650. *The Architecture of Sir Roger Pratt* ed. R. T. Gunther (Oxford 1928) pp. 132–4

25 Bradfer-Lawrence, *op cit* 125

26 *The Account Book of Nicholas Stone* ed. W. L. Spiers (Walpole Society vii 1919) p. 3

27 Baldwyn-Childe, *op cit* 53

28 For example, T34 and T141. See *The Book of Architecture of John Thorpe* ed J. Summerson (Walpole Society xl 1966) p. 29

29 T71–2 and T75–6 *Ibid* pp. 67–8

30 R.I.B.A. Library: Drawings Collection, Smythson Collection, 1 /25. See also *The Smythson Collection* ed. M. Girouard (*Architectural History* v 1962) p. 38

31 Devon County Record Office: 404 M /61–2

32 Summerson, *op cit* pp. 7–8

33 The only account of Stickell's life is in J. Summerson, 'Three Elizabethan Architects', *Bulletin of the John Rylands Library* xl (1957) 216–21

34 British Museum: Additional MSS, 39831 ff. 3–4

35   British Museum: Landsdowne 84 /10
36   *The Loseley Manuscripts* ed. A. J. Kempe (London 1836) p. 304
37   *The Account Book of Nicholas Stone* ed. W. L. Spiers (Walpole Society vii 1919) p. 104
38   Longleat Archives: R.O.B., I, 121, 18 June 1547
39   *Ibid* R.O.B., I, 19. 16 April 1547
40   *Ibid* R.O.B., I, 70. 7 May 1547
41   *Ibid* R.O.B., I, 120. 18 June 1547
42   *Ibid* R.O.B., I, 141. 22 June 1547
43   In June 1547, for example, he sought clarification of Thynne's wishes for treating the roof of a tower. *Ibid*, R.O.B., I, 127
44   *Ibid* R.O.B., I, 199. Undated, but probably 1546
45   *Ibid* R.O.B., III, 197
46   *Ibid* 213
47   *Richard Carew of Antony; The Survey of Cornwall etc.* ed. F. E. Halliday (London 1953) p. 175
48   Girouard, *Smythson* p. 68
49   Sandeen, p. 178
50   British Museum: Additional MSS. 27, 278, f. 24v
51   J. R. Wigfull, 'Extracts from the Note-Book of William Dickenson', *Transactions of the Hunter Archaeological Society* ii (1921) 189−200
52   J. A. Gotch, 'The Renaissance in Northamptonshire', *Transactions of the Royal Institute of British Architects* new series vi (1890) 104−6
53   Essex County Record Office: D /DP Q13 /3 /11
54   Willis and Clark, ii, 172
55   'Extracts from the Registers of the Parish of Much Wenlock', *Transactions of the Shropshire Archaeological Society* xi (1888) 15
56   H. Avray Tipping, 'Condover Hall' *Country Life* xliii, (1918) 513
57   Mrs Baldwyn-Childe, 'The Building of the Manor-House of Kyre Park, Worcestershire' *The Antiquary* xxi−ii (1890)
58   For Stickells and Adams see J. Summerson, 'Three Elizabethan Architects', *Bulletin of the John Rylands Library* xl (1957) 202−28. Bradshaw, who was Surveyor of the Royal Works, 1547−64, provided plans for Sir William Petre at East Thorndon, Essex in 1550, Essex County Record Office: D /DP A10 f. 81 & f. 85
59   D. J. Gordon, 'Poet and Architect: the Intellectual Setting of the Quarrel Between Ben Jonson and Inigo Jones' *Courtauld and Warburg Journal* xii (1949) 152−78
60   For an excellent discussion of Dee's preface see F. A. Yates, *Theatre of the World* (London 1969)
61   H. M. Colvin, *Biographical Dictionary of English Architects, 1660−1840* (London 1954) p. 171
62   *'Brief Lives' Chiefly of Contemporaries, set down by John Aubrey, between the years 1669 & 1696* ed. A. Clark (Oxford 1898) i, 78
63   *The Architecture of Sir Roger Pratt* ed. R. T. Gunther (Oxford 1928) p. 60
64   Colvin, *op cit* p. 382
65   *Ibid* p. 418
66   W. J. Williams, 'Wills of Freemasons and Masons' *The Masonic Record* xvi (1936) 171−236
67   *Ibid* 223
68   *Ibid* 234
69   *The Book of Architecture of John Thorpe* ed. J. Summerson (Walpole Society xl 1966) p. 4
70   R.I.B.A. Library Drawings Collection, Smythson Collection, I /3−4, 7, 9−15, 17, 20, 24
71   *Ibid* III /6−8, 13
72   Williams, *op cit* 204
73   *Ibid* 234
74   Girouard, *Smythson* p. 200

75 Noting his intention to see 'every place of mark where curiousities are used' before starting to build at Petworth. Historical Manuscripts Commission, *Cecil* xv, 383
76 Willis and Clark, ii, 490
77 G. Batho, 'Notes and Documents on Petworth House, 1574–1632' *Sussex Archaeological Collections* xcvi (1958) 108–34
78 British Museum: Additional MSS 7097, ff. 175, 175v, 178, & 192v

4 Methods of Undertaking

In 1681, Sir Christopher Wren advised the Bishop of Oxford that 'There are 3 ways of working: by the Day, by Measure, by Great',[1] an observation that could have been made with equal validity for the period with which this study is concerned. Before he began the detailed planning of his building enterprise, the builder had to decide which of these three main methods he was going to employ, for his administrative arrangements depended on the decision, as did, indeed, the degree of personal involvement that he was going to have in the work.

The most direct method of organisation was for the builder to supply all the materials himself, arrange for their carriage, provide the necessary equipment and accommodation for the working of the materials, and to hire workmen by the day to simply work on his materials in accordance with instructions. This method of direct labour, which was synonymous with Wren's first category of working, was suited to projects where the size of the labour force was comparatively small and could be effectively administered by a household official, or even the builder himself. Many country houses were built by this method throughout much of the 16th century, but by the early 17th century it had been largely superseded by other methods and its use was mainly confined to minor repair work on existing fabrics. Although it was a practical system for smaller houses, such as William Dickenson's house at Sheffield in 1575 and Dr William Griffith's house at Carreglwyd, Anglesey, in 1636, or for those houses which were built over a long period of time with a small labour force, such as Old Thorndon Hall, Essex, the builders of larger houses were faced with considerable administrative problems. Responsible officials were necessary to arrange for the supply, transport, storage, and issue of materials and equipment, the workmen had to be closely supervised and instructed, their attendance checked and their wages paid. Sometimes they had to be accommodated and fed. Accounts had to be kept, and the whole enterprise had to be co-ordinated and planned so that it would not be delayed through lack of labour or materials, or so that expenditure did not exceed the money currently available. All these functions were capable of being discharged by one or two household officials on smaller country house sites, although it must have meant an inconvenient disruption of their more regular duties, but where the labour force was large and the materials had to come from varied and sometimes more distant sources, the number of administrative officials invariably increased and the overall supervision became more complex. The majority of country house builders only built one house in their lifetime, and the temporary establishment of a large administrative body must have seemed impractical to many of them. Thus in 1530, when Sir Thomas Kytson decided to enlarge Hengrave Hall, Suffolk, he partly abandoned the direct labour method that he had exclusively employed for the previous five years and put much of the new work out to contract.[2] Similarly, Sir John Thynne contracted with a mason for a large new range at Longleat in 1559 rather than undertake it on the direct labour basis that had characterised his earlier, less ambitious, work.[3]

The Royal Works were predominantly carried out by direct labour, but the existence of a permanent administration and the power of coercion available to the crown enabled it to overcome the problems that the system posed to the private builder. Somerset, who was building Somerset House, Syon House, and Wolfhall between 1548 and 1551, in addition to work at Banbury, Odiham, and Reading, also largely relied on direct labour, but his powerful public position allowed him to set up a works organisation similar in its hierarchical complexity to that of the Royal Works.[4] There were not many other private builders who possessed such power or who built in so many different places simultaneously, to justify such an organisation. By the time that the Cecils came to engage in their building activity in the late 16th and early 17th centuries, the advantages of the contract and piece work systems had been recognised, and their reliance on direct labour was correspondingly less.

One way by which a builder could avoid the administrative problems of the direct labour system, was to let the work out to contract. This might take the extreme form of an agreement with a single contractor for a complete building, by which the latter was responsible for every aspect of the work in return for a sum of money agreed in advance. Such was the contract made by Joseph Wood with a builder for a new wing to his house at Illingworth, near Halifax, in April 1648,[5] but most private builders seem to have been reluctant to make comprehensive contracts for all the work with one contractor, and generally they entered into separate agreements with contractors from each of the crafts involved. There certainly were craftsmen who were capable of organising a complete building enterprise, such as the glazier Bernard Dinninghof, who offered to undertake all the work including the provision of designs for the rebuilding of Sheriff Hutton Castle, Yorkshire, in 1618 for Thomas Lumsden,[6] and Gilbert Wigge and Ralph Simons, who built the second court of St. John's College, Cambridge, between 1598 and 1602 for £3,605,[7] but the opportunities available to them on country house sites were almost invariably restricted to their own trades. Thus Henry Hunt, an Arundel freemason, contracted with Giles Garton for all the stone and brickwork for a new wing to his house at East Lavington, Sussex, in 1586, but no mention was made in the contract of the necessary carpentry, plastering, and roofing, which were clearly arranged by separate agreements with other craftsmen.[8] Hunt subsequently executed both the stonework and the woodwork for the Earl of Northumberland's new work at Petworth in 1595 and 1596, but again the plumbing, plastering, and tiling were undertaken by other craftsmen.[9] Most of the other surviving contracts relate to a single craft, such as that made by Roger Palmer, mason, for 'alle . . . masons worke' on Mount Edgcumbe, Cornwall, in 1547,[10] or William Spicer's contract at Longleat in 1559 for

'almaner of stone worke fremasonrye Rowmasonrye and bryckworkes'. [11]

47

Sometimes the responsibility was divided even further by making separate contracts with different craftsmen within the same trade. This seems to have been the case at Thorpe Hall, Northamptonshire, in 1653, when two masons agreed to make the thirty-eight windows for the house, the other masonry presumably being carried out by other masons,[12] and at Harrold House, Bedfordshire, between 1608 and 1610, where the fabric was executed by Thomas Harris, and some of the decorative masonry by Thomas Grumbold.[13]

Within the framework of the system there was a great deal of variety between the conditions attached to individual contracts. Most contractors bound themselves to provide all the necessary labour, and, in view of the difficulty that some builders experienced in attracting sufficient skilled workmen, it is possible that this was one of the prime motives for many builders to place part of their work in the hands of contractors. Materials were sometimes provided by the contractor and sometimes by the builder. Generally, masons supplied their own stone, while the builder arranged for the supply of more easily accessible materials, such as timber or sand for mortar. Clearly, where the builder was able to provide the necessary material from his own estates, he did so. Most contracts contained a clause specifying the date by which the work was to be completed, but it was only rarely that this was accompanied by a penalty for failure. In the few cases where a specific financial penalty was written into the contract it usually represented a substantial proportion of the total payment, as at Illingworth, Yorkshire, where the house was to be finished by 31 May 1649 under penalty of £2 on the £11 contract,[14] and at Hengrave Hall, Suffolk, in 1538, where Sir Thomas Kytson retained £20 out of an agreed sum of £116 until the joiner had successfully completed his contract.[15] In addition to a time limit for the completion of the work, some contractors also entered into a maintenance clause for the restitution of any defects that might appear within a specific period of time. Thus Henry Hunt was to be responsible for the new wing at East Lavington for twelve months after its completion.

In 1662, Sir Balthazar Gerbier warned that if

'Builders put their design to Master Workmen by the Great, or have it Wrought by the Day, either the Workmen will over-reach themselves, or the Builder will be over-reached.'   [16]

Although he perhaps over emphasised the financial danger to the builder of the direct labour system, adequate costing of the proposed work must have been a very arbitrary process when it was to be carried out either by contract or direct labour, and a number of contractors seem to have got into difficulties through unrealistic estimating. Spicer failed to complete his contract at Longleat, although he received most of the money for the work, and at Hardwick Old Hall, Derbyshire, Rauff Smith, a carpenter who had contracted to make the roof of the Great Chamber in March 1589, was forced to mortgage his house to Bess of Hardwick in November of that year, when another craftsman was paid for the 'bargain that Smith should have done'.[17] The massive contract undertaken by Wigge and Simons for St. John's College, Cambridge, was completed within the specified time, but 'in a manner ruinous to the undertakers and not over advantageous to the college'. A year after the end of the work, the contractors were still in debt to the College to the sum of £200, and a further £156 had been spent by the College in repairing some of the defects already apparent in the building.[18]

The builder was unlikely to obtain adequate recompense from a contractor who had got into financial difficulties during the course of the work, and he invariably had to make alternative arrangements at his own expense for the completion of the contract. A similar situation was liable to arise should the contractor decide to leave the site before the work was finished. At Ashley Park, Surrey, in the early 17th century, the builder contracted all the carpentry for the house with a carpenter called Parsons for £90. Having received £78 16s 0d on the contract, Parsons suddenly disappeared and the builder was forced to employ direct labour for the remainder of the work at a cost of £36 3s 0d. A contract which had been originally estimated at £90, therefore cost the builder £114 19s 0d before the work was successfully completed.[19]

Another deficiency inherent in the contract system was the possibility that the chosen contractor should prove to be incompetent. If his shortcomings did not become apparent until the work was well under way, the builder was faced with a considerable dilemma as to the action he should take to remedy the situation. Whatever he did invariably involved additional expenditure before a satisfactory result was obtained. The problem is well illustrated by the documentation for Little Saxham Hall, Suffolk, where Thomas Lucas contracted most of the bricklaying and masons' work to John Bronde, a mason of Bury St. Edmunds. The contract of 1505 for the foundations of one range seems to have been successful for in the following year Bronde was given a further contract for completing that range and building another. By 1508, however, the standard of his work was giving cause for concern and various parts of it were given to other craftsmen to complete. Lucas seem to have been reluctant to dispense with Bronde, possibly because of a shortage of masons in the area, but, significantly, the fresh contracts that he negotiated with him in 1508 and 1509 for further parts of the work were to be overseen by Thomas Loveday, the principal carpenter on the site. This attempt at increased supervision failed to have the desired effect, and in June 1510. Bronde was dismissed with 'moch of his said werk. . . not yet fynyshed'. Lucas then had to send to Cambridge to get workmen who were sufficiently competent to complete the work, and four years later parts of the building erected by Bronde were already being strengthened.[20]

The third method of working mentioned by Wren, payment by measure, overcame many of the problems associated with contract work. Instead of agreeing a lump sum for the whole, the work was broken down into all the separate operations which could be measured, and payment was made to individual craftsmen on the basis of a fixed price for each completed unit. This method was highly sensitive to the unequal degrees of skill and complexity involved in the different tasks carried out by the workmen. For example, the masons' work on the bay windows at Longleat in 1572 was paid for at the rate of 5s for each of the capitals, 3s for the base of each pilaster, 2s the foot for the cornice, frieze, and architrave, 1s a foot for window-heads and sills, 10d the foot for jambs, 6d a foot for the base of the pedestals, and 11s 6d for every hundred feet of plain ashlar work.[21] Even the price for more straightforward work could be varied according to the stage that the building had reached. At Chantmarle in Dorset, the masons were paid 1s 8d a perch for the walling of the ground storey, and 2s a

49

One of the bay windows at Longleat House, Wiltshire, for which the workmen were paid piece rates varying from 5s for each of the capitals to 6d per foot for the base of the pedestals

perch for the two upper storeys; the increased rate being due to the greater difficulties of working at a height above the ground.[22]

Although some work had been undertaken on a piece rate basis earlier in the century—for example, at Chevet Hall, Yorkshire in 1516[23]—it was only in the latter part of the 16th and the early part of the 17th century that it became the predominant method of working for most country house builders. By using piece rates, a much more acceptable pricing of the proposed work could be achieved, but it presupposed fairly sophisticated skills in calculating realistic rates and consequently the acceptance of the system was accompanied by the emergence of specialised building surveyors, generally from craft backgrounds, who began to play an increasingly important role in the administration of building projects. Such a development corresponded to the more professional approach characteristic of the later country house builders.

The advantages of the piece rate system were not confined to financial considerations, or to the more specialised administration that it required. The craftsmen could be left to carry out their work as instructed with the minimum of supervision, and it was to their own advantage to do it as speedily as possible for they were not being paid on a time basis. A close check could be made on their workmanship at the measuring stage, and as each workman's responsibility tended to be smaller than the collective responsibility of a contractor, the consequences of incompetence on the part of any one man could be effectively minimised. Similarly, the sudden departure of a craftsman was less likely to disrupt the work than if he were the sole contractor. The system also retained to the builder some of the personal control of the work that would have been sacrificed had he placed substantial parts of it in the hands of a contractor.

In practice it was rare for all the workmanship on a country house to be undertaken at piece rates. Some tasks, such as labouring and the routine craftsmanship, were more easily arranged on a direct labour basis, and as the numbers involved were smaller than if the whole enterprise had been carried out in this way, they could be easily administered. All the more skilled craft work, however, was invariably paid for at piece rates from the late 16th century onwards. The method by which the building of Trentham Hall, Staffordshire, was undertaken in the 1630s can be taken as a typical illustration of the situation by the end of the period.[24] All the labouring, apart from such easily measured work as trenching, was paid for by the day. All the joinery, glazing, and smith's work were at piece rates. The masonry and carpentry were predominantly carried out at piece rates between 1630 and 1635, although a small group of masons also worked at day rates during the same period. By 1636 the shell of the house had been largely completed, and the three masons and a similar number of carpenters who remained on the site for the final three years of the account were employed at day rates. Clearly during the early years of the enterprise all the specialised work had been executed at piece rates, whilst a nucleus of direct labour had been employed on the more routine tasks.

Sir Christopher Wren, in advising the Bishop of Oxford on the three ways of working, suggested that 'the best way in this business is to worke by measure'.[25] Twenty years earlier, two other prominent practitioners in the building world had pointed the same conclusion. In 1663, Sir Balthazar Gerbier wrote,

'It is best for the Builder to . . .
have his works done by the Rod or square',   [26]

and in 1665, Sir Roger Pratt offered similar advice.[27] During the previous hundred years many country house builders had discarded the traditional direct labour and contract systems and had adopted this way of working, but its acceptance had been dependent upon the emergence of a new type of building worker who was sufficiently literate to be able to understand and administer the sophisticated techniques of quantity surveying.

4 Notes

1   *Wren Society* v (1928) 20
2   Cambridge University Library: Hengrave Hall Deposit 80
3   Longleat Archives: R.O.B., ii, f. 117
4   British Museum: Egerton MSS 2816
5   J. Lister & W. Brown, 'Seventeenth Century Builders' Contracts', *Yorkshire Archaeological Journal* xvi (1902) 109-10
6   S. D. Kitson, 'The Heraldic Glass of Gilling Castle, Yorkshire, and Bernard Dinninghof' *Journal of the British Society of Master Glass Painters* iii (1929) 55-8
7   Willis and Clark, ii, 248-63
8   W. H. Godfrey, 'An Elizabethan Builders Contract' *Sussex Archaeological Collections* lxv (1924) 219-24
9   G. R. Batho, 'The Percies at Petworth, 1547-1632', *ibid* xcv (1957) 12
10 Cornwall County Record Office: Mount Edgcumbe MSS MTD /48 /10
11 Longleat Archives, R.O.B., ii, f. 117
12 British Museum: Additional MSS 25302, f. 153
13 Bedfordshire County Record Office: TW818
14 Lister & Brown, *op cit* 109-10
15 Cambridge University Library: Hengrave Hall Deposit 81
16 B. Gerbier, *A Brief Discourse Concerning the Three Chief Principles of Magnificent Building*. . . (London 1662) p. 26
17 B. Stallybrass, 'Bess of Hardwick's Buildings and Building Accounts', *Archaeologia* lxiv (1913) 366
18 Willis and Clark, ii, 257-8
19 Surrey County Record Office: Acc. 1030, f. 99v
20 British Museum: Additional MSS 7097, ff. 174-200
21 Longleat Archives: T.P., lxciii, Bk. 60, f. 43
22 Dorset County Record Office: MW /M4, f. 24v. See Sir Roger Pratt; '. . . it is to be observed, that the higher they go, the greater the price will be, by reason of the trouble of the materials, which are carried up to them. . .', *The Architecture of Sir Roger Pratt*, ed. R. T. Gunther, (Oxford 1928), p. 52
23 W. E. Preston, 'A Sixteenth Century Account Roll of the Building of a House at Chevet' *Yorkshire Archaeological Journal* xxxii (1934) 326-30
24 Staffordshire County Record Office: D593 R /1 /2
25 *Wren Society* v (1928) 20
26 B. Gerbier, *Counsel and Advise to All Builders*. . . . (London 1663) p. 61
27 Gunther, *op cit* pp. 87-88

5 The Administrative and Executive Labour Force

One of the most crucial steps in the building operation was the assembling of an adequate administrative and executive labour force. The efficient conclusion of the operation depended on the competence of the officials appointed to oversee the everyday details and to co-ordinate labour and materials so that the most economical use was made of the available resources. On most houses of any size it was physically impossible for one man to discharge all the administrative duties himself, and in practice the responsibility was usually divided up between a number of officials. When the house was relatively small and the builder was not active in national affairs which might take him away from the site for months at a time, he often administered the building himself, with the assistance of his relatives or his household steward. Francis Farrar, who built Harrold House in Bedfordshire between 1608 and 1610, was helped at various periods during the course of the building by his son-in-law, Thomas Boteler, and his brother-in-law, Humphrey Layton. Farrar acted as his own clerk and accountant, and supervised the administration on the site, but the purchase of materials and the arrangements for their carriage from distant sources such as King's Lynn and Northamptonshire was carried out as the occasion required by Boteler or Layton.[1] Farrar's administrative task was eased by employing his craftsmen by contract, and consequently the only part of his labour force which required close daily supervision was his labourers, and they never numbered more than fourteen in any one week. At Carreglwyd, Anglesey, in 1636 the total daily labour force never exceeded twenty-four, and was administered by the unnamed brother of the builder, Dr William Griffith, with the assistance of the principal mason. Griffith, a distinguished lawyer and chancellor of the dioceses of Bangor and St. Asaph, was presumably too busy to directly concern himself with the management of his own affairs, for the same brother who drew up the building accounts was also responsible for the running of his household and his estate.[2]

It was of course, only possible for the builder to administer his own building operation personally when the scale of that operation was relatively small, and when he was free from other commitments. Sir Edward Pytts, who in June 1611 began to make additions to his house at Kyre Wyard under his own supervision, was made sheriff of Worcestershire for the following year, and consequently in November he was forced to lay off part of his weekly labour force 'till my Sheriff work ended'. He then appointed a Staffordshire mason as 'Survey'r of the work & workmen', leaving his bailiff, Richard Turvill, free to undertake the remaining administrative duties.[3] This was a practical and common solution to the problem of organising the building operation on many of the smaller sites. The principal officer of the gentleman's household was, after all, trained in the administering of his master's estates and in the handling of his finances, while a leading craftsman could usually be trusted to supervise other workmen and to ensure adequate standards of craftmanship. It was an administrative system that was adopted for many of the documented buildings throughout the period, and can probably be considered as the most common method of organisation used by those men who only engaged in building once in their lifetime. The houses that they built were governed more by considerations of domestic comfort than by a desire for ostentatious architectural display, and consequently it was the simplest and most effective method available to them. It was not necessary to look further than their own household for a general administrator and clerk of the works. The work that they would be called upon to do could be seen as little more than an extension of their normal duties. If a competent craftsman was known, or could be found, he could be expected to be capable of dealing with the more specialised and technical side of the operation and would possibly be able to advise on sources of labour and materials.

Documentation for the early part of the 16th century is relatively sparse, but the system was employed by Thomas Lucas, Henry VII's Solicitor-General, for his house at Little Saxham, Suffolk, in 1505–14, and by Sir Thomas Kytson for the early years of his work at Hengrave, *circa* 1525–9.[5] It had been used in the medieval period, and was employed by Lord Hastings for Kirby Muxloe Castle in 1480–4. Nicholas Bacon used it in a modified form for the modest house that he built at Redgrave in 1545–54. Instead of a household servant he used a distant relative, John Bacon, to oversee his work with the assistance of the London mason John Gybbon.[7] Sir John Petre's work on Old Thorndon Hall, Essex, between 1573 and 1595, was organised by his steward, John Bentley, and a carpenter called Walter Madison.[8] Neither Madison nor Gybbon worked as craftsmen on the building that they supervised, but generally the supervising craftsmen were expected to execute work associated with their craft in addition to their other duties.

The principal craftsman was generally subservient to the administrative officer, and usually only concerned with matters confined to the technical side of the work. He was responsible to him for his actions, and seldom deputised for him when he was absent. Sir Thomas Tresham's building operations, for example, were administered by his steward, George Levens. He was away from the site for the week ending 22 June 1595, but his duties were temporarily carried out by another official of Tresham's household, John Androweson, and not by any of the principal craftsmen.[9]

The administrative combination of household servant and craftsman was occasionally employed on some of the more extensive building projects. The construction of Hill Hall, Essex, was organised for Sir Thomas Smith by John Dighton, the 'steward of his house', who was assisted by Richard Kirby, a bricklayer, as 'his chief architect'.[10] The work carried out at Syon House, Middlesex, for the ninth Earl of Northumberland, was supervised by a gentleman officer of his household, Christopher Ingram, aided by John Dee, Northumberland's estate carpenter,[11] and the organisation for the early years at Longleat was administered in a similar fashion, with the main burden falling on Sir John Thynne's stewards, John Dodd in the 1540s and '50s, George Walker in the early 1560s, and then Thomas Vyttery.[12]

However, it was usual to employ a more diverse and sophisticated method of administration for buildings of this size. The necessity for a greater division among the administrative staff is well illustrated by the situation at Hengrave, Suffolk, between 1525 and 1540. In the early years the work was carried out by a small local labour force employed on a daily basis, and mainly using local material. The annual expenditure was modest, only exceeding £200 in 1527 and 1528, and the work was effectively administered by one man, Thomas Shethe, who seems to have been a member of Sir Thomas Kytson's household. In 1530 Kytson's plans for his house seem to have undergone a radical revision, and the scale of his building works was considerably increased. Only in 1532 did the annual expenditure again fall below £200, and by 1535 it was running at the level of £350 a year. Although the local labour force continued to be employed, the majority of the work was now being executed by outside contractors who were responsible for providing their own workmen. A new administrative officer, Robert Watson, was appointed to be 'ruler of bylding', Shethe's duties now being confined to the boarding arrangements for the outside workmen and supervising the carriage of materials. Watson made all the contracts, both with the craftsmen and for materials. He travelled extensively to Brandon, Cambridge, and even as far as London seeking materials and craftsmen. He made regular trips to London to consult Kytson, and also supervised those workmen who were working away from the site cutting timber and digging stone. On the regular occasions when he was absent from Hengrave, Shethe deputised for him. In addition to Watson and Shethe, and the principal contractors responsible for their own men, a separate clerk of the works was also employed to check the workmen and draw up the accounts. This position was filled up to March 1535 by Myllis Mason, the parson of the neighbouring village of Flempton, and then subsequently by Thomas Aldaye.[13] Mason was presumably employed on the clerical work because of his literacy, in the same way that the accounts of Chatsworth and Hardwick Old Hall in Derbyshire were kept by Bess of Hardwick's chaplain, the Reverend Henry Jenkins.[14]

Some powerful magnates, such as Somerset in the middle of the 16th century and Robert Cecil at the end of the century, built several houses and were occasionally engaged on work simultaneously on more than one site. It was necessary for them to have separate administrative staffs at each of their sites, but these were generally subordinate to a central group of officials who co-ordinated the works as a whole and ensured that there was no unnecessary duplication of resources at a local level. In this respect their organisations were analogous to the Royal Works, and, on occasion the officials that they used for their private purposes were employees of the Works. Between 1548 and 1551, Somerset employed separate supervisors, comptrollers, and clerks at Somerset House in the Strand, Syon House, Odiham, and Reading, in addition to the agents and bailiffs in charge of the preparations for his projected house at Great Bedwyn in Wiltshire. But all these officials reported to, and took instructions from a few of Somerset's principal stewards, in particular Sir John Thynne, and the financing of all the works was centrally controlled by John Pickarell, the Duke's cofferer.[15] Only in this way was it possible for the work on the various scattered sites to proceed unhindered by the absence of a key official who might be attending another site, yet by having a centralised administration ensure that materials, money, and men were directed to the place where they were most needed.

Robert Cecil, who in the opening decade of the 17th century was building Salisbury House and the New Exchange in the Strand, Hatfield House in Hertfordshire, and Cranborne House in Dorset, was faced with similar problems of organisation, and he solved them in a fashion that was broadly the same as that employed by the Duke of Somerset fifty years earlier. His three sites in or near London were under the financial control of Thomas Wilson, one of the leading officers in Cecil's household. Wilson was resident in Salisbury House, where he was able to closely supervise both operations being carried on in the Strand, and he rode down to Hatfield at frequent intervals to arrange for the financing of the work there. He also dealt with the carriage of material, much of which was shipped through London. For the early work at Salisbury House between 1599 and 1602, Cecil engaged the comptroller of the Royal Works, Simon Basil, as the site administrator. Basil was subsequently employed as general administrator and technical adviser for the New Exchange and Hatfield House. The everyday supervision on these sites was carried out by men with craft backgrounds who, in addition to their organising ability, were capable of dealing with technical problems arising on the site. Cecil filled this post for the New Exchange with another employee of the Office of Works, William Southes, who was later to be appointed Master Mason at Windsor Castle. At Hatfield he employed a relatively unknown carpenter, Robert Liming, whose administrative and designing talents were subsequently patronised by Sir Henry Hobbart for his house at Blickling in Norfolk. Wilson and Basil formed the nucleus of the centralised co-ordinating administration, playing an active role on all three sites but leaving the close supervision in the hands of Southes and Liming and their subordinates.[16] Cranborne was a considerable distance away from London, and consequently it was impractical for Wilson and Basil to pay close attention in person to the work there. They were able to arrange for the shipment of materials through London and to send money and men where necessary to Dorset, but for all practical purposes, the building was administered by William Arnold, a west-country mason whose reputation was such that he was known to Sir Edward Hext as 'the absolutest & honestest workeman in Ingland'.[17]

Although on the majority of major building works in the 16th century the supervisors with craft backgrounds were generally subordinate to the household and financial administrators, the latter part of the century saw the emergence of a small group of professional surveyors capable of directing the whole operation, and frequently employed as the principal administrative officer to whom all the other officials were responsible. Almost without exception these surveyors had originally been practising craftsmen or were descended from craftsmen. Their emergence, and the consolidation of their position in the 17th century, can be seen as a process of acceptance of the qualified building specialist similar to that which took place with regard to the architect over the same period. They were men who were capable of mastering the more specialised administrative techniques demanded by the growing predominance of piece work as the method of working, and who were knowledgeable about such diverse things as the current prices of materials and the sharp practices that could be perpetrated by deceitful workmen. Occasionally they were responsible for the preparation of the design in addition to their administrative duties, but in general they never achieved the status that was accorded to the gentleman-architect of the type epitomised by Sir Roger Pratt. They remained basically artisans and, with a few notable exceptions, their relationship with the builder was that of employee rather than adviser. During the period when their roles were being evolved, the distinction between architects and surveyors was often very confused, but by the later 17th century it was possible to define more precisely their separate functions. To Sir Roger Pratt, the surveyor organised the everyday administration of the building in response to the instructions that he received from the architect who had designed it.[18] The surveyor was the agent who enabled the architect's intentions to be satisfactorily fulfilled. In essence it was the crucial intellectual and social distinction between the liberal and mechanical arts.

In the absence of any information about the background of Robert Watson, the 'ruler of bylding' at Hengrave, William Spicer, the Somerset mason who had been employed at Longleat between 1554 and 1563, seems to have been one of the earliest examples of a craftsman employed to direct a building operation in the period with which we are concerned. He was clearly a man with exceptional organising ability for within five years of beginning work at Longleat as a junior craftsman he had been given a contract worth £300 to build all the new work begun in 1559, and in addition was appointed bailiff and rent collector of Thynne's manor of Lullington in Somerset.[19] His building contract was not a success, and in 1563 he left Longleat with much of the work unfinished. Whatever his shortcomings as a building contractor, however, his administrative ability continued to be recognised. A letter preserved in the archives at Longleat shows that by 1571 he was being employed by the Earl of Leicester in charge of the works at Kenilworth Castle where he was directly responsible to Leicester for the provision of materials, the hiring of the workmen, and the negotiating of contracts.[20] The tone of the letter suggests that his position was of more consequence than that of merely craft supervisor. He seems to have had direction of the whole enterprise, and his role was probably similar to that of the professional surveyor familiar later in the century. Spicer was to achieve even greater administrative distinction in subsequent years, being appointed Surveyor of the Queen's Works at Berwick in 1584 and Surveyor of the Royal Works in 1596.

Another craftsman who had spent part of his early career as a working mason at Longleat also became in later life a professional surveyor of building operations. Robert Smythson worked for Thynne for twelve years from 1568. He was employed as one of the two principal masons, and there are no indications in the very full documentation for the building that he took any part in the administration, other than supervising the other masons in his own gang. He was, however, a workman of considerable experience and reputation. Before working at Longleat he had been employed by Sir Francis Knollys, the Vice-Chamberlain, and he was personally recommended to Thynne by Humphrey Lovell, the Queen's Master Mason. In 1575, whilst still at Longleat he carried out work for Sir Mathew Arundell at Wardour Castle. On the death of Thynne in 1580, Smythson moved to the Midlands to work for Sir Francis Willoughby, where, as his tombstone records, he was employed as 'Architector and Survayor unto yee most worthy house of Wollaton'. The amount of mason's work actually carried out by Smythson was minimal. His principal job was to direct the building operation, and to prepare the designs in consultation with Willoughby. The status of his position is marked by the appellation of 'Mr' accorded him in the building accounts.[21] Smythson remained at Wollaton for the rest of his life, and after the house had been completed he seems to have been employed by the Willoughby family in a general administrative capacity connected with their coal-mining enterprises. During the same period, he continued to prepare architectural designs for other patrons, and to supervise some of the building operations of the Cavendish family. An entry in the Hardwick accounts for 1597 refers to him as 'Mr Smythson the Surveyour'. By this date he was being assisted in his building activities by his son John who had been initially trained as a mason in the final years of the work at Wollaton.

In 1612, Sir Charles Cavendish began to build at Bolsover Castle, Derbyshire, and John Smythson was engaged to direct the work and supply the design. By 1615 he had become a permanent employee of Cavendish with the title of bailiff and was concerned with the general administration of part of his estates. His son, Huntingdon, who succeeded him as bailiff to the Cavendish estates, also seems to have been responsible for the direction of the works at Bolsover in 1629–30. Unlike his father, there is no evidence that he was ever trained as a working mason. His marriage into a gentry family is probably a fair indication of the status that the Smythson family had achieved within two generations of their craftsman origins.

Craftsmen who had achieved positions of responsibility in the Royal Works were especially experienced in the directing of building operations. The Surveyor of the Works and the various Master craftsmen were more concerned with the administration of the Works than with the actual practice of their trade. Despite the lack of any major new building projects under Elizabeth, the Royal Works was the only body organised to consistently give a training in the specialised job of supervising a large building operation. It is not therefore surprising that the administrative experience of men trained in the Works was sought by private patrons for employment on their own enterprises. As has already been noted, Robert Cecil made extensive use of Simon Basil to supervise three important building operations early in the 17th century. His father, Lord Burghley, had used the services of Henry Hawthorne, Purveyor to the Royal Works, at Theobalds, and later extensively patronised John Symonds, another leading Works craftsman, employing him as surveyor in charge of all his London houses.[22]

Robert Stickells, who had been employed in the Works since the 1580s, was appointed by the London Grocers Company in 1591 to direct the work of wainscoting their Hall,[23] and John Thorpe, whose early training had been as a clerk in the Office of Works, was paid £5 as 'surveir of ye contractinge' for supervising the erection of a gallery at Belvoir for the Earl of Rutland.[24] Nicholas Stone, was another employee of the Works whose expertise was sought by private patrons. In addition to his flourishing private practice as a monumental mason, he was employed by the Earl of Danby in 1631 'to desine a new hous for him at Corenbury in Oxfordsheer and to dereckt the workmen', and later in the decade he was appointed surveyor of the building of the new Goldsmith's Hall, and superintended the additions to Tart Hall, St. James's Park, for the Countess of Arundel.[25]

The majority of building surveyors who had been connected with the Works were based in London, but the provincial surveyors who were increasingly coming into prominence in the early 17th century invariably emerged from a similar craft background. William Arnold, for example, who had directed the works for Cecil at Cranborne in Dorset, and was employed in a similar capacity at Wadham College, Oxford, in 1610, and for George Luttrell at Dunster Castle, Somerset, in 1617, was a Somerset mason,[26] as was Gabriel Moore, who was employed by John Strode 'to survey & direct the building' of Chantmarle House, Dorset, in 1619.[27] Lawrence Shipway, who 'sett forward the worke' at Condover Hall, Shropshire, in the 1590s, had previously been employed as the Master mason working on the Shire Hall at Stafford.[28] Robert Liming, the carpenter who had been employed by Cecil at Hatfield, was described in the parish register at Blickling Norfolk as 'the architect and builder of Blickling Hall', and, in view of his administrative experience at Hatfield, it is probably safe to assume that he supervised the work carried out there between 1616 and 1627 for Sir Henry Hobart. Insufficient biographical details survive for the majority of early 17th-century craftsmen, but what is known about men such as the masons John Chaunce,[29] and Ralph Symons[30] suggest that they, too, were often principally employed as administrators.

Once the builder had decided on the form of administration that he was going to adopt for his work, he was faced with the problem of assembling sufficient labourers and craftsmen to carry it out. The size of his executive labour force obviously depended largely on the size of the project and the speed with which it was intended to carry it out. Sir William More employed little more than a total of fifty workmen between 1560 and 1569 to build his house at Loseley, near Guildford. Although it was not a large house, it was sufficient to receive the Queen on three of her progresses.[31] The accounts only survive for the last six years for Trentham Hall, Staffordshire, built by Sir Richard Leveson between 1630 and 1639; but during the period for which we have documentation he employed a total of one hundred and fifty-six workmen, and it was only during the last three years of the enterprise that his annual labour force fell below one hundred. It is difficult to know how many of these men were working on the site at the same time because much of the work was carried out at piece rates. However, the maximum number of workmen paid at day rates rarely exceeds thirty in any one week and it is probably reasonable to assume that the total weekly labour force was somewhere in the region of fifty men.[32] At the other end of the scale, Harrold House, Bedfordshire, was built between 1608 and 1610 with a weekly labour force of under twenty,[33] and the average weekly labour force employed at Carreglwyd, Anglesey, in 1636 was approximately twenty-four.[34] In general, few private building operations seem to have employed a weekly labour force greatly in excess of sixty men. A maximum of fifty to sixty workmen can be traced in the fortnightly accounts for the work at Bolsover Castle, Derbyshire, 1612–24,[35] whilst no more than sixty men were ever employed at one time by Sir Roger Townshend on Raynham Hall, Norfolk, 1619–25.[36] Sir Thomas Tresham's weekly labour force working on the much smaller Triangular Lodge in Northamptonshire was usually less than forty workmen in 1594 and 1595, and had dwindled to well below twenty in 1597 when the building was nearing completion.[37]

In contrast, royal projects, especially those built during the reign of Henry VIII, were often constructed on a vastly larger scale and usually at a speed that was beyond the resources of the private builder. The number of workmen employed in September 1538 on the palace of Nonsuch was five hundred and sixteen,[38] and we are told that over two thousand craftsmen and labourers were engaged on erecting temporary buildings at Guisnes in 1520 for the meeting of Francis I and Henry VIII.[39] The labour force used to build the palaces of St. James's, Whitehall, and Hampton Court must have been of considerable proportions.

Defensive works, naturally, had to be built with the greatest possible speed, and consequently they necessitated the employment of large numbers of workmen. Sandgate Castle, Kent, one of a number of South-Coast forts built in 1539 and 1540 in response to the invasion scare, took only eighteen months to complete. At the height of the work, in May 1540, over nine hundred workmen were engaged on the site.[40] The employment of so many men on royal works was not confined to the reign of Henry VIII. There was a work force of four hundred and twenty-eight men at Berwick in June 1557, for example.[41] Such voracious demands put an intolerable strain on the supply of building labour over the country as a whole, and the only way the Royal Works was able to maintain a labour force of the required size was by exercising its right of impressment.[42]

The only private builders who built on a scale and at a speed comparable with the Royal Works were a few figures prominent in the government and at the Court. Holders of the most influential public offices, they often had access to some of the resources of the Royal Works. They built vast private palaces, far in excess of their personal needs. Many of them still survive, symbols of their builders' power and position; and, later in the period, symptoms of their dependence on the monarch. Most of them were built late in the 16th century and early in the 17th century when the establishment of the royal progress under Elizabeth and James I gave those with sufficient resources the opportunity to seek favour at Court, and to acquire the rewards that accompanied it, by providing what were virtually occasional residences for the monarch. But the pattern had been set earlier in the century by the principal ministers of state. The labour force employed by Wolsey on his several buildings must have rivalled at times that employed by his sovereign, while Somerset in the following reign had almost three hundred workmen engaged on the preliminary preparations for the house that he proposed to build at Great Bedwyn, Wiltshire.[43] The expenditure on labour for that house between 1548 and 1551, as recorded by his paymaster, was under £20. This, clearly, is a very incomplete figure, but in comparison with the sums of over £6,500, that are recorded as being spent on labour for Somerset House, and £4,000 for Syon, it suggests that the number of workmen employed on his major works was remarkably high.[44]

Sufficient evidence exists to suggest that many builders experienced considerable difficulty in assembling enough skilled craftsmen for their works. The building craftsmen released from the permanent staffs of the larger ecclesiastical establishments by the dissolution of the monastries were probably insufficient to meet the increased demands for labour created by the expansion of the activities of the Royal Works during the later years of Henry VIII. Masons for the Royal Works at Nonsuch were sought in Gloucestershire, Wiltshire, Herefordshire, Worcestershire, Northamptonshire and Bedfordshire as well as in Surrey and Sussex.[45] At least three separate tours into the West-Country were necessary in 1539 and 1540 to impress sufficient masons for Sandgate Castle, Kent,[46] and on another of the Royal Works, at Berwick in 1557, masons were impressed from as far away as Kent.[47] The impressment of workmen was a royal prerogative which continued to be used well into the 17th century, and which enabled the Crown to overcome temporary shortages and to assemble a sufficient labour force as and when needed. Occasionally commissions of impressment were granted to collegiate bodies, such as that for Christ's College, Cambridge, in 1510,[48] and those for Trinity College,

Cambridge in 1554 and 1560,[49] but they were not generally available for private builders. By taking workmen away to work on royal sites, they must have considerably increased the labour problems of the private builder on occasion. Sir John Thynne was prepared to use his influence at Court to frustrate the commissioners should they threaten his labour force at Longleat,[50] but other builders were not so fortunate. We are told that William Jackson, a freemason, was unable to complete his contract of 1529 for work at Orby Church, Lincolnshire, because he had been pressed for the King's Works.[51] Understandably, such peremptory conscription was not always welcomed by the craftsmen themselves. The disciplining of Robert Short, a London carpenter, was recorded in 1504 'for he would not goo to the Kynges workes',[52] and no doubt there were other cases of evasion which have not been recorded because they were more successful.

The impressment of labour for major Royal Works produced only temporary shortages in the private sector, but there are indications of a more permanent shortage of skilled building labour, and especially masons, throughout much of the 16th century. It has already been noted that masons were invariably the subject of royal commissions of impressment. A dearth of good masons in north Berkshire and Oxfordshire has been postulated for the period from 1530 onwards,[53] and in other parts of the country there is reason to suppose that builders experienced some difficulty in getting the masons that they required. Robert Cecil recruited masons from Oxfordshire, Gloucestershire, Worcestershire, Warwickshire, Berkshire, and Northamptonshire for his New Exchange in 1608. Even so, he found it difficult to get enough, and was forced to advance money 'to som of the masones which were stubburn'.[54] In 1590 a mason for the Shire Hall, Stafford, was summoned from Bridgnorth, Shropshire, twenty-three miles away,[55] and many of the masons employed at Kyre Park, Worcestershire, 1588–1618, came from distances of over twenty-five miles.[56] One of the masons working at Loseley House, Surrey, in 1562, had been brought from Oxford,[57] and thirteen masons and their labourers employed by Sir Nicholas Bacon at Redgrave, Suffolk, in 1551 came from London. There are several other examples in the building accounts of the period of masons being sought at a considerable distance even on sites which were fairly close to areas of building stone, and consequently areas which can be assumed to have had a higher number of resident masons. In 1561, for example, a mason living at Ruscombe, near Reading, Berkshire, was engaged to work at Burghley House, Northamptonshire.[58] No doubt some of the examples were the result of builders seeking the services of specific craftsmen of skill and repute, as when Sir John Thynne requested the carver, John Chapman, from Sir William Sharington of Lacock Abbey, Wiltshire, only to be told that Chapman was first 'going to Dudley, to be sent thither by my Lord of Northumberland, to do things there of like effect'.[59] But there are too many examples for them all to be explicable in this way.

In addition there is evidence from the Longleat archives of some builders attempting to entice masons away from the service of other builders. In the summer of 1547 Andrew Baynton, son of Sir Edward Baynton, seems to have temporarily persuaded Sir John Thynne's principal mason, Berryman, to work for him before he had completed the work that he had agreed to do at Longleat. Baynton owned the lease on Berryman's house, and used this to force him to transfer his allegiance. Thynne rapidly made Baynton fully aware of his wrath, and assured Berryman that Baynton would 'do him no wrong nor yet put him to any troble' over his lease 'for though he threten him never so muche I am suer he wol take better advisement or ever he do anything', and Berryman was soon back at Longleat.[60] It is clear from Thynne's letter to his steward, that he was prepared to use the full force of the law to secure the return of his mason. It is possible to explain the vigour of Thynne's reaction by the slight on his power and position, but in combination with the examples of masons being sought from a distance it does seem to indicate that there were insufficient masons of the required skill to easily meet the needs of all the builders in the 16th century.

This shortage also applied to a certain extent to the other trades connected with building. At Redgrave in 1552, Nicholas Bacon paid the expenses of his joiner while 'seeking for woorkmen to help hym', and his glazier and several of his other joiners came from London.[61] In 1576 he sent his son, Nathaniel, two pairs of sawyers from London to work at Stiffkey in Norfolk.[62] Edward Batten, the joiner employed on fitting out John Strode's new chapel at Chantmarle, Dorset, in 1617, came from Salisbury, a distance of forty-five miles.[63] The plumbers used by Sir Richard Leveson for his house at Trentham, Staffordshire, in 1633 and 1635 came from Bridgnorth, thirty-six miles away,[64] whilst those plumbers working at Petworth, Sussex, in 1595–6 came almost fifty miles from London.[65] This evidence must be seen against the background of the itinerant nature of the specialised building crafts, but it does seem to indicate a continual difficulty in finding a sufficiently skilled labour force close at hand.

Labour was recruited in several ways. Some of the craftsmen and most of the labourers were invariably local men and their recruitment was presumably by word of mouth. Craftsmen from a distance were sometimes summoned by messenger. In 1594 a boy was sent to Witham to fetch a plumber to work at Old Thorndon Hall, Essex,[66] and the Oxford mason who was employed at Loseley in 1562 had been recruited by the master mason's boy, who travelled to Oxford for the purpose.[67] The masons who had been temporarily laid off work on Sir Thomas Tresham's Triangular Lodge, in 1595, were recalled by the despatch of a labourer to their homes at Weldon.[68] When the craftsman being sought was sufficiently important, the supervisor of the works would personally go and negotiate with him. The supervisor at Old Thorndon Hall, which was built largely of brick, travelled up to London by boat in August 1581 to arrange for a mason to carry out some work at the site,[69] and his counterpart at Trinity College, Cambridge, rode to Thaxted in Essex 'to bargen wth the glasier for the wyndowes yet to glase' in the chapel.[70]

Sometimes workmen were summoned by letter, as when Sir Richard Leveson paid one of his building officials 3s 'for money he laid out to send a letter to the masons the first journey' in June 1635. In the previous month Leveson had sent the local cobbler to Burton-on-Trent with a letter 'to stay a dutch masons journey'.[71] No doubt those craftsmen who were literate replied in a similar fashion. Thomas Accres, a skilled mason who had worked at Chatsworth in the 1570s and Wollaton in the 1580s, sent a letter to the supervisor at Hardwick in August 1594, and by the following spring he was working at the site.[72]

The builders themselves seem to have frequently solicited craftsmen of exceptional reputation from each other. Sir John Thynne's request of a carver from Sir William Sharington has already been noted. An unnamed plasterer employed by Thynne was the subject of a similar request from Sir William Cavendish, who wrote, probably in 1555,

'Sr I understand that you have A connyng plaisterer at Longlete wch hath in yor hall and in other places of yor house made Dyvse pendaunts and other ptye thyngs. Yf yor busynes be at An ende or wilbe by the next somer after this that comyth in I woold p[ra]y you that I myght have hym in to Darbyshere ffor my hall is yet on made And therefore nowe myght he devyse wt my carpenter howe he shuld frame the same that it myght s[er]ve for his worke'.   73

Thynne presumably was unwilling to part with him at that date for five years later the widow of Cavendish, then married to Sir William St. Loe, and more familiar as Bess of Hardwick, wrote,

'Thies are even to desire you to spare me your plaistere that flowered your halle whom I wold gladly have forthwith to be sent either to my howse at Chattesworthe . . . Or elles to London that I may sende him downe with all spede myselfe'.

She added that if he was unavailable she would be grateful if Thynne would send her another plasterer.[74]

Conversely, craftsmen were often engaged on the direct recommendation of builders for whom they had previously worked. Robert Smythson was almost certainly brought to the notice of Sir Francis Willoughby of Wollaton by his brother-in-law, Sir Matthew Arundell, for whom Smythson had executed some work at Wardour Castle, Wiltshire, in or before 1576.[75] William Arnold, the mason, had been commended to Dorothy Wadham by her 'good frend and lovinge neighboure Sr Edward Phelipps', the builder of Montacute House, Somerset, and she, in turn, requested Lord Petre to employ him on the building of Wadham College, Oxford.[76] Sir Francis Newport, the builder of High Ercall and Eyton-on-Severn, wrote in 1595 to the Bailiffs of Shrewsbury, who were proposing to build a market hall,

'I pray you let mee comende a Mason of approved Skyll and honestye, one Walter Hancock, unto yo for the doing thereof. I think it is not unknowne to you that I have great cause to make tryall of workmen, and therefore can well write unto you of myne owne knowledge and experience that you cannott match the man in these parts (with any of that occupacon)',

adding that if Mr Justice Owen, the builder of Condover Hall, Shropshire, 'were in the country he would say as much on Hancock's behalf as I have done'.[77] A mason working at Chatsworth in 1560 had been recommended by 'Sur James' and two of the plasterers there in 1579 had been sent from Kenilworth by the Earl of Leicester.[78] Sir Thomas Gresham provided Lord Burghley in 1567 with the highly experienced Flemish mason, Henryk, who had previously been in charge of the building of Gresham's Exchange in London,[79] and Edmund Withypoll, the builder of Christ Church Mansion, Ipswich, sent Nicholas Bacon a number of freemasons to work at his house at Redgrave in Suffolk.[80]

Craftsmen were also recruited on the recommendation of other craftsmen. It seems to have been common practice for the builder to consult with his surveyor or principal craftsman over the appointment of craftsmen. John Strode, for example, let the building of his house at Chantmarle to John, Joseph and Daniel Rowe, masons from Ham Hill, Somerset, who were 'prferred to me by Gabriell Moore my Surveyor'. Moore, who was also a mason by trade, came from Chinnock which was only a few miles from Ham Hill.[81] Inigo Jones, who designed a garden gateway for Beaufort House, Chelsea, wrote to Lionel Cranfield on 4 April 1620,

> 'According to yor honours desire I have sent you a Mason for your worke at Chelsea; his name is John Medhurst, hee is a yard stone man, and will fytt yor turne well'. [82]

A number of the leading craftsmen at Wollaton in the 1580s had previously worked at Longleat and clearly owed their positions to the influence of Robert Smythson, surveyor at Wollaton and formerly one of the principal masons at Longleat. Similarly, some of the craftsmen from Wollaton later worked at Hardwick where Smythson was also concerned in an executive capacity.[83]

Some of the more influential builders were able to approach officers of the Royal Works to find competent craftsmen for their own works. Humphrey Lovell, the Queen's Master Mason, sent Robert Smythson and his men to Longleat in 1568 'accordenge to his promes' to Sir John Thynne.[84] Somerset and the Cecils undoubtedly recruited part of their labour force in this way, as well as using leading personalities from the Works as administrators.

Once a builder began to make preparations, news of the impending work must have spread fairly rapidly and no doubt some of his labour force was made up of workmen arriving at the site in search of work. By its nature, this form of recruitment has left very little documentary record and it can often only be traced in its most extreme form of casual workmen employed for short periods of a few days. However, the accounts of Kyre Park, where preliminary work began in the autumn of 1588, contain an entry for December of 12s given 'to two masons that came to seek work from Richmond',[85] and a letter of 1618 survives from Bernard Dinninghof, a glazier and building contractor, to Thomas Lumsden, offering to rebuild Sheriff Hutton Castle, Yorkshire, which begins,

> 'Sir,—if it may please your worship, my being with you in York in Sir Arthur Ingram's garden at that time having some compliment concerning the building the which your worship would have done at the gatehouse at Sherif Hutton Castell . . .' [86]

In addition to offering to undertake all the work, Dinninghof also submitted architectural designs for the building. His letter was more of an attempt to solicit a commission for the whole project than an enquiry for work, but it is an interesting illustration of how craftsmen sometimes must have taken the initiative in seeking employment.

5 Notes

1   Bedfordshire County Record Office: TW 818
2   D. Knoop and G. P. Jones, 'The Carreglwyd Building Account, 1636' *Transactions of the Anglesey Antiquarian Society* (1934) 27—43

3   Mrs Baldwyn-Childe, 'The Building of the Manor-House of Kyre Park, Worcestershire, 1588–1628' *The Antiquary* xxi–ii (1890) pp. 202–264 and 24–50

4   British Museum: Additional MSS 7097, ff. 174–200

5   Cambridge University Library: Hengrave Hall Deposit 80

6   See D. Knoop and G. P. Jones, *The Medieval Mason* (3rd edition, Manchester 1967), pp. 38–9

7   E. R. Sandeen, 'The Building of Redgrave Hall, 1545–54' *Proceedings of the Suffolk Institute of Archaeology* xxix, pt. 1 (1961) 1–33

8   Essex County Record Office: D /DP A 18–22

9   British Museum: Additional MSS 39832 f. 47

10   J. Strype, *The Life of the Learned Sir Thomas Smith, kt., D.C.L.* (Oxford 1820) p. 171

11   G. R. Batho, 'Henry, Ninth Earl of Northumberland, and Syon House Middlesex, 1594–1632' *Transactions of the Ancient Monuments Society* new series iv (1956) 104

12   Longleat Archives: R.O.B., i & ii

13   Cambridge University Library: Hengrave Hall Deposit 80

14   B. Stallybrass, 'Bess of Hardwick's Buildings and Building Accounts' *Archaeologia* lxiv (1913) 359

15   For the house at Great Bedwyn see J. E. Jackson, 'Wulfhall and the Seymours' *Wiltshire Archaeological Magazine* xv (1875), 178–186; for the remainder of Somerset's building, see British Museum: Egerton MSS 2815

16   For Salisbury House see *Survey of London, xviii, The Strand* (1937) pp. 120–3; for the New Exchange see L. Stone, 'Inigo Jones and the New Exchange', *Archaeological Journal* cxiv (1957) 106–21; for Hatfield House see L. Stone, 'The Building of Hatfield House', *ibid* cxii (1955) 100–28

17   N. Briggs, 'The Foundation of Wadham College, Oxford' *Oxoniensia* xxi (1956) 67–8

18   *The Architecture of Sir Roger Pratt* ed. R. T. Gunther (Oxford 1928) p. 48

19   Girouard, *Smythson* p. 54

20   Longleat Archives: R.O.B., iii, 161. William Spicer to the Earl of Leicester, 15 July 1571

21   Nottingham University Library: Mi A 60 /1–7. For the other details of his career, and that of John and Huntingdon Smythson, see Girouard

22   J. Summerson, 'Three Elizabethan Architects' *Bulletin of the John Rylands Library* xl (1957) 201

23   *Ibid* 216

24   *The Book of Architecture of John Thorpe* ed. J. Summerson (Walpole Society xl, 1966) p. 11

25   *The Account Book of Nicholas Stone* ed. W. L. Spiers (Walpole Society vii, 1919) pp. 70, 10, & 11

26   A. Oswald, *Country Houses of Dorset* (2nd edition London 1959) pp. 25–30

27   Dorset County Record Office: MW /M4 f. 24v

28   William Salt Library, Stafford: D1721 /1 /4; Shrewsbury Public Library: Deeds 6885

29   Mrs Baldwyn-Childe, 'The Building of the Manor-House of Kyre Park, Worcestershire' *The Antiquary* xxi–ii (1890)

30   Willis and Clark, ii, 475n

31   J. Evans, 'Extracts from the Private Account Book of Sir William More of Loseley . . .' *Archaeologia* xxxvi (1855) 284–310

32   Staffordshire County Record Office: D593 R /1 /2

33   Bedfordshire County Record Office: TW 818

34   D. Knoop and G. P. Jones, 'The Carreglwyd Building Account, 1636' *Transactions of the Anglesey Antiquarian Society* (1934) 27–43

35   D. Knoop and G. P. Jones, 'The Bolsover Castle Building Account for 1613' *Ars Quatuor Coronatorum* xlix (1939) 24–80

36   H. L. Bradfer-Lawrence, 'The Building of Raynham Hall' *Norfolk Archaeology* xxiii, pts. 1 and 2 (1927) 93–146

37   British Museum: Additional MSS 39832

38   J. Dent, *Quest for Nonsuch* (London 1962) p. 261

39   *The Chronicle of Calais* (Camden Society 1846) p. 17

40   W. L. Rutton, 'Sandgate Castle, A.D. 1539–1540' *Archaeologia Cantiana* xx (1893) 228–57

41 Public Record Office: E101/483/16

42 Salzman, pp. 37—9

43 J. E. Jackson, 'Wulfhall and the Seymours' *Wiltshire Archaeological Magazine* xv (1875) 181

44 British Museum: Egerton MSS 2815

45 J. Dent, *Quest for Nonsuch* (London 1962) pp. 263—4

46 Rutton, *op cit*

47 Public Record Office: E101/483/16

48 Willis and Clark, ii, 198

49 *Ibid* 469—70

50 Longleat Archives: R.O.B., i, 117. Thynne to Dodd, 18 June 1547

51 Salzman, p. 575

52 *Records of the Worshipful Company of Carpenters* ii, 155

53 P. S. Spokes and E. M. Jope, 'The Priory, Marcham, Berkshire', *Berkshire Archaeological Journal* lvii (1959) 93—4

54 L. Stone, 'Inigo Jones and the New Exchange' *Archaeological Journal* cxiv (1957) 114

55 William Salt Library, Stafford: D1721/1/4

56 Mrs Baldwyn-Childe, 'The Building of the Manor-House of Kyre Park, Worcestershire' *The Antiquary* xxi—ii (1890)

57 J. Evans, 'Extracts from the Private Account Book of Sir William More of Loseley . . .' *Archaeologia* xxxvi (1855) 296

58 J. A. Gotch, 'The Renaissance in Northamptonshire' *Transactions of the Royal Institute of British Architects* vi, new series (1890) 105

59 Longleat Archives: R.O.B., ii, 31. Sharington to Thynne, 25 June 1553

60 *Ibid* R.O.B., i, 135. Thynne to Dodd, 21 June 1547

61 Sandeen, *op cit* p. 40

62 *Ibid* p. 186

63 Dorset County Record Office: MW/M4 f. 23

64 Staffordshire County Record Office: D593 R/1/2

65 G. R. Batho, 'The Percies at Petworth, 1574—1632' *Sussex Archaeological Collections* xcv (1957) 14

66 Essex County Record Office: D/DP A22

67 J. Evans, *op cit* 296

68 British Museum: Additional MSS 39832

69 Essex County Record Office: D/DP A19

70 Willis and Clark, ii, 571

71 Staffordshire County Record Office: D593 R/1/2

72 B. Stallybrass, 'Bess of Hardwick's Buildings and Building Accounts', *Archaeologia* lxiv (1913) 378

73 Longleat Archives: R.O.B., ii, 87. Cavendish to Thynne, 30 March (1555?)

74 *Ibid* ii, 129. Elizabeth St. Loe to Thynne, 25 April 1560

75 Girouard, *Smythson* pp. 75 and 77

76 A. Oswald, *Country Houses of Dorset* (2nd edition, London 1959) p. 26

77 H. A. Tipping, 'Condover Hall, Shropshire' *Country Life* xliii (1918) 513

78 Stallybrass, *op cit* 352 & 356

79 J. W. Burgon, *The Life and Times of Sir Thomas Gresham* (London 1831) ii, 257

80 E. R. Sandeen, 'The Building of Redgrave Hall, 1545—54' *Proceedings of the Suffolk Institute of Archaeology* xxix, pt. 1 (1961) 23

81 Dorset County Record Office: MW/M4 f, 24v

82 Cranfield Papers. Quoted in J. Harris, 'A History of the Burlington-Devonshire Collection & an Analysis of the English Drawings' (typescript catalogue of the collection in the R.I.B.A. Library, 1969) p. 90

83 Girouard, *Smythson* pp. 80—1

84 Longleat Archives: R.O.B., iii, 61

85   Mrs Baldwyn-Childe, 'The Building of the Manor-House of Kyre Park, Worcestershire', *The Antiquary* xxi (1890) 202–5. The masons had probably been working at Weston Hall, Warwickshire, for Ralph Sheldon whose steward, R. Richmond, had travelled to Kyre earlier in the month

86   S. D. Kitson, 'The Heraldic Glass of Gilling Castle, Yorkshire, and Bernard Dinninghof' *Journal of the British Society of Master Glass Painters* iii (1929) 55–8

6 Preparation of the Work

The preparation of the site and the accumulation of materials were frequently put in hand before the builder had considered the design of his projected building or begun to recruit the bulk of his labour force. Sir Edward Pytts, who paid 40*s* in December 1588 'To John Symons of London for drawing my first platt for my house' and who had only begun to recruit workmen in the autumn of that year, recorded in his notebook that he 'Began to provide Stone Brick Timber Wainscott, and other necessaries ... anno Domini 1586 ... mense Augusti', the same year that he had purchased the property. For the two years from 1586 the only building workmen that he employed were a mason and a labourer, engaged on opening up a quarry in the park and roughly dressing stone.[1] Similarly, Sir William More of Loseley, Surrey, spent the fourteen months from Michaelmas 1560 to Christmas 1561 accumulating stone and timber, digging sawpits, and burning bricks and lime. During that period his labour force consisted of a few stone-diggers, masons, carpenters, and labourers engaged on preparatory work

> 'for such buildynge as I made, viz. a bruehowse & ye stone wall goynge from the same to my mylkehowse, and the stone wale goyng ffrom my stable to the garden, as also my pricons [provisions] then had for my buldyng to cum'.   [2]

The documents relating to many other building projects of the period show a similar pattern of initial preparation. The accounts for Gawthorpe Hall, Lancashire, commence on 1 February 1600 with the opening up of stone pits, felling of timber, and purchase of tools and materials. It was early August before workmen began levelling the ground for the hall, and the 16th of that month before the first stone was laid.[3] The preparations for Harrold House, Bedfordshire, were begun in May 1608, but it was February 1610 before the labourers started the foundation work,[4] and in Shropshire, Thomas Owen began accumulating large quantities of building materials as soon as he acquired the manor of Condover in 1586, some twelve months before the 'trencheinge of the plott' was recorded in the accounts.[5]

A more detailed idea of the nature of the preparations carried out by the builder can be derived from the Bacon papers relating to Stiffkey Hall, Norfolk. Sir Nicholas Bacon bought the manor in 1571 for his son Nathaniel who was to be married the following year. In the autumn of 1573 Nathaniel and his bride moved from Norwich to the neighbouring manor of Cockthorpe, and preparations were put in hand for building. Already in March 1573 he had begun negotiating with the Dean and Chapter of Norwich for the purchase of timber from

Hindolveston Wood, near Melton Constable. In September the following year he obtained a twenty-one year lease of the oaks in the wood. In November 1575 one of his servants 'bowght for my lord and honor a gret bargenye of tymbere of Mr Gorge Thembetthorpe of Fellshme' which was already sawn into lengths and had been seasoned. In the following year Bacon bought more timber from his father-in-law, Sir Thomas Gresham. Thus by the time that he was ready to commence the actual building he had probably made arrangements for the provision of most of the timber that he would require. He had also been accumulating other basic materials from an early date. The house is largely constructed of brick, but he had initially determined to use stone for the dressings, and had accordingly sought to buy monastic stone from his neighbour, Edward Paston of Binham Priory. Meeting with a refusal from this source he bought a small amount of stone from Sir Henry Clinton and Christopher Wray. But the quantities that he was able to acquire were insufficient for his purposes so, inspired by the example of Clement Paston, the uncle of his neighbour, he altered his plans and used brick rendered with plaster for his dressings.

At the same time as he was accumulating materials, work was going ahead with the preparation of designs for the house. In April 1574 Sir Nicholas Bacon had written to his son asking for the exact measurements of the proposed site. The Lord Keeper had designs based on these measurements drawn up in London. In August of the following year he sent 'the plat that I drewe for Styfkey to the end that you showlde set out theise thinges followyng wch I cannot do by the instruccons I have alredy receyved'. By April of 1576 the plans were sufficiently corrected for Nicholas to return them to his son 'to thentent that they and the grownd may be compared together'. This was clearly the preliminary step to the laying out of the foundations, and in August the construction of the house was finally begun; some five years after the original purchase of the site.[6]

House building, of course, represented a large capital investment, and it was in the interest of the prospective builder to spend a considerable period of time in his preparatory arrangements to ensure that he got the best return on his outlay and avoided any serious delays during the course of construction. The absence of any documentary reference in particular building accounts to a period of preparation cannot be taken to imply a lack of preparation, but should perhaps rather be interpreted as an indication that separate accounts were only begun when the actual building work commenced. For it is impossible to imagine any country house being built without any preliminary accumulation of material or preparation of the site. Most of the major decisions concerning the general design, type of materials, and method of undertaking the work, must have been considered at length before the first sod was cut. A good deal of thought, too, must also have been given to the costing of the work, although it is difficult to see how this could have been achieved with any precision where the building was to be carried out by direct labour.

As Gerbier advised in 1662 'Builders ought to calculate the charge of their designed building, and especially with what sum of money they are willing to part'.[7] There is very little extant evidence from the 16th century to show how builders estimated the costs of their intended work. When in September 1578 Sir Nicholas Bacon expressed his intention to provide sufficient money to build a new chapel for Corpus Christi College, Cambridge, a rough plan was prepared, and on the basis of its dimensions estimates of the cost of the work were drawn up by working craftsmen. 'The charges of ye chappell as they were estemed by the artificers' came to £202 12s, but the basis of their estimation was thoroughly inadequate, excluding as it did such essential items as the wages of the labourers, and the cost of making the foundations. In addition, the plans were subsequently altered but the original estimate for the work continued to be adhered to. Needless to say, it was grossly exceeded.[8] Peculiar considerations applied to the Oxford and Cambridge colleges, for potential benefactors wished to know fairly precisely the extent of their financial liability, as when Fulke Greville wrote to the Master of Jesus College, Cambridge, in 1617 confirming his intention to finance the provision of new lodgings:

> 'Let me therfore entreat you, with all speed, fullie and particularly to enforme your selfe by some honest and skilfull workman what the charge will be of convertinge the west end of your Chappell into lodginge chambers. And I pray you send me a bill of all particulars, viz. of the precise height, length, and breadth of the platt; of the certayne number, cizes, and prices of the Sommers, Juistes, and Bordes . . . for the floores; of the transomes and studdes for the partitions; of the lights with theyr irons, casements, and glasse; of bricke for chimneyes, and all other materialles, with the severall charges of the workmanshippe.' [9]

Domestic builders seem to have been less concerned with a precise costing of their work. It is probable that this was partly due to their method of financing their building out of current revenue over an indeterminate period of time, the overall cost being subordinate to the amount of money readily available at any given moment. In addition, for some builders, such as the builders of the prodigy houses, considerations of cost were clearly secondary to the powerful motives that inspired them to build in the way that they did.[10] Estimates were certainly made for the purposes of calculating the amount of materials necessary in subsequent years, such as that for bricks at Hatfield,[11] and for lead at Redgrave,[12] but there is very little evidence for the preliminary costing of the total work, although there are occasional examples of specific jobs being costed while the work was in progress, as at Burghley in 1564 when the mason was instructed to

> 'make a profe of v foote square, what the chardges wilbe, to take ye grounde out of yor garden to the loones [lowness] of the flower in yor lower gallerie, so as you may have an estimate of the rest . . .' [13]

However, by the 17th century there seems to have been a growing awareness of the benefits of adequate costing, which can possibly be related to the emergence of specialised building surveyors who must invariably have been expected to have been capable of preparing estimates with a reasonable degree of accuracy. This is certainly the implication behind Chancery proceedings instituted by George Luttrell against the surveyor and mason William Arnold in 1619. Luttrell was claiming against Arnold for the unsatisfactory way in which he had fulfilled an agreement made in 1617 to oversee the work at Dunster Castle, Somerset, and part of the indictment was that work originally estimated at £462 was now likely to amount to £1,200.[14] A contributory factor must have been the growing acceptance of piece work as a desirable method of working, which enabled preliminary estimates based on quantities to be made. The only document of any length relating to the costing of a proposed building enterprise that survives from the period under discussion was only able to achieve its remarkably precise calculations by assuming that the materials were to be worked on a piece rate basis. It was drawn up in 1615 by the principal carpenter and a leading household official of the Earl of Northumberland when the Earl was contemplating building a palatial new house at Petworth, a project which he subsequently abandoned in favour of extensions to the existing house. Their calculations, based 'according to a Plotte thereof and directions therunto given by the said Earle', cover some eleven pages of detailed analysis before they arrive at the exact sum of £25,572 18s 4d for the total work. Significantly they emphasise that,

'wheras wee make computacon as the rates of all matterialls may be now bought, hearafter may be risen and therfore to trust at all tymes to nothing but quantitie which wee thinck to be true'.

It is a most impressive document, of which a sample entry relating to the ashlar work for the gatehouse towers must suffice to give an indication of the thoroughness with which they carried out their task:

'The working of 4736 foote of Ashler at iiii*d*. the foote beinge the six inches surface of those towres with the Battlements at iiii*d*. the foote, lxxviii *li*. vi*s*.
The stones for the rough wale of 325 rodd 486 loades, the digginge and caringe at x*d*. ye Loade. xx *li*. v *s*.
The sixe inches Ashelere wille take 95 loades digginge and caryinge at xviii *d*. the loade, vii *li*. ii *s*. vi *d*.
Both which will require 116 loade of Lyme at ix *s*. iiii *d*. a Loade, liiii *li*. ii *s*. viii *d*.
And of sande for the same lyme 560 at vi *d*. the loade digginge and caryinge xii *li*. x *s*.' [15]

Northumberland is known to have taken great care over the preparations for his building work. The letter that he wrote to Cecil in 1603 expressing his intention, 'now that I am a builder', to visit 'Copthall . . . Tibballs . . . and every place of mark where curiosities are used' was not just a gratuitous compliment to Cecil's own building, for in the same year his carpenter was indeed sent to look at Theobalds, and bound together with the Petworth estimates of 1615 are a collection of notes on the sizes of the main rooms of ten important contemporary buildings and a memorandum on 'materialls for buildinge'.[16] For his work at Syon earlier in the century, Northumberland had been amongst the first English builders to have used architectural models, and his correspondence with his officials and friends throughout the country regarding the right choice of materials still survives.[17] Amongst his papers preserved at Syon are some undated calculations in his own hand for rebuilding the wine cellar at Petworth at a cost of £97 17s 6d, using 50,000 bricks.[18]

From the evidence that is available, it is clear that Northumberland was an exceptionally well-prepared builder but it is highly improbable that he was alone amongst his contemporaries in taking adequate precautions before actually commencing to build. However, there must still have been builders in the 17th century who rashly embarked on their work without sufficient preparations, for as late as 1672 Sir Roger Pratt was able to write,

> 'How though it cannot well be supposed that any rational man should put himself upon building without having first made in his purse some competent provision, yet are the examples but too many of the sufferings of those who have not first laboured to make of their expenses some near calculation . . .' [19]

Although the preliminary planning must have been of paramount importance it was still necessary to exercise a considerable degree of forethought in the advance preparation of material throughout the course of the work. A lack of sufficient materials at any particular point could lead to an underemployment of parts of the labour force and consequently added expense. It was specifically written into the contract of 1547 between Sir Richard Edgecumbe and Roger Palmer for the building of Mount Edgcumbe, Cornwall, that Sir Richard was

> 'by the warnyng of xii dayes to have in redynes all maner of stuff necessary or for lake of suche preparation the seyd Roger and hys company shall have from tyme to tyme their Jorney Wages as they use to take of other men'. [20]

At St John's College, Cambridge, in 1598, where it was the contractors' responsibility to provide materials, they were bound to have accumulated sufficient material on the site by the beginning of August each year for the whole of the following year's work,[21] and the two masons who were making windows for Thorpe Hall, Northamptonshire, in 1653 were bound by a clause in their contract to deliver them from time to time at the site so that building 'shall not at any time be hindered for want of ye sd: windowes'.[22]

The instructions that Sir Thomas Tresham issued to his steward in the autumn of 1597 make explicit some of the reasons for stock-piling materials in advance. He ordered as much stone as possible to be got from the quarries while the weather held so that in the following spring building could begin four to six weeks before the state of the ground would allow carts to be used, and he also instructed his steward to ensure that there were always sufficient jambs and other works of freestone in store for eight weeks use, otherwise the freemasons would·in summer 'loyter and linger out ther worke to needless charge and encumbrance many ways'.[23] As a result of the weather, construction work usually came to a halt during the worst of the winter months, but with the sort of planning shown by Tresham the effects of this could be minimised. However, if building was to make a prompt start as soon as the weather improved, and if craftsmen were to be able to prepare their materials under cover while the weather was still bad, it was essential that sufficient quantities of materials had been accumulated before the winter had set in. Consequently, Bernard Dinninghof, in his letter of October 1618 to Thomas Lumsden offering to rebuild Sheriff Hutton Castle, Yorkshire, advised that,

> 'if you be aminded to build I would set on in the quarry to get stone for window stones and hew the same this winter against the spring', [24]

and at Old Thorndon Hall, Essex, sand was being dug in October 1580 'in redynes agaynste the next yeare'.[25] In October 1547, Sir John Thynne wrote at length to his steward with instructions for preparing against the winter. They included a request for him to enlist the aid of Thynne's friends during the present fine weather to carry stone to Longleat from the quarries in readiness for the next year, and to ensure that sufficient laths were made during the winter so that a plasterer could be employed at the beginning of the following year.[26]

In the early weeks of the new building season there was not always sufficient construction work to occupy the assembled labour force, especially if the weather was poor. The situation could be alleviated by putting the craftsmen to work on preparing materials only if there were sufficient materials already in store on the site. Thus William Cecil's steward at Burghley was able to write to him on 16 May 1562 'yor masons sence they came have ben yet hetherto onestlye occupied in making reyde of suche stone as is nedfull furste to be ocupied'.[27]

Where work on a particular building was continuously in progress over a number of years much of the material was probably accumulated well in advance of its use, being acquired as the availability of the material and the finance allowed. Sir John Petre, who had begun to remodel Old Thorndon Hall, Essex, in 1573, bought the slate for the roof of his banqueting house in 1587 although he did not actually use it until 1594[28] and Sir Thomas Smith who began rebuilding Hill Hall, Essex, in 1568 refers in his will of 1576 to 'all the brick, timber, chalk, sand and all other stuff that I have prepared' for the house.[29]

6 Notes

1   Mrs Baldwyn-Childe, 'The Building of the Manor-House of Kyre Park, Worcestershire, 1588—1618' *The Antiquary* xxi (1890) 202—5

2   J. Evans, 'Extracts from the Private Account Book of Sir William More of Loseley. . .' *Archaeologia* xxxvi (1855) 296

3   *The House and Farm Accounts of the Shuttleworths* ed. J. Harland (Chetham Society xxxv 1856) pp. 126—30

4   Bedfordshire County Record Office: TW 818

5   Shrewsbury Public Library: Deeds 6883

6   Sandeen, p. 157 *et seq*

7   Sir Balthazar Gerbier, *A Brief Discourse Concerning the Three Chief Principles of Magnificent Building. viz. Solidity, Conveniency, and Ornament* (London 1662) p. 26

8   E. R. Sandeen, 'The Building of the Sixteenth-Century Corpus Christi College Chapel' *Proceedings of the Cambridge Antiquarian Society* lv (1961) 23—35

9   Willis and Clark, ii, 172

10 See, for example, the abandonment of the economy measures proposed at Hatfield in 1609. L. Stone, 'The Building of Hatfield House' *Archaeological Journal* cxii (1955) 115—6

11 *Ibid* 107n

12 Sandeen, pp. 318—9

13 J. A. Gotch, 'The Renaissance in Northamptonshire' *Transactions of the Royal Institute of British Architects* new series vi (1890) 108

14 H. C. Maxwell Lyte, *A History of Dunster* (London 1909) ii, 366

15 G. R. Batho, 'Notes and Documents on Petworth House, 1574—1632' *Sussex Archaeological Collections*, xcvi (1958) 113—29

16 *Ibid* 108 & 109
17 G. R. Batho, 'Henry, Ninth Earl of Northumberland and Syon House, Middlesex, 1594–1632' *Transactions of the Ancient Monuments Society* new series iv (1956) 102–4
18 G. R. Batho, 'The Percies at Petworth, 1574–1632' *Sussex Archaeological Collections* xcv (1957) 16
19 *The Architecture of Sir Roger Pratt* ed. R. T. Gunther (Oxford 1928) p. 46
20 Cornwall County Record Office: Mt. Edgcumbe MS MTD /48 /10
21 Willis and Clark, ii, 253
22 British Museum: Additional MSS 25302 f. 153
23 Historic Manuscripts Commission, *Various* iii, p. li
24 S. D. Kitson, 'The Heraldic Glass of Gilling Castle, Yorkshire, and Bernard Dinninghof' *Journal of the British Society of Master Glass Painters* iii (1929) 55–8
25 Essex County Record Office: D /DP A 19
26 Longleat Archives: R.O.B., I, 287–9. Thynne to Dodd, 2 October 1547
27 J. A. Gotch, 'The Renaissance in Northamptonshire' *Transactions of the Royal Institute of British Architects* new series vi (1890) 106
28 Essex County Record Office: D /DP A 20 & A 22
29 J. Strype, *The Life of the learned Sir Thomas Smith* (Oxford 1820) p. 171

7 Aspects of Construction

Although this book is not primarily concerned with the technology of the building industry, there are important aspects connected with the construction work that have to be examined. In particular, it is necessary to consider how detailed technical information about the design of a house was communicated to the ordinary workmen who were entrusted with its execution. In their various writings, Sir Henry Wotton, Sir Roger Pratt and Sir Balthazar Gerbier all laid particular emphasis on the necessity of making a wooden or pasteboard model of the building before the work should begin, but there is little evidence for any widespread use of architectural models in England during the 16th and early 17th centuries. The earliest documentary mention of the construction of a model was by a French joiner for Longleat in 1568.[1] It seems probable that this was in conscious imitation of current continental practice. Robert Adams, later to become Surveyor of the Royal Works, possibly made a model for the Earl of Southampton's house at Dogmersfield, Hampshire, sometime before 1581, but there are no other examples known from the 16th century.[2] Models for details, such as staircases and roofs, became more frequent in the following century, but there are still very few known for complete buildings.[3] Ralph Symons probably made one for the hall of Trinity College, Cambridge, in 1604,[4] and Inigo Jones was paid for making two models for the Queen's House at Greenwich during the accounting period, 1616–18, and for the Banqueting House in 1619,[5] but the only documented model made for a country house was in 1622 when a mason and a joiner made one for Sir Roger Townshend's house at Raynham, Norfolk.[6] Even the few models that are known to have been made in England were primarily intended to solve details of planning and to show the clients what their completed work would look like, and would not have been of any real value in communicating precise technical information to the stonecutters and masons.

Detailed written specifications, such as were incorporated in a number of building contracts of the period, would have been useful in providing the contractor with a general conception of the work that he was to carry out. The contract with John Atkinson for the Legge Building at Gonville and Caius College, Cambridge, in 1618, for example, contains sufficient instructions for the erection of the shell of the building,[7] but it nevertheless omits any mention of such details as the mouldings, and precise measurements for features like the sills and the jambs. A similar criticism can be made against all the other written specifications that survive. Where these specifications were combined with plans and drawings, as in the contract of 1586 for Woollavington, Sussex,[8] their usefulness was considerably increased, but they still failed to

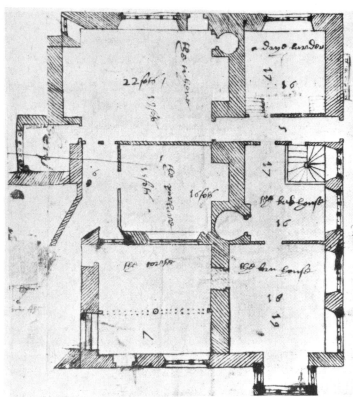

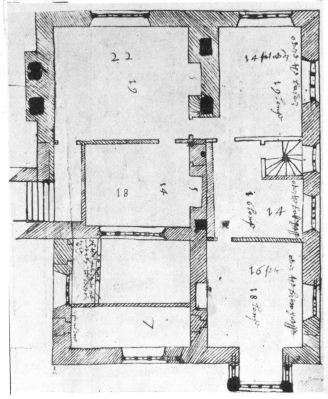

Ground and first-floor plans attached to a building
contract of 1586 for Woollavington, Sussex

provide the necessary detailed technical information. None of the surviving plans and elevations could have been used as blue-prints for construction, for they rarely show more than the most general overall dimensions, and omit entirely the detailed measurements and such essential information as the jointings of the stones and precise details of the mouldings. The function of many of the drawings was clearly similar to that of the architectural models; they were made to give some indication of how the building would look. But it must be remembered that these were the drawings that were most likely to survive, for generally they were the presentation copies intended for show and not subject to continual handling on the site. On the other hand, there is no evidence from those that survive to suggest that the working drawings appreciably differed in the amount of information that they contained.

Despite the objections that have been made about their usefulness as complete blue-prints, however, it is evident that they fulfilled a practical function in the building process. They were used, for example, in costing the proposed work and calculating the necessary quantities of materials, as John Smythson's annotated drawings for the marble room at Bolsover graphically illustrate.[9] They were also used on the site for the laying out of the foundations. Sir Nicholas Bacon sent the plans for Stiffkey Hall to Norfolk in April 1576 'to thentent that they and the grownd may be compared together',[10] and in 1549 one of the Duke of Somerset's agents at Wulfhall in Wiltshire wrote to Sir John Thynne that he would

'trace and set forth my lords grace's house according to the plat which my lord's grace resolved upon the last time, and so be ready to lay the foundation'.   [11]

Furthermore, drawings were made of separate features such as windows and panelling, and, although few of these have survived, there are sufficient documentary references to show that they were used as working guides by the craftsmen. This is evident from the references to 'plattes' for battlements, pinnacles, and vaults in the masons' contracts for King's College Chapel, Cambridge, in 1512 and 1513,[12] and from a contract whereby the joiner at Chatsworth, Derbyshire, was 'to seall the . . . parloure . . . according to a patterne drawne for the same'.[13] Similar examples could be cited for masons making windows, carpenters framing roofs, and even painters concerned with interior decoration. The important part played by drawings in the execution of the work is emphasised by a letter that Sir Thomas Gresham wrote to Lord Burghley in February 1568 informing him that

'Henricke hath lost the patrone of the pillors for your galerie in the country, so, he can procede no further in the workinge thereof, untill he have another'.   [14]

So despite the apparent deficiencies of contemporary drawings, they clearly were used in connection with construction work, and it follows that the details they lack were provided in other ways. Mouldings seem to have been made by providing the craftsmen with full-size templates from which to work; a practice which had been in use throughout the medieval period, and which was to continue well after the end of the period under consideration. The templates, or 'moulds', were usually drawn out by the surveyor or master craftsmen, or whoever had been appointed to oversee the technical details of the design. When Nicholas Stone contracted to build Cornbury Park, Oxfordshire, in 1631, it was stipulated that he was to direct the workmen, and to make all their moulds,[15] and at Raynham Hall, Norfolk,

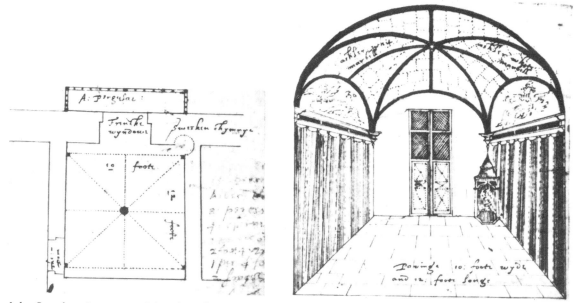

John Smythson's annotated drawings for the marble room at Bolsover Castle, Derbyshire

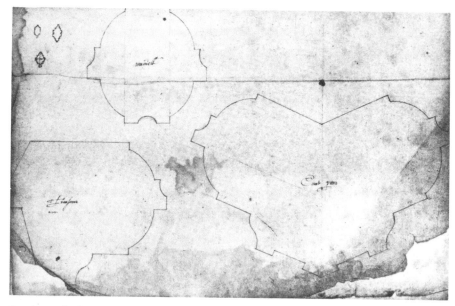

Sections of mouldings drawn full-size by John Thorpe

William Edge, the principal mason, was engaged in July 1621 on drawing 'patterns for mowld'.[16] The sort of drawings that they made must have been similar to the sections and profiles in the Thorpe Collection.[17] These were then made up into templates, usually by a joiner, but occasionally by workmen in the crafts concerned. The moulds at Raynham were made of oak, but it was more common for them to be made of deal. A few were made from pasteboard[18] or paper.[19] They were employed by masons, carpenters, plasterers, bricklayers, and even, on occasion, by plumbers. Once a set of moulds for a particular feature had been made, they could be used for similar features in other parts of the building, and there is even evidence that they were used on other buildings. When a plasterer was hired to work at Old Thorndon Hall, Essex, in 1577, the carriage of his moulds to the site was paid for,[20] and in 1575 Nathaniel Bacon expressed his intention of borrowing the moulds that Clement Paston had used for the windows of his house in Norfolk to use as models for the work at Stiffkey.[21]

Additional technical information could have been supplied to the workmen by verbal instructions from the surveyor or the leading craftsmen. Consequently the realisation of the design of a building was basically achieved through the supervisor of the work, who received his instructions from consultations with the builder and from written specifications and drawings, and who passed these on to the relevant workmen through working drawings, full-size templates, and by word of mouth. It was a method which relied for its success on close and continuous site supervision, and this partly explains the importance attached to the position of surveyor and was one of the factors responsible for the emergence towards the end of the 16th century of specialised building supervisors.

Given this method of working, it is apparent that work was begun on many buildings with only a very general conception of the finished design. This has already been suggested from some of the evidence relating to the process of design, and it can be inferred in other cases from documentary examples. One of the inherent dangers of working in this way was that insufficient initial planning could result in mistakes in the design of the building that would only become apparent when the construction was at an advanced stage, and the alterations necessary to rectify the fault could lead to considerable extra expense. Work on the Triangular Lodge for Sir Thomas Tresham was disrupted in October 1594 when the top floor had to be removed and set higher to allow of 'convement coveyance' of the stairs,[22] a basic mistake of planning that suggests that not enough care had been taken in the preparation of the initial design. In the following year it was decided that twelve decorative letters which had already been carved were too small, and they had to be discarded.[23]

Alterations while the work was in progress are frequently met with in the building accounts. Sometimes this was the result of a revision of the requirements of the builder caused by factors such as over expenditure, but more commonly they resulted from the imprecision of the initial planning procedures and the practice of improvising solutions to questions of detail as they arose. The design of Hatfield House, where work had commenced in August 1607, was altered in 1609 because of the Earl of Salisbury's mounting debts, but major revisions had already been made in 1608 and further alterations were carried out in 1610 as a result of the particular consideration of details of the plan and design. It appears that the detailed designs of the principal front at Hatfield were not commenced until as late as October 1609,[24] when work had already been in progress on the house for over two years. Alterations to the original design of Little Saxham Hall, Suffolk, for Thomas Lucas, took place in almost every year that the work was in progress, and ranged from raising the foundations by an extra foot in 1501, to enlarging the chapel in 1509 and 1510.[25]

In addition to the inconvenience and delays caused by alterations to the fabric while the work was in progress, the builder was also likely to incur additional expenditure. When Sir Richard Leveson decided to raise the height of three chimneys at Trentham Hall, Staffordshire, in 1635, he had to pay for the re-slating of part of the roof as well as for the actual work on the chimneys,[26] and the fellows of St. John's College, Cambridge, paid an extra £205 to their contractors in 1599 for altering the height of the buildings that they had commenced the previous year.[27] An endorsement on the contract of 1547 between Sir Richard Edgecumbe and Roger Palmer for the building of Mount Edgcumbe, specifically bound the former to pay for any extra work resulting from changes made to the initial plan,[28] but sometimes alterations seem to have been initiated by the building contractor or surveyor without authorisation from the person for whom the building was being constructed. William Arnold, the mason, agreed in 1617 to supply the designs and supervise the building at Dunster Castle, Somerset, for George Luttrell, but within two years the two parties were in dispute, Luttrell claiming that Arnold had so altered the original plans in execution, that work initially estimated at £462 was likely to cost £1,200.[29]

Although some examples of alterations carried out after the work had been begun can be attributed to the changing circumstances or the growing pretensions of the builders, such as those at Theobalds which, as Cecil wrote 'was begun by me with a mean measure but encrease by occasion of her Majesty's often coming',[30] many of the examples resulted directly from the method of working whereby the details of the design were only fully resolved on the site while the building was actually under construction. The architectural theorists of the 17th century were largely paraphrasing Italian and French practice in their advocation of the construction of models, but they were also suggesting a solution to what must have been a common problem; that of working out in three-dimensional terms the details of the design before commencing to build. It was a problem that was eventually to be solved by improvements in draughtsmanship and in the technical expertise of the building industry, but in 1660, the advice of Sir Roger Pratt must have been particularly appropriate:

'get a model of wood to be most exactly framed . . . . and as you shall then like it, so go on with your building, or change it till it please you, but resolve after you have once laid one stone never to alter your design, except it may be done without pulling down anything; for if you be once irresolute in that, your alterations may chance to cost you half as much as your whole building . . .' [31]

7 Notes

1 Longleat Archives: T.P. Box lxviii, Book 59, f. 59. The first payment to Adrian Gaunt, the joiner, was in December 1567 and the model seems to have been completed in June 1568. It is doubtful whether 'the frame' mentioned in a mason's contract of *circa* 1530 for Hengrave Hall, Suffolk, was anything more than a drawing or plan. Cambridge University Library: Hengrave Hall Deposit 81

2 Public Record Office: PROB 11/65/45. Will of Henry Wriothesley, 2nd Earl of Southampton, dated 29 June 1581, refers to the 'modell made by Adams . . . for the buildinge of the saide house'

3 At Syon House in 1602 the carpenter made a model for the staircase; G. R. Batho, 'Syon House: The First Two Hundred Years' *Transactions of the London and Middlesex Archaeological Society* xix (1958) 13. In Oxford a model was made of a proposed staircase to the library in 1632–4; I. G. Philip, 'The Building of the Schools Quadrangle' *Oxoniensia* xiii (1948) 47. During the alterations to Kirby Hall, Northamptonshire, a model for a staircase was made in 1639; *The Account Book of Nicholas Stone* ed. W. L. Spiers (Walpole Society vii, 1919) p. 125

4 Willis and Clark, ii, 475

5 G. H. Chettle, *The Queen's House, Greenwich* (14th Monograph of The London Survey Committee, 1937) p. 102: Public Record Office: SP 14/108, no. 55

6 H. L. Bradfer-Lawrence, 'The Building of Raynham Hall' *Norfolk Archaeology* xxiii (1927) 135

7 Willis and Clark, i, 206–8

8 W. H. Godfrey, 'An Elizabethan Builder's Contract' *Sussex Archaeological Collections* lxv (1924) 201–23

9 R.I.B.A. Library: drawings collection, Smythson Collection, III/1(2). I am grateful to Dr Mark Girouard for pointing out the significance of this drawing

10 Sandeen, p. 178

11 J. E. Jackson, 'Wulfhall and the Seymours' *Wiltshire Archaeological Magazine* xv (1875) 180

12 Willis and Clark, i, 608–13

13 B. Stallybrass, 'Bess of Hardwick's Buildings and Building Accounts' *Archaeologia* lxiv (1913) 357

14 J. W. Burgon, *The Life and Times of Sir Thomas Gresham* (London 1831) ii, 257

15 *The Account Book of Nicholas Stone* ed. W. L. Spiers (Walpole Society vii, 1919) p. 70

16 H. L. Bradfer-Lawrence, 'The Building of Raynham Hall' *Norfolk Archaeology* xxiii (1927) 128

17 Sir John Soane's Museum: Thorpe Collection T1–9. Illustrated in *The Book of Architecture of John Thorpe* ed. J. Summerson (Walpole Society xl, 1966) plates 1–4

18 Trentham Hall, Staffordshire; Staffordshire County Record Office: D593 R/1/2, 5 April 1634

19 Trinity College, Cambridge, 1566; Willis and Clark, ii, 570

20 Essex County Record Office: D/DP A 18

21 Sandeen, p. 189

22 British Museum: Additional MSS 39832, f. 26

23 *Ibid* f. 50

24 L. Stone, 'The Building of Hatfield House' *Archaeological Journal* cxii (1955) 114–8

25 British Museum: Additional MSS 7097, ff. 176v & 195v

26 Staffordshire County Record Office: D593 R/1/2 13 June 1635

27 Willis and Clark, ii, 155

28 Cornwall County Record Office: Mt. Edgcumbe MS MTD/48/10

29 H. C. Maxwell Lyte, *A History of Dunster* (London 1909) ii, 366

30 J. Nichols, *The Progresses and Public Processions of Queen Elizabeth* (London 1823) i, 205

31 *The Architecture of Sir Roger Pratt* ed. R. T. Gunther (Oxford 1928) pp. 60–1

8 Financing and Expenditure

It is necessary to exercise the greatest caution in drawing conclusions about comparative expenditure on building between 1500–1640. Because of the erratic methods of accounting it is never possible to be certain that the total outlay on a particular building had been recorded in the accounts that survive. Even when the documentation is apparently complete there is always the possibility that substantial items, especially materials, had been entered under a separate account. Occasionally, where the account for the last year of building survives, the accountant would make a general statement about the total cost of the work, such as that for Trentham Hall, Staffordshire, that

> 'The whole charge of all the worke for the building of the mannor house at Trentham with stables, barnes in the feilds and others neere the house & all other houses of office wth gardens, orchards & panns thereunto belonging wth conveyanse of water to all the houses of office, wch said workes began the twelfte day of june 1630 & ended the second of march 1638 as more at large may appeare by 3 severall bookes of Accompt subscribed wth Sr Richard Levesons owne hand now at this pr'sent delivered unto him—6165 *l* 17*s* 4*d*.' [1]

More frequently, however, the account abruptly stops with no clear indication that the fitting-out of the building had been fully completed. Consequently there are very few country houses for which the total building cost is definitely known. Even where summary accounts exist, it is inadvisable to accept them uncritically, as is shown by an examination of the entries relating to the Duke of Somerset's house of Wolfhall, near Great Bedwyn, Wiltshire, in the account roll of his Paymaster of the works. During the period from 1548 to 1551 the account records that only £45 6*s* 8¼*d* was spent on work at the house, of which sum almost a quarter was devoted to the purchase of nails and ironwork while less than £8 was paid in wages to the labourers.[2] However the fragments of correspondence that survive for 1549 from the Duke's agents and bailiffs in Wiltshire to Sir John Thynne reveal that in that year alone over five hundred and eighty-five acres for the estate were surveyed, enclosed and ditched; quarries were opened up, brick earth dug and brick-making begun; a conduit house and a brick conduit some one thousand, six hundred feet in length and fifteen feet in depth were constructed; the foundations of the house were laid, and the craftsmen working on the site included masons and bricklayers as well as brickmakers and lime-burners. The total labour force in May was in excess of two hundred and eighty men, and twenty carts were in use solely to serve the brickmakers.[3] Clearly a large part of the expenditure on Wolfhall failed to get recorded on the central Paymaster's summary account.

Given the unreliability of the available figures, and the incompleteness of the majority of accounts it is difficult to make any meaningful comparisons between individual expenditure on building at specific points during the period. It is clear that the court nobility spent a greater proportion of their resources in the late 16th century and the early 17th century on ostentatious building than their predecessors, but even at this level of society, it is difficult to substantiate this assertion with precise figures. In 1610 Robert Cecil, Earl of Salisbury, was in debt to the sum of £42,395,[4] and a large part of this must have been due to the building work that he was engaged upon in the first decade of the 17th century. Hatfield House alone cost him nearly £39,000 between 1607 and 1612, and during the same period he made extensive additions to Cranborne House in Dorset and built the New Exchange in London as well as continuing the work on Salisbury House, London, begun in 1599. Professor Stone has similarly attributed a large part of the responsibility for the debts of £46,000 left by the Earl of Winchester to his ambitious building at Basing and Chelsea.[5] The £200,000 that the Earl of Suffolk is reputed to have told King James I that he spent on building Audley End[6] was undoubtedly an exaggeration, but nevertheless the cost was probably in excess of that spent by Salisbury on Hatfield, and when Suffolk died in 1626 his estate was heavily encumbered with debt. Such excessive expenditure, however, was not universal amongst the aristocracy. The Earl of Northumberland for example abandoned his plans for building a new house at Petworth in 1615 on receipt of an estimate for the project in excess of £25,000. His landed income at the time was in the region of £11,000 per annum and the building could have been financed without much difficulty out of current revenue, but as his obligations included the composition of £11,000 on his fine in Star Chamber and dowries for two daughters, he contented himself with making less expensive additions to the existing house.[7] Northumberland's sympathy for the Catholic cause denied him any political ambition and consequently he seems to have had little incentive to build on a scale ruinous to his financial stability. In general it was established political figures and those seeking preferment who built the prodigy house.

Few houses of the nobility built before the reign of Elizabeth were conceived on such an excessive scale, and it is unlikely that their cost, as a proportion of the builder's estate, bore any comparative relation to that expended by later builders such as Burghley, Salisbury, and Suffolk. Precise details of expenditure are lacking, but the £994 spent between 1480 and 1484 by Lord Hastings on Kirby Muxloe Castle, Leicestershire, was well within his income over the same period.[8] He proclaimed his noble status by building in brick, a material almost unknown in the Midlands at the time, and not by a conspicuous display of size and costly decoration. In the first half of the 16th century the initiative in ostentatious building was taken by Henry VIII and few of his subjects were willing to compete. Lord Marney's grand mansion at Layer Marney in Essex got no further than the eight-storeyed gatehouse before work stopped with his death in 1523, and the inadvisability of building on a princely scale seems to have been one of the lessons drawn from the fall of Wolsey. Thomas Cromwell, signficantly, built nothing comparable with Wolsey's palaces in Whitehall and at Hampton.

The death of Henry VIII heralded the end of royal leadership in palatial building. The Duke of Somerset, principal minister during the minority of Edward VI, was responsible for the most impressive buildings of the middle of the century. During the period between 1548 and 1551 he spent at least £10,000 on Somerset House in the Strand and £5,000 on his country house at Syon in Middlesex, whilst a further £2,000 were spent on building at his other houses in Oxfordshire, Hampshire, Wiltshire and Berkshire.[9]

Elizabeth I, pre-occupied with restricting royal expenditure, built very little and positively encouraged the initiative in palatial building to remain with her leading ministers of state. William Cecil led the way with Burghley House and Theobalds, and some of his fellow peers were not slow to follow. At one stage his annual expenditure on Theobalds was well in excess of £2,000;[10] by the time that his son came to build Hatfield House under James I this figure was comfortably exceeded in every year that building was in progress. As has already been suggested, the building of noble palaces fit to entertain the monarch on summer progresses often left the builder deeply in debt. A growing awareness of the disastrous financial effects of ostentatious building combined with a decline in the practice of royal progresses under Charles I resulted in a greater restraint in the scale and opulence of noble building after the first quarter of the 17th century. The reduction of Crown patronage and the increasing isolation of the Court in the decade before the Civil War were further factors that tended to diminish the necessity for building in a way that was designed, in part at least, to secure preferment.

The general pattern of aristocratic expenditure on building during the period under consideration is fairly clear, even if the precise figures remain largely obscured. There was little ostentatious expenditure while the Crown was sensitive to anything that could be construed as personal rivalry in a field where it had consciously chosen to demonstrate its primacy; but once the dominant figure of Henry VIII had been succeeded by the minority of Edward VI and the parsimony of Elizabeth, the impetus, and ultimately the necessity, for lavish building passed to the leading courtiers and ministers of state. Noble expenditure on architecture reached its height in the early years of James I, but after about 1620 dramatically declined.

This pattern of expenditure was largely confined to the nobility and the politically ambitious courtiers, whom it must be emphasised, formed only a small proportion of the country house builders of the period. For the remainder there are few indications of a general rise in expenditure on building. The picture is necessarily incomplete. There are few figures available for the period up to the middle of the 16th century, and it must be remembered that there are too many variables involved for any precise parallels to be drawn between the expenditure on particular houses. Few of the houses for which accounts survive are strictly comparable in size, and this reservation is further complicated by the fact that only some accounts include payments for such things as food and drink for the work force, or estimated costs of material deriving from the builder's own estate, or the value of materials and carriage given by friends. In addition many of the accounts are incomplete and only a few of them contain entries relating to landscaping and the general clearing up of the site after the actual construction work had been completed. In the latter part of the 16th century and the early part of the 17th century the prevailing architectural fashion was for a wealth of applied decoration and

Hengrave Hall, Suffolk, on which Sir Thomas Kytson spent more than £3,500 between 1525 and 1539

Loseley House, Surrey, built in the 1560s for less than £1,700

this must have necessarily increased expenditure on building during that period. Individual expenditure also varied according to the availability of the chosen material. Should a material be sought that was not available locally, its expensive carriage to the site would have considerably increased the cost of the building; but on the whole the smaller country houses seem to have been built largely of local materials with only the small quantities used for special effects being brought great distances. This was the policy adopted by Sir John Petre when he rebuilt Old Thorndon Hall in Essex in the second half of the 16th century. He used local brick for the main shell of the house, but he bought small quantities of Purbeck stone from Dorset and Beer stone from Devon for special dressings, and he roofed his tiny banqueting house with Devon slate.[11]

Despite the almost infinite number of variables, the conclusions that can be cautiously drawn from the figures that remain are difficult to reconcile with the assertion of Professor Stone that there was a startling rise in building costs in the early 17th century that appears to have far outstripped the 'price revolution'.[12] The expenditure of a small minority of country house builders increased in that period, but there were particular social and political reasons for this which were unrelated to any rise in costs. Given the lack of reliable statistics it is only possible to comment on expenditure on building and not on comparative costs. Nevertheless, it is probable that there was an approximate relationship between the two. If the figures of the large prodigy houses are excluded, the general picture that is presented is of a fairly stable level of expenditure throughout the 16th century, with a noticable but by no means startling rise beginning around the second decade of the 17th century.

Little Saxham Hall, Suffolk, built between 1505 and 1514 by Sir Thomas Lucas, secretary to Jasper, Duke of Bedford, and subsequently Solicitor-General to Henry VIII, cost £1,425.[13] Sir Thomas Kytson, the London merchant, spent something over £3,500 between 1525 and 1539 on building his larger and more ambitious house at Hengrave in the same county,[14] while Redgrave Hall, also in Suffolk, built by Sir Nicholas Bacon when he was Solicitor to the Court of Augmentations, cost just over £1,250 between 1545 and 1554.[15] Bacon's rise in political prominence was reflected in his expenditure of £3,177 11s 9¼d on building Gorhambury House, Hertfordshire in 1563–1568.[16] However, during the same decade Sir William More, a highly experienced parliamentarian, Deputy Lieutenant and twice Sheriff of the county of Surrey, built Loseley House near Guildford for a recorded cost of only £1,660 19s 7½d.[17] Little credence can be attached to the enormous sum of £40,000 said to have been spent by Sir Henry Cheney on his house at Toddington, Bedfordshire, in the 1560s. The house itself no longer exists, but, judging by the sketch in the Thorpe Collection, it was not of exceptional size or opulence. No comparable figures are extant for country houses built in the 1570s and 1580s, but it is instructive that when William Dickenson, bailiff to the Earl of Shrewsbury, built himself a house in Sheffield between 1575 and 1576 it cost him less than £50,[18] and in the 1590s Sir Thomas Tresham spent less than £1,000 on his extensive minor building works in Northamptonshire.[19] In the 17th century it was still possible to build a country house of moderate size for a comparatively small sum, as the incomplete accounts for Harrold House, Bedfordshire, show. During the two years between 1608 and 1610 when the shell of the house was erected, Francis Farrar spent little over £160 on the work.[20]

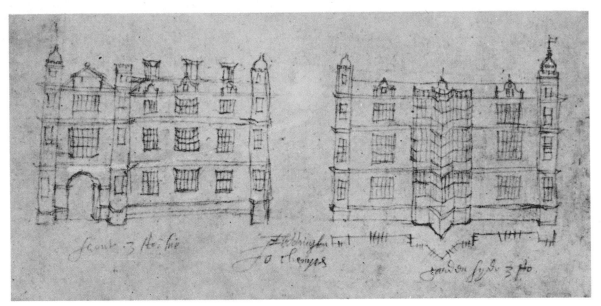

Toddington, Bedfordshire, improbably said to have cost £40,000

Harrold House, Bedfordshire, largely erected between 1608 and 1610 for little more than £160. Now demolished

The cost of larger houses, however, had almost certainly risen. The accounts for 1619–22 show the expenditure of £3,500 on Raynham Hall, Norfolk for Sir Roger Townshend,[21] while a contemporary estimate of the cost of building Fountains Hall, Yorkshire in the second decade of the century, was £3,000.[22] Between 1602 and 1607, a similar sum was spent on building Ashley Park, Surrey,[23] and Irmingland Hall, Norfolk, built at about the same time, was said to have cost Sir Nathaniel Bacon £3,991.[24] Sir John Strode built himself a house at Chantmarle in Dorset for £1,142, but this sum excluded 'much stone, many timber trees, and a very great number of carraiges of stones'.[25] Trentham Hall, Staffordshire, built between 1630 and 1639, cost Sir Richard Leveson just over £6,000,[26] and Sir Basil Dixwell spent £8,000 by his own account on building Broome Park, Kent, between 1635 and 1638.[27] In 1638–40 the addition of a new wing and the building of a splendidly decorated coach-house and stable block at Holland House, Kensington, cost £6,584 9s 4d. These figures suggest an appreciable rise in expenditure in the 1630s, but even so they are only approximately twice the sum spent by Sir Thomas Kytson a century earlier, and as late as 1669 Sir Roger Pratt was able to build a handsome if modest house for himself for £2,800.[28] There clearly was a rise in building expenditure in the 17th century, but it is equally clear that it was nowhere near as steep as the general rise in food prices.

The money expended on building was one of the largest capital sums laid out by the majority of country house builders. The estates of a few noble families were plunged into debt as a result of building, but for the builder of the smaller country house the consequences were rarely so disastrous The heaviest expenditure on building usually took place in the first few years of the work, when large quantities of material were assembled, the executive labour force set up, and the shell of the building begun. At Trentham Hall, Staffordshire, for example, where the total expenditure between 1630 and 1639 was £6,165 17s 4d, the sum laid out in the first three years was £2,817 8s 2d, or nearly half the total.[29] With foresight it was possible to mitigate the difficulty of raising sufficient funds for the initial expenditure. If materials had been stockpiled for some years prior to starting work, or if surplus profits had been accumulated for the purpose, then the estate of the builder would not have been subject to undue strain when building began. Such advance planning, however, was probably rarely thorough enough to obviate the need for a certain amount of short-term manipulation of the resources of the builder. Leases would have to be granted for low rents and large entry fines, woodlands farmed, and rent charges sold to raise extra capital, and the prospective builder would call in any money that he might have out on loan. In 1668, when Sir Roger Pratt was considering rebuilding his house at Ryston, Norfolk, he wrote a memorandum to himself

'To see what moneys I have out & to consider well in what hands, & to adjust all interest due to mee, & to speedily call in what moneys I shall think fitt for my intended building.'   [30]

Following the accumulation of sufficient funds to meet the initial expenditure, many builders seem to have been largely successful in financing the bulk of their works out of current revenue. Special conditions, again, apply to the ostentatious courtier houses where excessive expenditure made deep inroads into capital, but the majority of builders appear to have allocated certain items from their annual income for building expenses and the amount of work executed in that year would be fairly loosely related to the product of those items. Sir Thomas Tresham largely organised the financing of his building work in this fashion. In 1594, for example, he set aside £112 18s 10d made up of certain rents and the proceeds of selling timber and livestock, to pay for his work on the Triangular Lodge.[31] His expenditure over the same period was £114 6s 10½d, leaving a deficit of only £1 8s 0½d to be made up from other sources.[32] The pattern of his expenditure seems to have varied little in subsequent years, with much of the finance for his various building works being provided by rent money supplemented by the occasional sale of superfluous materials,[33] horses,[34] sheep,[35] and on one occasion a cottage.[36] Sir Francis Willoughby used his resources in a similar way in the 1580s when he largely financed the building of Wollaton Hall, Nottinghamshire, out of the income from his rents and coalmines.[37] In the building accounts for 1586 for example, receipts, including over £600 for 'collmoney', were in excess of £1,700 while the recorded disbursments totalled just over £990.

Few of the builders of smaller country houses had a surplus income as large as that of Sir Francis Willoughby, and the amount of money that they would have been able to put into their building every year must have been comparatively small. It was probably as a result of limited investment capital that many of the buildings that they erected took so long to complete. Chantmarle in Dorset was begun in April 1612, but it was 1623 before the work was finished; the modest Redgrave Hall, built at the outset of Sir Nicholas Bacon's career, took nearly ten years to complete; and Sir Thomas Tresham spent four years building the minute Triangular Lodge at Rushton. It usually took something like ten years to build a small country house, whereas, by way of contrast, the Earl of Salisbury's mansion at Hatfield was built, and the gardens laid out, within five years of the work commencing. It was certainly technically feasible to build at a faster rate, and given the domestic inconvenience while building was in progress, it was probably highly desirable to do so. Several factors could have been responsible for the slow pace of erection. The shortage of skilled building craftsmen has already been mentioned, and this clearly would have been reflected in the speed with which the less influential builders were able to build. However, a more important limitation was probably that imposed by the amount of money available from year to year. The annual income of the builder was liable to fluctuate, and where the building was being financed out of current revenue, the effects of this would be apparent in the accounts. At Loseley, Sir William More spent approximately £180 and £220 respectively on the first two years of building, but for the next three years, between 1563 and 1566, his annual expenditure dropped to an average of £65. In 1567 his expenditure rose to £292 and it remained around that higher level for the final two years of the work.[38] In default of any other evidence, the drastic fall in expenditure at such a crucial stage of the work could be reasonably explained by a reduction in his income over the same period. A similar explanation can be postulated at Redgrave where Sir Nicholas Bacon's expenditure in 1548 dropped to £101 following the outlay of £268 in the previous year, but rose again to £170 in 1550 and £200 in 1551.[39] Although many of the accounts are uninformative on the method by which the work was financed, it would seem a reasonable assumption that where progress was slow and the annual expenditure was subject to otherwise inexplicable fluctuations the building was probably being financed largely out of current revenue.

Throughout the period, few builders seem to have made use of commercial loans to help finance their work. There are no examples of money borrowed at interest being employed on any of the surviving 16th-century accounts, and the very few examples from the 17th century are for comparatively small amounts and date from well into the century. In the early years of his work at Trentham, Staffordshire, when his expenditure was at its highest, Sir Richard Leveson was using two separate loans of £200 to help finance the building. He paid the interest on the loans at six-monthly intervals, at the statutory rate of 8 per cent per annum. By the Summer of 1633 he had paid off one of the loans, but the remaining loan was continued until January 1635.[40] The £400 that he was borrowing in 1633 was equal to a third of his total expenditure in that year, and it seems likely that he was using it in an attempt to finish the building at a faster rate than his ordinary resources would allow. By the end of 1635, when he was no longer borrowing extra capital, he had paid off the majority of his masons and carpenters, and the fitting out of the building over the next four years proceeded at a more leisurely pace. Sir Roger Pratt also borrowed money to assist him in the rebuilding of Ryston Hall, Norfolk. The exact details of the transaction are unknown, but in 1670 he owed £20 in 'Interest money to Piggot & Grene'.[41] It is uncertain what period this interest covered, but as the total cost of the house was only £2,800, it is unlikely that the capital borrowed was very large.[42] Pratt, himself, had lent £1,300 at interest in 1650 to his relative Sir George Pratt, to enable him to build Coleshill House, Berkshire.[43]

The difficulties of raising sufficient capital were solved for a few builders by generous gifts from their relatives. Stiffkey Hall, Norfolk, built to provide a suitable home for the newly-married Nathaniel Bacon, was largely paid for by his father, Sir Nicholas Bacon. At the time of its erection, Nathaniel was clearly incapable of financing such a project. In a letter of 1576 he wrote to his father that 'ye charg is too great for my present estat'. Sir Nicholas bought the manor, paid for the building materials, supplied some of the skilled labour force, and in his will he bequeathed the estate to his son together with £200 towards the cost of finishing the house.[44] Bess of Hardwick gave £300 in 1593 to her son, William Cavendish, when he was building Oldcotes in Derbyshire, and in 1599 she contributed a further £100 to the building expenses.[45] Another of her sons, Charles Cavendish, similarly received £300 from his mother in 1597 and another £100 in 1599 to help pay for the house that he was building at Kirkby-in-Ashfield, Nottinghamshire.[46] Harrold House, Bedfordshire, was partly financed by Sir Thomas Boteler, the son-in-law of the builder, Francis Farrar. The accounts for 1608–10 show the expenditure of £162 8s 4d, of which £65 had been contributed by Boteler.[47] This was probably more in the nature of an investment than a gift, for in 1614 Farrar settled the property on the heirs of Sir Thomas and Dame Alice, his wife.[48]

8   Notes

1   Staffordshire County Record Office: D593 R /1 /2

Broome Park, Kent, cost £8,000 between 1635 and 1638

Trentham Hall, Staffordshire, built between 1630 and 1639 for a total cost of £6,165 17s 4d

2 British Museum: Egerton MSS 2815

3 J. E. Jackson, 'Wulfhall and the Seymours' *Wiltshire Archaeological Magazine* xv (1875) 178–86

4 L. Stone, 'The Building of Hatfield House' *Archaeological Journal* cxii (1955) 114n

5 L. Stone, *The Crisis of the Aristocracy, 1558–1641* (Oxford 1965) p. 554

6 Ministry of Public Buildings & Works, *Official Guide Book* (1965) p. 5

7 G. R. Batho, 'Notes and Documents on Petworth House, 1574–1632' *Sussex Archaeological Collections* xcvi (1958) 112

8 A. Hamilton-Thompson, 'The Building Accounts of Kirby Muxloe Castle, 1480–84' *Transactions of the Leicester Archaeological Society* xi (1913–14) 193–345

9 British Museum: Egerton MSS 2815

10 J. Summerson, 'The Building of Theobalds, 1564–1585' *Archaeologia* xcvii (1959) 110

11 Essex County Record Office: D/DP A18–22

12 L. Stone, *The Crisis of the Aristocracy, 1558–1641* (Oxford 1965) pp. 554–5

13 British Museum: Additional MSS 7097, ff. 174–200. The total cost recorded in this account book is £1,425 3s 0½d, and not £719 3s 0½d as stated in J. Gage, *Thingoe Hundred* (London 1838) p. 151

14 Cambridge University Library: Hengrave Hall Deposit 80. The recorded expenditure in these account books is £3,036 3s 8d, but the accounts for 1538 and 1539 are missing

15 E. R. Sandeen, 'The Building of Redgrave Hall, 1545–1554' *Proceedings of the Suffolk Institute of Archaeology* xxix, pt. 1 (1961) 1–33. The total expenditure shown in the building accounts was £1,253 2s 5¾d

16 J. C. Rogers, 'The Manor and Houses of Gorhambury' *Transactions of the St. Albans and Hertfordshire Architectural and Archaeological Society* new series iv (1933) 108

17 J. Evans, 'Extracts from the Private Account Book of Sir William More of Loseley . . .' *Archaeologia* xxxvi (1855) 284–310

18 The total cost given in the accounts was £48 6s 11½d. J. R. Wigfull, 'House Building in Queen Elizabeth's Days', *Transactions of the Hunter Archaeological Society* iii (1925) 68–73

19 M. E. Finch, *The Wealth of Five Northamptonshire Families, 1540–1640* (Northamptonshire Record Society xix, 1956) p. 183. Between September 1593 and May 1600 his recorded expenditure was £971 0s 11d

20 Bedfordshire County Record Office: TW 818

21 H. L. Bradfer-Lawrence, 'The Building of Raynham Hall' *Norfolk Archaeology* xxiii (1927) 93–146. These figures are incomplete but they include the cost of abandoning the original foundations

22 British Museum: Harleian MSS 6853, f. 450. It is possible that this sum was exaggerated as it was quoted to justify a price of £2,500 for the sale of the house

23 Surrey County Record Office: Acc. 1030. The actual cost including landscaping, was £3,119 4s 7½d

24 B. Cozens-Hardy, 'Some Norfolk Halls' *Norfolk Archaeology* xxxii (1961) 188

25 Dorset County Record Office: MW/M4, f. 24b

26 Staffordshire County Record Office: D593 R/1/2

27 British Museum: Additional MSS 54332

28 *The Architecture of Sir Roger Pratt* ed. R. T. Gunther (Oxford 1928) p. 14

29 Staffordshire County Record Office: D593 R/1/1

30 Gunther, *op cit* p. 167

31 British Museum: Additional MSS 39832, f. 32

32 *Ibid* f. 33

33 *Ibid* f. 90

34 *Ibid* f. 93v

35 *Ibid* f. 107

36 *Ibid* f. 110

37 Nottingham University Library: Mi A60/5

38 J. Evans, 'Extracts from the Private Account Book of Sir William More of Loseley . . .' *Archaeologia* xxxvi (1855) 294–310

39 Sandeen, pp. 32–3. Only £28 was spent in 1549, but this can be accounted for by Kett's rebellion of that year
40 Staffordshire County Record Office: D593 R /1 /2
41 *The Architecture of Sir Roger Pratt* ed. R. T. Gunther (Oxford 1928) p. 172
42 *Ibid* p. 14
43 *Ibid* p. 8
44 Sandeen, pp. 191–3
45 Girouard, *Smythson* p. 139
46 *Ibid* p. 139
47 Bedfordshire County Record Office: TW 818
48 *Ibid* TW 11 /110

Part III: Materials

9 Selection of Materials

Whether of timber, brick or stone, the majority of country houses were built of local materials. The difficulty, and above all the expense, of transporting bulky materials meant that all but the most extravagant builders were restricted to the materials close at hand. It was only those builders for whom costs were secondary to considerations of magnificence who were able to use distant sources for their basic materials.

Although choice of materials was to a large extent governed by the ease with which they were available, great care was often taken before selecting those which were most suitable. In December 1575, when Nathaniel Bacon had decided to use moulded brick dressings for his house at Stiffkey, Norfolk, he wrote to his father:

'in ye beginning of ye spring [I will] cause tryall to be mad how ye [ground] in Styfkey [will serve] for yt purpose'. [1]

At Rushton, Northamptonshire, when a new quarry of ironstone for Sir Thomas Tresham's Triangular Lodge was opened up in 1595 one of the masons spent a full working week making 'ashelers and a coyne of redstone wrought only for trial of the stone'.[2]

Experimentation was not confined to the basic materials of the fabric, and a similar care was exercised over the choice of the materials for the more important fittings. The joiner at Gawthorpe Hall, Lancashire, for example spent part of March 1605 in 'tryeinge of tymber' for the great table in the dining chamber.[3] The builders of the larger houses were equally selective in choosing their materials. In 1609, when the Earl of Northumberland was about to battle-ment Syon House, Middlesex, he sought the advice of his officers up and down the country and had tests made on various samples of stone from Northumberland before deciding to use Purbeck stone,[4] and the surviving correspondence concerning the preparations for the Duke of Somerset's house at Great Bedwyn, Wiltshire, in 1548 and 1549 is largely devoted to a discussion of the merits of various quarries. To help choose the most suitable quarry one of his agents in Wiltshire sent 'a wallet of stone to London, whereon I have written upon every stone where he grew'.[5] A proposal to add a colonnade to the river side of Salisbury House, London, in 1610, uncertain as to whether Caen stone or Beer stone would be the more suitable for the project, suggested that:

'all stones both for pillers and frontispice may lye roughe hewed at theyr quarryes two winters at the leaste and then a man shall assuredly see which be the stones will hold and he shall see a nomber that at the first he would have thought serviceable breake and moulder away'. [6]

However, it is doubtful whether many builders went to such expensive and time-consuming lengths before selecting their building stone. For most of them it was simply a choice between what they possessed on their own estates and what was available from outside sources in the surrounding area.

9 *Notes*

1   Sandeen, p. 189
2   British Museum: Additional MSS 39832, f. 40v
3   *The House and Farm Accounts of the Shuttleworths* ed. J. Harland (Chetham Society xxxv 1856) p. 160
4   G. R. Batho, 'Henry, Ninth Earl of Northumberland and Syon House, Middlesex 1594–1632' *Transactions of the Ancient Monuments Society* new series iv (1956) 103–4
5   J. E. Jackson, 'Wulfhall and the Seymours' *Wiltshire Archaeological Magazine* xv (1875) 181
6   Public Record Office: SP14/57, f. 108

10 Stone

Although brick was used to build a number of prestige buildings in the 16th and 17th centuries, the time-honoured popularity of stone was unaffected. For the majority of country house builders brick provided an alternative building material only in those areas where stone was not easily available. Even in these areas brick-built houses were often embellished with stone dressings, for finely dressed stone was still a material that was indicative of social status. If a builder was unable to obtain sufficient stone he was sometimes prepared to imitate its appearance in other materials. Clement Paston used moulded brick for the window dressings at Oxnead Hall in Norfolk in the 1570s, and 'yei shewe as freestone'.[1] Nathaniel Bacon followed his example at Stiffkey Hall in the same county and treated several of his brick windows with plaster in an attempt to achieve the same effect.[2] Other examples of similar practice in eastern England include the gatehouse at Giffords Hall, Stoke-by-Nayland, Suffolk, and Eastbury House, Essex. In London, Paul D'Ewes even specified that the wooden windows on the three houses that he was building at Charing Cross in 1626 were to be finished 'wth collour of whight lead like stone worke'.[3]

This imitation of stone was not just a stylistic conceit. There was clearly a very strong desire on the part of many builders for a prominent display of stone to adorn the principal elevations of their houses, but it was a desire that was limited by practical considerations. If they were not able to acquire stone on reasonable terms, they were prepared to use other materials that provided the form if not the substance. Mainly because of the difficulties and the heavy costs of transportation, it was only the influential and the wealthy who were able to bring stone from distant quarries to use on their buildings. The majority of builders chose to build in other materials if there was no building stone available in the vicinity of their proposed house, or easily accessible by water. They would, if it were possible, use small quantities of stone for decorative effect, but they were not prepared to go to excessive lengths to acquire it. Thus the distribution of stone-built country houses largely reflects the geological distribution of suitable building stone, and the exceptions to this pattern can usually be explained by good communications by water.

The majority of houses were built of local stone. Gawthorpe Hall, Lancashire, was largely constructed of red sandstone from quarries opened up on the site,[4] while the stone for the fabric of Loseley House, Surrey, came from Guildford, just over three miles away.[5] Sir Thomas Tresham's various building works of the late 16th and early 17th centuries mainly used stone from the local quarries at Rushton, Pipewell, and Pilton, although small quantities

Eastbury House, Essex, with brick windows treated to resemble stone

were brought from the highly regarded quarries at Weldon and King's Cliffe, both of which were within fifteen miles of the site.[6] The large quantities of stone required for Sir Richard Leveson's Trentham Hall, Staffordshire, in the 1630s were all dug in the neighbourhood of the house.[7]

The use of local stone was not confined to the smaller country houses. Some of the most ostentatious houses of the period exhibit a similar preference. Burghley House, the mansion of William Cecil, was built mostly of stone from Barnack, where the quarries were almost within sight of the house, although stone for some of the more exotic fittings was shipped from Antwerp by Sir Thomas Gresham.[8] Hardwick Hall, Derbyshire, the climax of Elizabeth of Shrewsbury's building career, is largely of local sandstone, and Sir Christopher Hatton's Kirby Hall, Northamptonshire, was built of stone from the quarries at Weldon, three miles away.

Some builders did use stone from more distant sources. Much of the stone for the early work at Longleat, Wiltshire, was quarried locally although it had been supplemented with Bath stone from Haselbury, twenty-five miles away. By 1567, however, when the design of the

97

house entered its third phase, Sir John Thynne was getting the bulk of his stone from the quarries near Bath. By this date considerations of architectural effect were probably of more importance to him than convenience of supply, but even so none of his stone was brought from a greater distance than the twenty-seven miles to his own quarries at Cheddar.[9] John Strode used stone from Ham and Whatley, respectively nineteen and twenty-six miles from the site of his house at Chantmarle in Dorset, but the expense was not great for 'a very great number of carraiges of stones . . . were freely given me by my neighbours'.[10] There were very few builders indeed who sought stone from such diverse sources as Robert Cecil, Earl of Salisbury. During the first decade of the 17th century, for his buildings at Hatfield and London, he was using stone from Kent, Oxfordshire, Derbyshire, Yorkshire, Devon, Dorset, Lincolnshire, Northumberland, and Normandy, in addition to a small quantity of marble from Italy.[11] His father, Lord Burghley, has already been noted as using stone brought over from Holland, and he also imported stone from Spain in 1584 'to helpe finishe a device in the grete chambr at tebolts',[12] but these were for fittings, and the fabric of both his principal houses was of local materials.

There were usually special circumstances involved when builders did use stone that had to be transported for some distance. Although some of the stone for Wollaton Hall, Nottinghamshire, was quarried locally,[13] most of it was brought thirty-five miles from Ancaster in Lincolnshire, and there is a persistent legend that Sir Francis Willoughby's pack-horses carried coal from his mines at Wollaton to the quarries and returned laden with stone.[14] Unfortunately, the books relating to materials and carriage are missing from the surviving building accounts for Wollaton and it is not possible to verify the story, but the arrangment would not seem to have been inherently improbable.

Sometimes the special reason for bringing stone from a distance was the opportunity of a good bargain, or the influence of an acquaintance at the source. Thus in 1594, Sir Edward Pytts paid the very reasonable sum of £6 15s

'for 10 tun of Hoscum hedd stone being so great that 10 Stones conteyned the 10 tun hadd from my cosen Pytts chamberleyn of Brystowe [Bristol] of the executors of one that hadd provided them for some great purpose'.

Although the stone was some eighty-five miles away from the house that Pytts was building in Worcestershire, the carriage was a relatively simple matter using the River Severn.[15]

Indeed, the availability of water transport seems to have been the crucial factor in considering the use of quarries further than a few miles from the site. Old Thorndon Hall in Essex, for example, was a brick-built house which incorporated small quantities of stone for decorative effect. For his gatehouse and terrace, Sir John Petre bought stone in Devon in 1594.[16] The quarries at Beer were conveniently situated close to the sea, as were those on the Isle of Purbeck from which he bought stone in 1581, and the only land transport involved was for the ten miles to the site from Grays Thurrock where the stone was landed. Similarly, the Merstham stone and Kentish Rag used in 1586 and 1594 were brought down the River Medway and then carried by sea to Grays. At Kyre Park, the principal sources of stone were from quarries opened up in the park and Madeley Quarry in Shropshire, some thirty-six miles away. The stone from the latter was carried down the Severn to Bewdley, and thence by land to Kyre, the overland stage of the journey costing only 5s the load.[17]

The great limestone quarries of the east Midlands were all accessible to the comparatively stone-less counties of East Anglia via the River Ouse, the River Nene, and the River Welland. Stone from Clipsham and Weldon, brought up the Little Ouse to Brandon, was used at Little Saxham Hall, Suffolk, between 1505 and 1514.[18] The upper storey of Hengrave Hall, Suffolk, was built of King's Cliffe stone in the 1530s, and again Brandon provided the collecting point.[19] In the early 17th century, the stone for Raynham Hall, Norfolk, came from Ketton and Clipsham and was carried by water to King's Lynn, where it was transferred to carts for the eighteen mile journey to the site.[20] The problems of transportation will be considered in more general terms elsewhere. As a factor in the distribution of stone away from the quarries they were of the highest importance. Transport by land of such a heavy and bulky material was generally difficult and consequently added greatly to the cost of stone delivered at the site. Water carriage was considerably easier and less expensive. As a result it was the quarries that were near to water that produced the most sought-after stone and which created the distribution pattern for those country houses of the 16th and 17th centuries that were not built of local stone.

Transport costs were only one factor in the price of stone; albeit a factor which disproportionately increased in importance the further the quarry was situated from the building site. But, as has already been emphasised, most houses were built of local stone, often from quarries opened up on the estate. These quarries, of course, belonged to the builder, and the only expense that he was put to was in digging the stone and moving it the short distance to where the house was being built. Some builders who used their own stone for the fabric of the building also bought small quantities of better stone for special effects. Thus Harrold House, Bedfordshire, was built of stone dug in Francis Farrar's own pits on the site, but the string-courses and some of the windows were of stone from the quarries at Olney and Warrington, six miles away, and the remaining windows and the porch were of Weldon stone.[21] The proposals for the new house at Petworth for the Earl of Northumberland in 1615 show that the house was largely to be built of stone quarried in two places in the park, but that Purbeck and Beer stone were to be bought for paving and lining the ovens.[22]

If the stone on the builder's own land was of insufficient quality, or if there was no stone at all, he sometimes bought a quarry to provide him with the necessary material. Sir John Thynne bought a quarry at Haselbury, near Box in 1573,[23] although this was only one of several sources of supply. When Sir Christopher Hatton bought the unfinished Kirby Hall from the executors of Sir Humphrey Stafford in 1575, he also bought the neighbouring quarry land at Weldon. After completing the house, he leased the quarries out to various local masons.[24] The agent for Robert Cecil even went to the length of buying a quarry at Caen in Normandy in the early 17th century to expedite the supply of that stone for the Earl's various building projects.[25]

However, most builders only required stone for a single building operation of limited duration, and their needs could be met by renting a quarry. Sir William More rented a quarry at Guildford for seven years between 1563 and 1569, and it provided almost all the stone that he required to build Loseley House.[26] William Dickenson, bailiff to the Earl of Shrewsbury, rented a quarry from his employer to provide the stone for the house that he built himself in Sheffield in 1575,[27] and Sir John Thynne had been renting quarries from the Duchess of Somerset and a farmer at Slaughterford for seven years before he bought his quarry at Haselbury in 1575.[28]

Both the purchase and the renting of a quarry meant that the builder had to arrange and to supervise the extraction of the stone himself. This meant setting up a separate administrative organisation away from the building site, and many builders preferred to buy direct from quarry owners and stone suppliers instead. The Weldon stone for Harrold House was bought from the Grumbold family who leased some of the quarry land in the village from Lord Hatton.[29] From the late 16th century, stone from the quarries at Little Barrington in Gloucestershire and Taynton in Oxfordshire was supplied by Timothy Strong, who

> 'had several apprentices, and kept several masons and labourers employed in those quarries, to serve the Country with what they wanted in his way of trade'. [30]

The business was continued with great success by his sons and grandsons in the following century. Both the Grumbolds and the Strongs were masons, as were many of the other stone suppliers, like Arnold Goversonne who provided the Ketton stone for Raynham Hall, Norfolk, 1621,[31] and Gabriel Caldam who owned quarries in Kent and supplied stone for the Royal Works in the 1530s and 1540s.[32] Quarrying must have provided alternative employment for masons resident in stone areas when they were not engaged on building work. The quarries that they worked often seem to have been small,[33] and they were probably only capable of supplying stone for dressings and not for the complete fabric of a large house. Rented quarries, or quarries owned by the builder, provided the bulk of the stone for the country houses.

Where a large amount of stone was required it was often quarried by the builder's own work force. Usually one of the principal masons on the site would be sent to the quarry to examine the stone and select that which would be most suitable for the building, and then the extraction would be undertaken by labourers and lesser skilled workmen. Thus the stone from King's Cliffe used at Hengrave Hall, Suffolk, in 1537 was chosen by two of Sir Thomas Kytson's masons in April and by the end of the month his labourers were working at the quarry.[34] When the stone was quarried within the estate, the total work force was usually provided by the builder himself, as at Trentham Hall, Staffordshire, in the 1630s[35] and at Harrold House, Bedfordshire, in 1608–10,[36] but when the stone came from some distance away from the site the builder's workmen were used to supplement the quarryman's labour force. When Sir Edward Pytts was about to start the rebuilding of Kyre Park, Worcestershire, in 1588, he gave the quarryman of Madeley Quarry, Shropshire, 5s 'toward hiring of workmen to uncover the quarry', and in addition sent two of his own labourers to the quarry to help extract the stone.[37] This must have been inconvenient for the builder for he would have to arrange for the boarding of his workmen while they were away from the site, but few quarries were capable of the independent production of large quantities of stone to satisfy an irregular demand. The organisation maintained by Timothy Strong at Little Barrington and Taynton was probably unusual.

Occasionally the quarrying was carried out by masons but usually it was a job reserved for unskilled labour. Where masons were employed at the quarry they were generally engaged on more skilled tasks, such as squaring and dressing the blocks of stone as they were quarried. The principal mason at Longleat in 1546 was occupied in working 'stone square at the quarrie',[38] and most of the stone for Trentham Hall, Staffordshire, was dressed by the masons at the quarry.[39] One very good reason for roughly squaring stone at the quarry was that a certain amount of surplus weight was thereby removed, and thus the problems and the cost of transport were not quite so great. Another reason, possibly of even more importance, was that freestones are more easily worked when first quarried, as they are comparatively soft. On exposure to the atmosphere they gradually harden, and as transport was slow, advantage could only be taken of their initial softness at the quarryface.

Usually it was only the blocks of stone for walling that were worked upon by the masons at the quarry, but there are a few examples of more finely carved work being executed. In 1563, the mason William Spicer contracted to make a number of windows for Longleat at the quarry at Oldford, Somerset,[40] and in 1570 another of Thynne's masons, Thomas Gregory, made sixteen chimney-shafts at Haselbury quarry.[41] The scutcheons for Sir Thomas Tresham's Triangular Lodge were made in the quarry at Pipewell in 1596,[42] and much of the masons' work for his lodge at Lyveden was executed in the quarry at Weldon.[43] Where the quarry was close to the site of the building, as at Bolsover Castle, Derbyshire, in 1613, the masons mainly worked at the quarry, but on the whole, detailed carving of stone from distant quarries was executed at the site.

In the 17th century, there is some evidence to suggest a growing practice of commissioning independent masons who were not employed directly as wage-earners by the builder to provide finished stone-work at the site. There was, of course, a long-standing medieval tradition of monumental masons carving figures and tombs in their own workshops for erection wherever they were required,[44] and this trade continued to flourish in the 16th and 17th centuries. In 1569, Sir William More bought three 'figures' in London to set over the porch at Loseley House, Surrey,[45] and the eighth Earl of Northumberland bought a fountain in London in the 1580s for erection at Petworth House, Sussex.[46] Chimney-pieces were also delivered ready made at the site. The Duke of Northumberland ordered a chimney-piece for Dudley Castle, Staffordshire, in 1552 from John Chapman, who made it at Lacock Abbey in Wiltshire where he was working for Sir William Sharington, and sent it up by cart the following year.[47] In the 17th century, Nicholas Stone made chimney-pieces and other interior fittings in his London workshop for clients as far away as Yorkshire and Norfolk,[48] and he was also able to provide craftsmen if necessary to arrange for their erection. All these masons, however, were skilled carvers who specialised in decorative work; but there were other masons towards the end of the period who were providing ready made structural stonework. In 1608 Francis Farrar bought 'wyndowe stuffe & corbell table' from a mason at Olney and in 1610 the Grumbolds of Weldon provided him with 'stone reddy wrought' including 'toppstones' for his house at Harrold, Bedfordshire.[49] A similar service was provided by John Ashley and Sampson Frisbey,

Ketton freemasons, who agreed to supply thirty-eight windows ready made to the site, for Thorpe Hall, Northamptonshire in 1653.[50] There are even examples of finished stonework being sent overseas to Ireland, as when Sir Richard Boyle, first Earl of Cork, was preparing to build a house for his son at Gill Abbey, near Cork, in 1637, and 'employed Robert Belcher, into England, to supplie me with ffree stone chymneis, doores, and lightes, readie made at the ffree stone quarries at donderry Hill, neer Bristoll'.[51] Generally, however, stone arrived on the site in a roughly dressed condition and all the freemasons' work on it was carried out by the builder's own craftsmen.

10   Notes

1   E. R. Sandeen, p. 189
2   *Ibid* p. 190
3   British Museum: Harleian MSS 98/16
4   *The House and Farm Accounts of the Shuttleworths* ed. J. Harland (Chetham Society xxxv 1856) 125–74
5   J. Evans, 'Extracts from the Private Account Book of Sir William More of Loseley . . .' *Archaeologia* xxxvi (1855) 284–310
6   British Museum: Additional MSS 39832
7   Staffordshire County Record Office: D593 R/1/2
8   G. Patrick, 'Burghley House and the First Lord Burghley' *Journal of the British Archaeological Association* xxxv (1879) 265
9   Longleat Archives: R.O.B., i, ii, and iii
10   Dorset County Record Office: MW/M4 f. 24b
11   L. Stone, 'The Building of Hatfield House' *Archaeological Journal* cxii (1955) 108–9; L. Stone, 'Inigo Jones and the New Exchange', *ibid* cxiv (1957) 115; *Survey of London xviii: The Strand* (1937) p. 121
12   British Museum: Landsdowne MSS 43/14
13   Nottingham University Library: Mi A60/2, f. 10v
14   Girouard, *Smythson* p. 78
15   Mrs Baldwyn-Childe, 'The Building of the Manor-House of Kyre Park, Worcestershire, 1588–1618' *The Antiquary* xxi (1890) 263
16   Essex County Record Office: D/DP A22
17   Mrs Baldwyn-Childe, *op cit* p. 205
18   British Museum: Additional MSS 7097, ff. 174–200
19   Cambridge University Library: Hengrave Hall Deposit 80
20   H. L. Bradfer-Lawrence, 'The Building of Raynham Hall' *Norfolk Archaeology* xxiii (1927) 93–146
21   Bedfordshire County Record Office: TW 818
22   G. R. Batho, 'Notes and Documents on Petworth House, 1574–1632' *Sussex Archaeological Collections* xcvi (1958) 113–29
23   Longleat Archives: R.O.B. iii, f. 173
24   H. M. Colvin, 'Haunt Hill House, Weldon' in *Studies in Building History*, ed. E. M. Jope (London 1961) p. 224
25   L. Stone, 'The Building of Hatfield House' *Archaeological Journal* cxii (1955) 109
26   J. Evans, 'Extracts from the Private Account Book of Sir William More, of Loseley . . .' *Archaeologia* xxxvi (1855) 284–310
27   J. R. Wigfull, 'House Building in Queen Elizabeth's Days' *Transactions of the Hunter Archaeological Society* iii (1925) 68
28   Longleat Archives: R.O.B., iii, f. 79 & f. 169

29 Bedfordshire County Record Office: TW 818
30 From a MS history of the family compiled by Edward Strong in 1716 and printed in R. Clutterbuck, *The History and Antiquities of the County of Hertford* (London 1815) i, 167n
31 H. L. Bradfer-Lawrence, 'The Building of Raynham Hall' *Norfolk Archaeology* xxiii (1927) 128. It is interesting to note that the father of William Arnold, the West Country mason, was also called Arnold Goverson
32 D. Knoop & G. P. Jones, 'The Sixteenth-Century Mason' *Ars Quatuor Coronatorum* l (1937) 199n
33 *Idem* 'The English Medieval Quarry' *Economic History Review* ix (1938) 30
34 Cambridge University Library: Hengrave Hall Deposit 80
35 Staffordshire County Record Office: D593 R /1 /2
36 Bedfordshire County Record Office: TW 818
37 Mrs Baldwyn-Childe, 'The Building of the Manor-House of Kyre Park, Worcestershire, 1588—1618' *The Antiquary* xxi (1890) 204
38 Longleat Archives: R.O.B. i, f. 228
39 Staffordshire County Record Office: D593 R /1 /2
40 Longleat Archives: R.O.B. ii, f. 179
41 *Ibid* iii, f. 39
42 British Museum: Additional MSS 39832, f. 85
43 *Ibid* f. 93
44 D. Knoop & G. P. Jones, *The Mediaeval Mason* (3rd edition, Manchester 1967) pp. 12 & 71
45 J. Evans, 'Extracts from the Private Account Book of Sir William More of Loseley . . .' *Archaeologia* xxxvi (1855) 308
46 G. R. Batho, 'The Percies at Petworth, 1574—1632' *Sussex Archaeological Collections* xcv (1957) 11
47 Longleat Archives: R.O.B. ii, f. 31. Sharington to Thynne, 25 June 1553
48 *The Account Book of Nicholas Stone*, ed. W. L. Spiers (Walpole Society vii, 1919) pp. 42, 68, 82, 101—2, 104, 105 & 134
49 Bedfordshire County Record Office: TW 818
50 British Museum: Additional MSS 25302, f. 153
51 *The Lismore Papers* ed. A. B. Grosart (v, 1886) p. 37. I owe this reference to the kindness of Dr Mark Girouard

11 Brick

The early part of the 16th century has been called with some justification the first great age of English brickwork.[1] As a material, brick was of considerable status throughout the century. The decorative properties inherent in the material were exploited to the full during the reign of Henry VIII, especially in the use of elaborately moulded and rubbed bricks for such prominent features as chimneystacks and gable ends. It is clear that by the 16th century the craft of bricklaying had reached a high level of technical perfection, although the most virtuoso effects were still largely confined to the eastern counties. By the end of the century, it had become an important building material in Hampshire and Berkshire, as well as in the counties surrounding London and in the south-east and eastern parts of the country, but brick was still rarely used in the Midlands and apart from the isolated example of Stevenstone, near Torrington, in Devon, rebuilt in the early 16th century by George Rolle, a London lawyer, it does not seem to have been adopted in the south-west until well into the 17th century.[2] The pattern of its distribution was largely imposed by geological factors, for in areas where building stone was easily obtainable the local material was generally preferred.

Although the use of brick in areas where suitable clay was available was no longer a novelty by the 16th century, it was still a material that was almost solely confined to important buildings. Very few houses of a social level below that of the country house were built wholly of brick during the period. This meant that there must have been a very erratic demand for the material, and that the making of bricks was almost always closely associated with the construction of the building that was to use them. This generalisation is less valid, of course, for the eastern counties, particularly Norfolk, Suffolk, and Essex, where there was a longer tradition of brick-making and where building in brick had passed further down the social scale; but even in this part of England there is little evidence for the independent manufacture of bricks on any scale. The large quantities of bricks required to build a country house were almost invariably made on the site or within a very short distance of it. Besides enabling the builder or his agents to closely supervise the process, this had the added advantage of reducing to a minimum the costs of transporting the heavy finished material.

In the 16th century brick-making was largely a seasonal activity, with all the stages of manufacture being spread over twelve months. The accounts for Sir Nicholas Bacon's house at Redgrave, Suffolk, give a full description of how the process was carried out at the middle of the century. The clay was dug in the autumn or early winter, and then spread out in an open field to be broken up by the moisture and frost. In the spring it was watered and trampled under foot. Any pebbles which would be liable to cause the clay to split in the course of firing were removed at this stage. The clay was then cut to size using wooden moulds, and left to dry in stacks for a period of about a month. The bricks were burnt in kilns or clamps, and by the time the process had been completed it was ready to start digging the clay for the following year.[3] The bricks used for the building of Kyre Park, Worcestershire, between 1588 and 1594, were made in a similar way, with an annual firing in the late summer extending over a fortnight.[4]

Weather conditions were important to the success of the operation. It was, for example, crucial that there should be little rain during the time that the unburnt bricks were drying. The comments made by Sir Edward Pytts at the end of each year's brick-making at Kyre Park clearly illustrate the effects of the weather on production. In 1588 his brickmaker had contracted to make 200,000 bricks, but in the event produced only 57,000 'for no more colde be made this yeare because the continuall rayne letted', and again in 1592 only 100,800 bricks were made because 'the beginning of sommer proved very wett and unseasonable for making thereof'.

The clamps, which often seem to have been very temporary affairs and were rebuilt each year, were generally wood-fired. Brush-wood and 'gren', or unseasoned, wood were used at Little Saxham, Suffolk, in 1507,[5] although coal was in use on the site for burning lime. It appears that there was a definite preference in the 16th century for wood-fired brick, for Sir Edward Pytts also made use of substantial amounts of coal at Kyre Park but only burnt wood at his brick-kilns. By the 17th century, however, there is evidence of an increasing use of coal. The Earl of Salisbury initially had the bricks for Hatfield House made in wood-fired kilns, but towards the end of the enterprise coal was being used,[6] and the brick-kilns at Raynham Hall, Norfolk, used both coal and wood for fuel between 1619 and 1622.[7] It is unlikely that the change was wholly due to a shortage of timber. Possibly it was being realised that the predictable burning qualities of coal could take some of the uncertainty out of the firing process.

Complaints about insufficiently burnt bricks are frequently met with. The contract with a brickmaker for 200,000 bricks at Little Saxham Hall in 1505 specifically excluded any bricks from the total that were not thoroughly burnt,[8] and bricks from 'the evill burned clampe' at Redgrave Hall, Suffolk, were only fit for use as rubble.[9] At Loseley House, Surrey, in 1561 a clamp of over 120,000 bricks had to be fired again because the bricks had been insufficiently burnt,[10] although it was more usual for only part of the bricks in any particular batch to be unsatisfactory, as with the clamp burnt by Sir Edward Pytts at Kyre Park in 1594, where

'the side toward the meddowe is worst burnt because the winde lay allwaies in that end: the other side is throwlie burnt'.   [11]

Although the bricks measuring $9\frac{1}{2} \times 4\frac{1}{2} \times 2\frac{1}{4}$ inches in use at Eton College in 1543–4 were said to be 'of a lawfull scantlyng'[12] there was, in fact, little uniformity in the size of bricks in use during the period. Given the way that they were made to order as required, this is hardly surprising. Those at Little Saxham Hall in 1505 were 'to be x inch in length, v inch in brede, and ij inch & di in thiknesse when it is wele and sufficiently brent',[13] while the bricks used at

Redgrave Hall measured $9 \times 4 \times 2$ inches.[14] Eastbury House, Essex, was built in the 1560s with $10 \times 4\frac{1}{2} \times 2\frac{1}{2}$ inch bricks.[15] In the early 17th century Ince Castle, Cornwall, used bricks with the comparatively small dimensions of $8 \times 4 \times 2$ inches,[16] and later in the century Sir Balthazar Gerbier advocated an ideal size of $9\frac{1}{2} \times 4\frac{5}{8} \times 2\frac{3}{4}$ inches.[17]

The overall picture that emerges of brick-making in the 16th and early 17th centuries is of a largely localised activity. There were specialised brick-makers who travelled some distance for employment, such as the two brick-makers from Essex working at Raynham Hall, Norfolk, in 1619,[18] but on the whole brick-makers tended to be local men who could be called upon during the fairly short periods of the year when their services were necessary. It is unlikely that the manufacture of bricks provided them with a full-time occupation, but in the eastern counties at least, there was probably enough building taking place to provide them with some work during most years. For over twenty years from 1573 to about 1595 the requirements of Old Thorndon Hall, Essex, provided annual work for Walter Guy of Great Warley and George Bowes of East Horndon.[19] It is significant that neither of these men had their own kilns. They were employed only to make bricks at the various kilns set up around the site of the house. This was the usual arrangement for most of the brick-built houses of the period. The builder supplied the equipment, including the moulds, and the brick-maker provided only his labour and his skill.[20] There are a few examples of ready-made bricks being bought, but they are generally of insignificant amounts, such as the 2,200 bricks bought in May 1635 for the stone-built Trentham Hall, Staffordshire, and used 'for the topping of a chymney in ye evidence house'.[21]

As most of the bricks were made on the site it was possible for many of the stages in the manufacturing process to be carried out by unskilled labour. The expertise of the brick-maker was only really necessary to select the clay and to supervise the moulding and firing of the bricks. Consequently brick-makers tended either to be employed on a part-time basis, working only in the autumn and the spring, in which case they could only be regularly available if they were local men, or they were capable of carrying out other tasks on the site during the periods when they were not making bricks. Thus, Hugh Hether, the brick-maker at Longleat between 1568 and 1576, was also employed as a labourer,[22] while the bricks for Kyre Park, Worcestershire, were made by Thomas Lem, who also acted as the principal mason.[23]

11   Notes

1   A. Clifton-Taylor, *The Pattern of English Building* (2nd edition, London 1965) p. 213
2   W. G. Hoskins, *Devon* (London 1954) p. 166
3   Sandeen, pp. 23–4
4   Mrs Baldwyn-Childe, 'The Building of the Manor-House of Kyre Park, Worcestershire, 1588–1618' *The Antiquary* xxi & xxii (1890) 263–4 & 24
5   British Museum: Additional MSS 7097, f. 184v
6   L. Stone, 'The Building of Hatfield House' *Archaeological Journal* cxii (1955) 107
7   H. L. Bradfer-Lawrence, 'The Building of Raynham Hall' *Norfolk Archaeology* xxiii (1927) 93–146
8   'no semel breke . . . to be told'. British Museum: Additional MSS 7097, f. 176
9   Sandeen, p. 27

10 J. Evans, 'Extracts from the Private Account Book of Sir William More of Loseley . . .' *Archaeologia* xxxvi (1855) 295

11 Mrs Baldwyn-Childe, *op cit* 24

12 Willis and Clark, i, 419n

13 British Museum: Additional MSS 7097, f. 176

14 Sandeen, p. 23

15 *Eastbury Manor House, Barking* 11th monograph of London Survey Committee (1917) p. 20

16 E. M. Jope, 'Cornish Houses, 1400–1700', in *Studies in Building History* (London 1961) p. 212

17 B. Gerbier, *Counsel and Advise* . . . (London 1663) p. 56

18 H. L. Bradfer-Lawrence, 'The Building of Raynham Hall' *Norfolk Archaeology* xxiii (1927) 103

19 Walter Guy had previously been making bricks for Sir William Petre at Ingatestone Hall in the 1550s; Essex County Record Office: D/DP A 10–11

20 In addition to Little Saxham Hall, Redgrave Hall, Loseley House, Old Thorndon Hall, Hatfield House, and Raynham Hall already mentioned, see also Gorhambury House, Hertfordshire (J. C. Rogers, 'The Manor and Houses of Gorhambury' *Transactions of the St. Albans and Hertfordshire Architectural and Archaeological Society*, new series iv (1933) 108). Kirkby-in-Ashfield, Derbyshire (*The Chamberlain Letters*, ed. E. M. Thompson (London 1966) p. 27), Condover Hall, Salop (Shrewsbury Public Library: Deeds 6885), and Broome House, Kent (British Museum: Additional MSS 54332)

21 Staffordshire County Record Office: D 593 R /1 /2. 30 May 1635

22 Longleat Archives: R.O.B., iii

23 Mrs Baldwyn-Childe, 'The Building of the Manor-House of Kyre Park, Worcestershire, 1588–1618' *The Antiquary* xxi & xxii (1890)

12 Timber

Although country houses in many counties were built of timber, the only extant documentary information for a house built of that material is a carpenter's contract of 1617 concerned with alterations to an existing house.[1] No building accounts are known to survive, and consequently timber will largely be considered here in its secondary role as a material for the framework of roofs and floors and as a medium for applied decoration.

The most common variety of wood used for structural purposes was oak. It seems to have been generally preferred, both for its qualities of strength and durability, and for its natural abundance. There are however, a few examples of other types of wood being used. A. W. Clapham found that almost all the woodwork of the Court House at Barking in Essex was of chestnut, including the frame, the roof, the stairs, and the windows.[2] It is no longer possible to test this assertion as the building has been demolished and the accounts for its construction do not specify what sort of timber was used.[3] It should be noted, however, that oak and chestnut became visually almost indistinguishable with age. The Court House was built in 1567, and at about the same time Clement Sysley was building Eastbury House, just over a mile away, where he is said to have similarly employed chestnut for a stair-case and some of the floor joists.[4] Elm was another timber sometimes used instead of oak. Francis Farrar employed it at Harrold House, Bedfordshire, in 1609,[5] and it was also used at Raynham Hall, Norfolk, in 1619 and 1621.[6] In addition, Sir Roger Townshend used a small quantity of maple at Raynham, as did Sir Nicholas Bacon at Redgrave Hall, Suffolk, in the mid-16th century.[7] These are isolated examples however, and generally oak was the preferred wood.

Oak was also used for interior fittings such as floorboards and panelling, but owing to its tendency to warp and crack it was necessary to season it carefully. Deal, which was easier to work and which seasoned more quickly, was growing in popularity. Walnut was used on occasion, generally for furniture as at Wollaton in 1587[8] where tables were made from it; but at Kyre Park, Worcestershire, in 1595, a quantity of eight feet planks were possibly used for floorboards.[9] Ash and elder were used for scaffolding poles, and at Loseley House, Surrey, in 1566, ash boards were used for flooring.[10]

Much of the structural timberwork seems to have been used unseasoned. It has been estimated that a trunk of oak requires a year's seasoning for each inch of thickness plus an additional year for every three inches of the total thickness,[11] and few builders would have been able to plan their complete timber supply that far in advance. In addition, unseasoned oak was much easier to work, and as it dried out it became harder, so that the strength of the work was not necessarily compromised by the wood's tendency to warp. Carpenters were generally conservative in their estimates of stresses and tolerances, although weaknesses in the design of the timberwork for the early 17th century Schools Quadrangle at Oxford were aggravated by the use of unseasoned timber.[12]

It was crucial, however, that the finer woodwork such as floors, doors, and panelling, should not warp. There was little margin for error in this sort of work, and generally it was specifically stated that the timber used should be properly seasoned. In the contract for the Perse Building at Gonville and Caius College, Cambridge, in 1617, the floorboards and the doors were to be of 'seasoned board of oake', but there were no instructions for the seasoning of the structural timbers.[13] Contracts for the Legge Building at the same college in 1618, for St. John's College in 1598, and for St. Catherine's Hall in 1611, were similarly selective in their instructions.[14] In June 1547, Sir John Thynne wrote from France to his steward at Longleat to ensure that he would

'not forget that there be plancks sawen for my dores so that they may be seasoned in tyme', [15]

and the only wood specifically stated to be seasoned at Trentham Hall, Staffordshire, in the 1630s was used by the joiners for panelling and flooring.[16] At Rushton Hall, Northamptonshire, in 1595, insufficient seasoning caused the gallery floor to warp in several places and in consequence it had to be replaced shortly after it had been laid.[17]

Sir John Thynne placed the responsibility for ensuring that the wood had been correctly treated on his joiners,

'for if I shall finde any faut with the workmanship or the seasoning of their stuf they shall make it agayn'. [18]

He recommended that when the wood had been sawn into planks they should be 'laid up drye with stikks betweene it so that it may season the better'.[19] Another method for seasoning panelling, similar to the modern technique, was that suggested by William Spicer to the Earl of Leicester in 1571. The trees at Kenilworth were to be cut to size and the pieces then immersed in water to remove the acid and the sap. The process was to be completed by the use of a drying kiln or oven.[20] It was a method that was far more sophisticated and quicker than that in use at Longleat twenty-four years earlier.

The sources of timber supply were generally local, although a number of builders seem to have experienced difficulty in accumulating sufficient quantities. Most builders possessed some woodland of their own but sometimes it was insufficient to meet the heavy demands of a building programme, and there are a number of documented buildings where timber had to be brought from a source well away from the site. There is evidence of difficulties of supply in certain parts of the country as early as the first decade of the 16th century. Timber, like stone, was a difficult material to transport, and the costs of carrying it were considerable; consequently it is not unreasonable to deduce that a builder who brought quantities of timber, other than soft-wood for internal work, from outside the neighbourhood of his building was unable to find enough local timber for his works. Although much of the timber used in the first few years for Little Saxham Hall came from within a radius of six miles of the site, by 1508 trees from Winfarthing Park in Norfolk, thirty-three miles away, were being used and other sources of supply were being sought at Hundon Park, eleven miles away and Rattlesden, thirteen miles away.[21] When Sir Thomas Kytson built Hengrave Hall, a few miles distant, he seems to have had similar difficulties over his timber supply. Some was brought the fifteen miles from Woolpit Wood, near Stowmarket, and in 1527 and 1528 he bought and dismantled two timber-framed houses and a barn, and had the timber transported to the site where, presumably it was re-used in an inconspicuous place in the new building.[22]

Most of the evidence for a shortage of building timber in the first half of the 16th century is confined to East Anglia, and particularly to Suffolk, but by June 1567 Sir John Thynne was writing from Longleat in Wiltshire to the Earl of Hertford thanking him for fifty trees and hoping for a similar number in the following year, 'timber being my only lack'.[23] In 1587, timber for Wollaton Hall, Nottinghamshire, was brought nearly forty miles from Kingsbury in Warwickshire,[24] and amongst Sir Francis Willoughby's other sources of supply were Middleton, Derbyshire,[25] twenty-five miles away, and West Hallam, seven miles away.[26] The difficulty of finding sufficient timber was as acute in Norfolk as it was in Suffolk. Sir Nathaniel Bacon began negotiating for timber for his house at Stiffkey early in 1573, although work on the building did not commence until 1576. In 1574 he secured a lease on the oaks in Hindolveston Wood, eleven miles from the site, and in the following year one of his agents bought 'a gret bargenye of tymbere of Mr George Thembetthorpe' of Foulsham, fourteen miles away, which was 'redye brocon so that it lake but the framyn'. Further timber was purchased in 1576 from Sir Thomas Gresham's wood at Mileham, eighteen miles from Stiffkey.[27]

Other areas where there is documentary evidence of a shortage of timber include Plymouth in the early 17th century, where the demands of the ship-building industry led the overseers for the building of the new Guildhall to import timber from Ireland,[28] and parts of Lancashire where the timber for Gawthorpe Hall was brought eight miles, and laths and boards had to be purchased in Halifax, twenty-seven miles away.[29] Clearly there was a scarcity of good building timber but it only seems to have been a major problem in certain parts of the country, and was not faced by all the builders of whom we have record. A large number of country houses, particularly in the south and in parts of the Midlands, were predominantly built of local timber. The builders of such houses as Hardwick Hall and Bolsover Castle in Derbyshire, Harrold Hall in Bedfordshire, Loseley House, Surrey, and Old Thorndon Hall, Essex, seem to have had little trouble in getting sufficient timber in the immediate neighbourhood of their building sites. When the estimates were drawn up in 1615 for the Earl of Northumberland's proposed new building at Petworth, Sussex, it was envisaged that the estate would be able to provide all the required timber apart from the soft wood for the panelling which was to be supplied by the joiner.[30]

It seems that the generally accepted thesis of a growing shortage of timber in the late 16th and early 17th centuries must be modified to a certain extent in its application to the building industry. In the first place there is evidence that it was affecting builders in Suffolk from the very beginning of the 16th century, and on the other hand it seems that a large number of country house builders, particularly in the south-east and in the north Midlands, completely escaped the effects of any shortage. It is instructive to note that much of the contemporary evidence for a shortage of timber was concerned with its use as a fuel.[31] There were few complaints of a scarcity of building wood before the 17th century. In the first edition of William Harrison's *Description of England* in 1577, 'lacke of wood' for building was noted 'in the fennie countries', but in the second edition of 1586 the reference was extended to include the 'northerne parts'.[32] John Norden expressed concern in 1607 about the depletion in Wealden timber that had taken place during the previous thirty years,[33] and Robert Reyce wrote in 1618, significantly with reference to Suffolk, of

> 'the carelesse wast of this age of our wonted plenty of timber, and other building stuffe . . .' [34]

In certain areas good building timber was in short supply, but this shortage was far from universal thoughout the country.[35]

The timber to be used in the building was generally selected by the principal carpenter who examined the standing trees in the wood. At Stafford in 1589, the carpenter responsible for the roof of the new Shire Hall was given a dinner 'at choosing the Trees',[36] and two carpenters at Condover Hall, Shropshire, were paid 1s each in February 1587 'for the veweinge of Timber in Longenoeswoodde'.[37] Saw pits were often constructed in the wood, and the trees were invariably sawn and roughly shaped on the spot as they were felled, both for convenience of transport and because they were easier to work in a 'green' state. The timber was then carried to the site, where the carpenters worked on it at the 'framing yard',[38] or 'framing place'.[39] Here the joints were made and the framework of features such as the roof assembled to check that the work was true. Adjustments could be more easily made at this stage than when the framework was in position on the building. The position of all the main members were marked by roman numerals, and the framework was then dismantled ready for re-erecting in the building.

The placing of the frame in position was a particularly difficult job, and often extra labour was employed on a casual basis to assist the regular carpenters. At Trentham Hall, Staffordshire, ten extra men were taken on for two days in July 1633, to help the carpenters erect the stable.[40] Gloves were provided for the men involved, as at the Shire Hall, Stafford, in 1590, 'to hale ropes with',[41] and there were occasionally accidents. At Stafford 3s 4d was spent 'ffor spices and fitt meates and other necessaries ministed to Tusle sore bruised with a fall in rearing', and at Trentham in 1637 one of the casual labourers was given 5s 'being hurt with a fall of the barne' that he was helping to erect.[42] The placing of the roof in position, marking as it did almost the final stage in the erection of the shell of the building, was often an occasion for celebration. Usually ale was provided for the workmen, but at William Dickenson's house in Sheffield in 1576, the substantial sum of £2 6s 8d was spent on 'meat and drinck that Day that the howse was Reared',[43] and at Gawthorpe Hall, Lancashire, the placing of the roof in June 1602 was celebrated with music when 6d was 'gyven to a pypper upon the rearing day'.[44]

12 Notes

1 W. A. Singleton, 'Traditional House-Types in Rural Lancashire and Cheshire' *Transactions of the History Society of Lancashire and Cheshire* civ (1952) 90–1

2 A. W. Clapham, 'The Court House, or "Old Town Hall", at Barking' *Transactions of the Essex Archaeological Society* xii (1912) 295–8

3 Bodleian Library: Rawl. MSS A195c, ff. 369–73

4 T. H. Clarke and W. H. Black, *Eastbury Illustrated* . . . (London 1834) p. 12

5 Bedfordshire County Record Office: TW 818

6 H. L. Bradfer-Lawrence, 'The Building of Raynham Hall' *Norfolk Archaeology* xxiii (1927) 106 & 127

7 Sandeen, p. 34

8 Nottingham University Library: Mi A 60 /6, f. 9

9 Mrs Baldwyn-Childe, 'The Building of the Manor-House of Kyre Park, Worcestershire, 1588–1618' *The Antiquary* xxii (1890) 25

10 J. Evans, 'Extracts from the Private Account Book of Sir William More of Loseley . . .' *Archaeologia* xxxvi (1855) 306

11 A. Clifton-Taylor, *The Pattern of English Building* (2nd edition, London 1965) p. 29

12 I. G. Philip, 'The Building of the Schools Quadrangle' *Oxoniensia* xiii (1948) 45

13 Willis and Clark, i, 205

14 *Ibid* i, 207; i, 252; ii, 111

15 Longleat Archives: R.O.B., i, f. 121. Thynne to Dodd, 18 June 1547

16 Staffordshire County Record Office: D 593 R /1 /2

17 British Museum: Additional MSS 39832, f. 68v

18 Longleat Archives: R.O.B., i, f. 135. Thynne to Dodd, 21 June 1547

19 *Ibid* f. 121

20 *Ibid* R.O.B., iii, f. 161. William Spicer to the Earl of Leicester, 15 July 1571

21 British Museum: Additional MSS 7097, ff. 174–200

22 Cambridge University Library: Hengrave Hall Deposit 80

23 Longleat Archives: R.O.B., ii, f. 263. Thynne to Hertford, 15 June 1567

24 Nottingham University Library: Mi A60 /6, f. 4v

25 *Ibid* Mi A60 /4, f. 8

26 *Ibid* Mi A60 /5, f. 4

27 Sandeen, pp. 183–5

28 *Plymouth Building Accounts of the Sixteenth and Seventeenth Centuries* ed. E. Welch (Devon & Cornwall Record Society new series xii, 1967) p. xiii

29 *The House and Farm Accounts of the Shuttleworths* ed. J. Harland (Chetham Society xxxv, 1856) 172

30 G. R. Batho, 'Notes and Documents on Petworth House, 1574–1632' *Sussex Archaeological Collections* xcvi (1958) 113–29

31 For example, the statute of 7 Ed. VI c. 7; *Tudor Economic Documents*, ed. R. H. Tawney & E. Power (London 1924) i, 238. The other examples of scarcity given by the same authors similarly relate to wood as a fuel or as a ship-building material

32 *Harrison's Description of England* ed. F. J. Furnivall (New Shakspere Society series vi, pt. i, 1877) p. 233

33 J. Norden, *The Surveyors Dialogue* (London 1607) p. 214

34 R. Reyce, *Breviary of Suffolk* ed. Lord Francis Hervey (London 1902) p. 50

35 On this point, see also G. Hammersley, 'The Crown Woods and their Exploitation in the Sixteenth and Seventeenth centuries' *Bulletin of the Institute of Historical Research* xxx (1957) 136–161

36 William Salt Library, Stafford: D. 1721 /1 /4

37 Shrewsbury Public Library: Deeds 6883, f. 12

38 Old Thorndon Hall, Essex; Essex County Record Office: D /DP A21

39 Redgrave Hall, Suffolk

40 Staffordshire County Record Office: D593 R /1 /2
41 William Salt Library, Stafford: D. 1721 /1 /4
42 Staffordshire County Record Office: D593 R /1 /2
43 J. R. Wigfull, 'House Building in Queen Elizabeth's Days' *Transactions of the Hunter Archaeological Society* iii (1925) 70
44 *The House and Farm Accounts of the Shuttleworths* ed. J. Harland (Chetham Society xxxv 1856) 143

13 Roofing Materials

Tiles, which were one of the most popular roof coverings were invariably made on the site or within the locality of the building. Their process of manufacture differed little from the methods used for making bricks. They were generally made by the same craftsmen using the same brick earth, and were fired in the same kilns, often together with the bricks, although specially decorated tiles which required more skill to manufacture were sometimes bought ready-made.

Recent research has produced a substantial body of documentary and archaeological evidence for the use of blue slate for roofing over a wide area of southern England in the Middle Ages.[1] The main sources of this slate were Devon and Cornwall, and it was sometimes even carried into areas where other local slates, such as the sandstone 'slates' of Horsham, were more readily available. One of the probable reasons for their extraordinary popularity was that they could usually be split much thinner than stone slates and consequently their use produced a much lighter roof covering. The advantages of this presumably out-weighed the necessity of transporting them over considerable distances. Much of the transport, in any case, was by sea and river which was comparatively less expensive and difficult than land carriage.

Despite some evidence for a decline in the trade of west country slates to Sussex after the middle of the 15th century, which can possibly be accounted for by a more vigorous exploitation of the local slates, they were employed on a number of important country houses in southern England in the 16th and 17th centuries. In 1529 the abbot of the monastery of Tavistock in Devon was instructed by Royal Commission to supply blue slate for use at Hampton Court,[2] and in 1574 Sir John Thynne bought 13,000 Cornish slates for Longleat.[3] Devonshire slate for Sir John Petre's banqueting house at Old Thorndon Hall, Essex, was carried by sea from Salcombe to Greys Thurrock in 1587.[4] In the 17th century, Lord Salisbury used small quantities of slate shipped from Plymouth on Hatfield House,[5] and Sir Francis Bacon roofed his curious banqueting house at Verulam with Cornish slate.[6] The Earl of Northumberland's intention in 1615 to use 667,000 'of blew slate to cover all the rooffes of them galleries' at Petworth suggests that the material continued to be used in Sussex for larger houses,[7] and at Ashley Park, Surrey, 'blue slate' was used to cover the entrance porch and three dormer windows.[8]

There are few references to blue slates from Wales being employed on English country houses during the period, but no doubt they were used on occasion for houses in the west Midlands, and in 1564 Welsh slate was sent to Dublin for work on the cathedral.[9]

Fissile limestones and sandstones were also used as roofing materials, although their distribution tended to be fairly local and there is no evidence for a widespread trade similar to that for blue slates. Where suitable deposits were close to the sea, as at Purbeck, there were difficulties of extraction,[10] and as the technique of frost splitting was not discovered until the end of the 16th century, the slates had to be laboriously split by hand along the natural bedding planes.[11] The considerable weight of a stone roof which necessitated a much heavier timber framework was possibly a further inhibition to any extensive use of the material away from its area of origin. It was necessary to mine the limestone slates of the Cotswolds around Burford, and of Northamptonshire at Collyweston, but existing buildings in the locality show that they were extensively used, especially in the 17th century, and the proximity of the universities of Oxford and Cambridge provided them with further outlets. The sandstone slates quarried near Horsham were used in Surrey and Sussex, and to some extent in Kent. Amongst the larger houses on which they were employed were Loseley House, Surrey, in 1569,[12] and it was intended to cover the main part of the Earl of Northumberland's house at Petworth in 1615 with them in contrast to the blue slate roofed galleries.[13] Sandstone slates were also used for roofing in parts of the west and north of England, and Bess of Hardwick employed them for Hardwick Old Hall, Derbyshire.[14]

Lead was used for a variety of purposes on the building site. Its malleable qualities and freedom from rust meant that it was extensively used for glazing and for rain-water systems. It was a highly expensive material. £500, out of a total expenditure of £8,000, was spent on lead for Broome Park, Kent, between 1635, and 1638.[15] High costs, together with its general unsuitability for the purpose, meant that lead was rarely used for steeply-pitched roofs, although it was often employed to cover the curved and ogee-shaped turrets so characteristic of many of the buildings of the period. Lead, however, was virtually the only material capable of providing a water-tight covering for roofs of a gentle or flat pitch, and its use for this purpose increased with the introduction of classical architectural motifs. Somerset House in London, built between 1547 and 1552, was amongst the first houses to extensively use lead in this way, and it was subsequently used for such great houses as Hardwick Hall and Hatfield.

The most important sources for lead were the mines of Derbyshire in the north, and of the Mendips in the south west, but in view of the high basic cost of the material together with its transportation costs, considerable amounts of lead seem to have been re-used, especially in the south and the east of the country. At Hengrave Hall, Suffolk, in 1526, one hundred and twelve pounds of lead were bought from the vicar of nearby Cavenham, and in 1537 sixty loads of lead were brought from the abbey at Bury St. Edmunds.[16] In 1509, long before the dissolution, the abbot of Bury had sold lead to Sir Thomas Lucas for Little Saxham Hall, Suffolk,[17] and after the dissolution of the monastries increased quantities of lead suitable for re-using came onto the market. Much of this was used by the Royal Works, as at Canterbury in 1542,[18] but, like other monastic materials, a large amount was available for the private sector. Sir John Thynne got some lead in 1547 from Amesbury Abbey, Wiltshire, which had been granted at the dissolution to his patron, the Earl of Somerset,[19] and in 1573 William Cecil paid £42 for lead from the dissolved college at Fotheringhay, Northamptonshire, for use at Burghley House.[20]

13 Notes

1 E. M. Jope & G. C. Dunning, 'The Use of Blue Slate for Roofing in Medieval England' *The Antiquaries Journal* xxxiv (1954) 209–217; E. W. Holden, 'Slate Roofing in Medieval Sussex' *Sussex Archaeological Collections*, ciii (1965) 66–78

2 Devon County Record Office: L1258 m /vol. i. D84 no. 73

3 Longleat Archives: R.O.B., iii, f. 175

4 Essex County Record Office: D /DP A20

5 L. Stone, 'The Building of Hatfield House' *Archaeological Journal* cxii (1955) 109

6 *'Brief Lives', Chiefly of Contemporaries set down by John Aubrey, between the Years 1669 & 1696* ed. A. Clark (Oxford 1898) i, 81

7 G. R. Batho, 'Notes and Documents on Petworth House, 1574–1632' *Sussex Archaeological Collections* xcvi (1958), 128

8 Surrey County Record Office: Acc. 1030, f. 101

9 J. Mills, 'Peter Lewys: His Work and Workmen' *Journal of the Royal Society of Antiquaries of Ireland* xxxi (1901) 100. Girouard mentions Welsh slate at Longleat *(Smythson,* p. 59) but I have been unable to check the reference in the documents

10 A. Clifton-Taylor, *The Pattern of English Building* (2nd edition, London 1965) p. 121

11 E. M. Jope in *Oxoniensia* xiv (1949) 94

12 J. Evans, 'Extracts from the Private Account Book of Sir William More of Loseley. . .' *Archaeologia* xxxvi (1855) 309

13 G. R. Batho, 'Notes and Documents on Petworth House, 1574–1632' *Sussex Archaeological Collections*, xcvi (1958) 124

14 B. Stallybrass, 'Bess of Hardwick's Buildings and Building Accounts', *Archaeologia* lxiv (1913) 366

15 British Museum: Additional MSS 54332

16 Cambridge University Library: Hengrave Hall Deposit 80

17 British Museum: Additional MSS 7097, f. 195

18 Bodleian Library: Rawl. MSS D781, ff. 170–8

19 Longleat Archives: R.O.B., i, f. 149

20 Public Record Office: E101 /463 /23, f. 1

14 Other Materials

The main structural materials have been considered in the preceding chapters, and it remains to say something about the other materials which went to make up the finished house. The mortar for binding together the stones or bricks was generally composed of lime and sand. It was made by a method similar to that in use in the building industry in recent times, whereby the lime is mixed, or 'slaked', with water and then thoroughly beaten before being covered with sand and left to stand for a period, usually over the winter. On the Royal Works at Dartford in 1543, the mortarmen, who were paid at the same rate as the common labourers, were

> 'Wurking in carrying of watr to slaike lyme wt & in slaikyng of the saide lyme wt sande. And moreover in seiftyng the saide lyme & sande for to make mortr wt . . .' [1]

A similar process was carried out at Sir Thomas Tresham's works at Rushton in 1596, where the labourers prepared a place for making mortar towards the end of July, spent most of the following two months burning lime and slaking it, and in October began to beat and temper it. In the first week of November they finished beating it and covered it with sand ready for use the following year.[2]

The lime for the mortar was made by burning chalk or limestone, and it was frequently manufactured on the site. At Little Saxham Hall in 1505 the lime kiln was constructed by the limeburner himself.[3] The limeburner also helped to make his own kiln at Loseley House, Surrey, in 1562, where he was assisted by three masons, two bricklayers, and two labourers. The kiln took almost two weeks to build and 10,000 bricks were used in its construction.[4] It must have been a fairly large structure, and it was used for burning bricks as well as lime. Some builders, unlike Sir William More, seem to have under-estimated initially the amount of mortar required for their works, and were forced to take remedial measures at a later stage to meet the increased demands. Sir Roger Townshend's lime kiln at Raynham, Norfolk, which was set up in April 1619, was demolished and rebuilt with a larger capacity in 1622,[5] and Sir Thomas Tresham had to considerably enlarge his lime kiln in 1596.[6]

The chalk or limestone used in the kilns was often found locally, although sometimes not without difficulty. At Trentham Hall, Staffordshire, in the 1630s, the first few weeks in each building season were spent seeking out new sources of supply, and in April 1634, twenty tons of lime were bought at Clayton, two miles away, 'to supply ye workemens wants when my quarrey was wrought out'.[7]

Where the raw materials were not easily available it was necessary to buy lime ready-burnt. Sir William Petre bought lime in Woodham Ferrers for repairs at East Thorndon in Essex in 1550,[8] and his son, Sir John Petre, crossed the Thames to Northfleet in Kent to find the necessary lime for his work at Old Thorndon Hall later in the century.[9] Lime was also used as an agricultural fertiliser, and when only small quantities were required for building purposes they were, no doubt, supplied by men such as George Feltwell and John Nybgrave, lime-burners of Little Hadham, Hertfordshire, who in 1548 rented 'a parcel of chalk ground with two lym kylles' for twenty one years from Sir Gyles Capell, the lord of the manor.[10]

The sand for the mortar was usually dug locally, although Sir Basil Dixwell, if the notes of Henry Oxinden are to be believed, spent the enormous sum of £500 on sand for Broome Park, Kent, between 1635 and 1638.[11] Black mortar was sometimes required for special effects, and this was achieved by introducing coal dust into the mixture, as at Old Thorndon Hall, Essex, in 1594, where it was used by the slaters working on the roof of the banqueting house.[12]

A cement made of wax and resin had been used instead of mortar in the medieval period for masonry that was particularly exposed to the influence of wet,[13] and the practice continued throughout the 16th century. At Little Saxham Hall in 1507, wax and resin were bought 'for my masons',[14] and at Loseley House in 1569 'oyle and rosen to syment wtall' were provided in connection with the glazing of the house.[15] Some of the purposes to which cement of this nature was put are made explicit in the accounts for Old Thorndon Hall. In March and April 1587, wax and resin were bought at Brentwood 'to make syment for the hall porche', and in August of the same year 'yellow wax' was provided to make cement for the great chimney.[16] Two pounds of resin and two pounds of wax were bought for Condover Hall, Shropshire, in 1592, 'to symmen the broken stones togeather',[17] and the builder of Grafton Manor, Worcestershire, used a mixture of linseed oil, resin and chalk 'for to symende the glase wyndowes from the wether beatinge into the Chambr' in 1569.[18] Another method used by builders to make their mortar resistant to damp was by the insertion of oyster shells[19] and quantities of these were purchased by the Protector Somerset for his various works between 1548 and 1551.[20]

Iron was used for a large variety of purposes, both functional and decorative, in building. Clamps for stonework, glazing bars, the workmen's tools, and, of course, vast quantities of nails were all made of iron, as were the more artistic fittings such as hinges and fire-backs. A moderately sized country house, such as Trentham Hall in Staffordshire, provided sufficient work to keep two smiths in almost full-time employment throughout the most active years of the building,[21] but few builders seem to have been prepared to set up a forge on the site. At Kirby Muxloe Castle, Leicestershire, a timber framed forge with a slate roof was constructed in 1481,[22] and at Kyre Park, Worcestershire, in 1589 a timber 'Hovell for . . . a Smith to work in' was made.[23] It is not altogether clear whether the latter was actually a forge, but at Raynham Hall, Norfolk, in 1622 a lock was bought 'for ye Dore of ye Smithes fforge',[24] and at Trentham Hall in August 1635 a carpenter and some labourers were engaged on 'taking downe the forge'.[25]

Lawrence Shuttleworth rented an anvil and other equipment from a smith of Burnley in 1601 when he was building Gawthorpe Hall, Lancashire,[26] but many builders seem to have employed local smiths who worked in their own workshops and who were paid at piece-rates both for the materials and for their workmanship. Hence at Bolsover Castle, Derbyshire, in 1613, the bulk of the metalwork was executed at piece-rates by a smith from Bolsover, and the door hooks, grates, and glazing bars were made on the same terms by a more skilled smith from Norton Cuckney, just over six miles away.[27]

Often the smith provided his own iron, but on those occasions when it was bought by the builder, the craftsman was usually entrusted with its choice, as at Rushton in 1594 when the two local smiths working on the Triangular Lodge were sent to Wellingborough to purchase iron,[28] or at Raynham Hall, Norfolk, in 1622, when the smith travelled as far as London to choose iron.[29] The original source of most of the iron used was rarely stated in the documents, except where it was of foreign origin. As in the medieval period, quantities of iron were imported from Spain,[30] and that chosen by the smith of Raynham at London was Spanish, as was the iron imported into Bristol by Sir John Thynne and used at Longleat.[31] Sir Nicholas Bacon provided his smith at Redgrave Hall, Suffolk, with iron from Amiens as well as from Spain,[32] and no doubt some of the iron used by other builders was also imported.

By the 16th century glazed windows were to be found in even the most minor rooms of the houses with which this study is concerned. The manufacture of glass is known to have been carried on in England on a small scale from at least as early as the 13th century,[33] but glass from the readily accessible centres in Burgundy, Lorraine, and Normandy seems to have been generally preferred for its higher quality. The English glass-making industry underwent a considerable expansion in the 16th century, especially after 1567 when the French merchant Jean Carré obtained a patent to manufacture window glass in the Weald and brought over glassmakers from Lorraine and Normandy. By 1579 there were sufficient French workmen at Wisborough Green, Sussex, to hold their own religious services, and this influx of foreign skill led to a great improvement in the quality of native window glass. The forests of the Weald probably provided most of the native glass used in the south east of the country, whilst the Midlands seem to have been largely supplied from Staffordshire.[34] Other glass furnace sites dating from the 16th century have recently been located in Hampshire and around the Bristol Channel, and further north in Lancashire, Cheshire and Yorkshire.[35] Early in the 17th century the growing use of coal for firing the furnaces meant that the glass industry moved to new sites on the coalfields, particularly at Newcastle and Stourbridge.[36]

Where there was sufficient fuel, the manufacturer of glass was a relatively simple process, but there is no evidence to suggest that temporary furnaces were set up solely to glaze a single house. Glass was bought ready-made and sometimes carried vast distances to the site. The builders of an orphanage in Plymouth, for example, sent all the way to London for their glass in 1618.[37] Despite the expanding native industry, many builders continued to specify imported glass. The windows of the chapel at Trinity College, Cambridge, in 1564, were to be glazed with Burgundy glass, and the time limit of the contract was to be dependent on when 'passedge by sea' could be arranged.[38] Normandy, Burgundy and Rhenish glass were supplied by a Worcester glazier for Grafton Manor in 1576, and 'French glasse' was used at Trentham Hall in 1634.[40] Even as late as 1660 Sir Roger Pratt was able to write that

'The best glass that we have here of our own, is that of Newcastle, but from abroad for windows, is that of Normandy.' [41]

However, the source of the glass was rarely noted in the building accounts, and much of it was undoubtedly English glass.

Although glass was in common use for country houses, it continued to be a highly valued material which was treated with economy. Faulty pieces of glass were used in garret windows, and the re-use of old glass was a common practice, especially in the 16th century. When extensions were made to the Hall of the Carpenters' Company in London in 1572 the glazier used forty-one feet of new glass and thirty-six feet of re-used glass,[42] and one of the towers at Hengrave Hall, Suffolk, was glazed 'wt old glasse' in 1536.[43] Considerable amounts of re-used glass were employed by Henry VIII's Office of Works, and monastic glass was carefully salvaged after the dissolution, as at the demolition of the college of Fotheringhay, Northamptonshire, in 1573 when all the glass and iron in the widows were sold for £12.[44]

There is little information specifically about plaster to be derived from most of the building accounts. It must have been used in fairly large quantities for wall surfaces and ceilings, but few of the accountants mention its purchase or its manufacture on the site. This was presumably because much of the plaster was simply composed of lime and sand strengthened with chopped straw or hair and no distinction was made between the purchase of the basic materials for this purpose or for making mortar. Robert Caldwell, however, who drew up the accounts for Grafton Manor, Worcestershire, was more forthcoming. In July and October 1569 he recorded the purchase at Worcester of lime from Bristol specifically for the use of the plasterers, and in November 1568 he differentiated between plaster of 'the best sorte' at 6s 8d the load and plaster of 'the worser sorte' for which he only paid 3s 4d the load.[45]

The finest plaster was made of gypsum, which was to be found chiefly in parts of Dorset, Yorkshire, and the Trent Valley. When it was used outside these areas it had to be transported, sometimes for great distances. Sir Robert Sheffield of Butterwick, Lincolnshire, gave Sir Thomas Lucas thirty-two tons of plaster in 1507 for Little Saxham Hall, Suffolk. It was almost certainly made from gypsum, and to reach its destination it had to be carried overland to Boston, shipped by sea to King's Lynn, taken up the River Ouse to Brandon, and finally transferred to carts again for the journey to Little Saxham.[46] The organisation of its carriage must have involved considerable administrative effort, and gives some indication that gypsum plaster was very highly regarded. Similar plaster for Hengrave Hall, a few miles away from Little Saxham, was bought by Sir Thomas Kytson in 1538 at Collyweston, Northamptonshire, although the price that he paid included transport as far as Brandon where his own carts were able to collect it for the final stage of the journey.[47]

The specialised and often exotic materials used by the decorative painters to make their colours were frequently supplied by the craftsmen themselves, the builders simply re-imbursing the painters when they submitted their bills. Thus Sir Thomas Tresham received a bill from his painter early in the 17th century for work carried out over a period of sixteen weeks and three days, and for

'ooille thre gaullens and a haulfe..23*s*
whit lead forti iiii pound...23*s* vi*d*
haulfe a boucke off gould..12*d*
bllu, black, yealou, read, grean, gouldsicse and all cind off coulles.....................20*s*.' [48]

The craftsmen bought their materials, apparently on credit, from tradesmen; an arrangement that could result in difficulties for the craftsmen if the builder was slow in settling his accounts, as Thomas Selby discovered when he executed a considerable amount of work for Lord Zouche at Bramshill House, Hampshire, between 1615 and 1617. By 1619 only part of the bill had been paid and Selby was forced to remind his former employer that

> 'The stuffe belonging to the worke cost 20 markes for which your peticioner is yet indebted to dyvers men who seeke daylie to arrest your said peticioner for the same, soe that for feare he cannot perform any busynes whereby to get his living beeing restrayned of libertie to his utter undoinge.' [49]

Some builders bought painting materials direct from the tradesmen in the larger market centres, but the distances that were sometimes involved make it clear why the majority preferred the craftsmen to supply their own materials. Much of the materials for the painter at Hardwick Hall, Derbyshire, were bought in London,[50] and although the builders of Little Saxham Hall and Hengrave Hall in Suffolk were able to obtain some of their materials from a 'grossor of bury' they also had to buy others in London.[51]

A large variety of other materials appear in the building accounts, such as coal for burning lime and bricks, ochre for enhancing the colouring of brickwork, and hair for mixing with plaster or cleaning tools. Candles were bought on a number of building sites, both to provide light for craftsmen working on the interior of the building during the winter months and to heat up solder for plumbers engaged on soldering lead pipes. Other materials included bracken for thatching unfinished walls to protect them from frost during the winter, moss for bedding stone roof slates, and a vast array of miscellaneous purchases such as ropes, glue, thread, charcoal, pitch and so on.

14   Notes

1   Bodleian Library: Rawl. MSS D784. 4 February—4 March 1543
2   British Museum: Additional MSS 39832, ff. 88–95
3   British Museum: Additional MSS 7097, f. 174v
4   J. Evans, 'Extracts from the Private Account Book of Sir William More of Loseley . . .' *Archaeologia* xxxvi (1855) 297
5   H. L. Bradfer-Lawrence, 'The Building of Raynham Hall' *Norfolk Archaeology* xxiii (1927) 110 & 137
6   British Museum: Additional MSS 39832, f. 86
7   Staffordshire County Record Office: D593 R/1/2
8   Essex County Record Office: D/DP A10, f. 48
9   Essex County Record Office: D/DP A22
10   W. Minet, *Hadham Hall* (Colchester 1914) p. 17
11   British Museum: Additional MSS 54332
12   Essex County Record Office: D/DP A22
13   Salzman, p. 153

14   British Museum: Additional MSS 7097, f. 182
15   J. Evans, 'Extracts from the Private Account Book of Sir William More of Loseley . . .' *Archaeologia* xxxvi (1855) 309
16   Essex County Record Office: D /DP A20
17   Shrewsbury Public Library: Deeds 6885, f. 8v
18   J. Humphreys, 'The Elizabethan Estate Book of Grafton Manor' *Transactions of the Birmingham Archaeological Society* xliv (1918) 22
19   E. A. Gee, 'Oxford Masons, 1370–1530' *Archaeological Journal* cix (1952) 56
20   British Museum: Egerton MSS 2815
21   Staffordshire County Record Office: D593 R /1 /2
22   A. Hamilton-Thompson, 'The Building Accounts of Kirby Muxloe Castle, 1480–84' *Transactions of the Leicester Archaeological Society* xi (1913–20) 203
23   Mrs Baldwyn-Childe, 'The Building of the Manor-House of Kyre Park, Worcestershire' *The Antiquary* xxii (1890) 25
24   H. L. Bradfer-Lawrence, 'The Building of Raynham Hall' *Norfolk Archaeology* xxiii (1927) 131
25   Staffordshire County Record Office: D593 R /1 /2
26   *The House and Farm Accounts of the Shuttleworths* ed. J. Harland (Chetham Society xxxv 1856) p. 139
27   D. Knoop & G. P. Jones, 'The Bolsover Castle Building Account, 1613' *Ars Quatuor Coronatorum* xlix (1939) 24–79
28   British Museum: Additional MSS 39832, f. 30v
29   Bradfer-Lawrence, *op cit* 133
30   Salzman, pp. 286–7
31   Girouard, *Smythson* p. 59
32   Sandeen, p. 35
33   Salzman, p. 182
34   D. W. Crossley, 'Glass Making in Bagot's Park, Staffordshire, in the Sixteenth Century' *Post-Medieval Archaeology* i (1967) 44–83
35   *Idem*, 'The Performance of the Glass Industry in Sixteenth-Century England' *Economic History Review* 2nd series xxv (1972) 429
36   The most detailed study of the English glass industry in the sixteenth and seventeenth centuries is G. H. Kenyon, *The Glass Industry of the Weald* (Leicester 1967). Some of his conclusions, however, have been modified by the recent researches of Mr Crossley
37   *Plymouth Building Accounts* ed. E. Welch (Devon and Cornwall Record Society, new series xii, 1967) p. 94
38   Willis & Clark, ii, 572.
39   British Museum: Additional MSS 46, 461, f. 46v
40   Staffordshire County Record Office: D593 R /1 /2. 25 January 1633 /4
41   *The Architecture of Sir Roger Pratt* ed. R. T. Gunther (Oxford 1928) p. 72
42   G. J. Eltringham, 'The Extension of the Carpenters' Company Hall, 1572' *Guildhall Miscellany* i, no. 4 (1955) 32
43   Cambridge University Library: Hengrave Hall Deposit 80
44   Public Record Office: E101 /463 /23, f. 1
45   J. Humphreys, 'The Elizabethan Estate Book of Grafton Manor' *Transactions of the Birmingham Archaeological Society* xliv (1918) 34, 40, & 17
46   British Museum: Additional MSS 7097, f. 182
47   Cambridge University Library: Hengrave Hall Deposit 80
48   British Museum: Additional MSS 39836, f. 363
49   W. H. Cope, *Bramshill* (London 1883) p. 121
50   B. Stallybrass, 'Bess of Hardwick's Buildings and Building Accounts' *Archaeologia* lxiv (1913) 383
51   British Museum: Additional MSS 7097, ff. 174–200; Cambridge University Library: Hengrave Hall Deposit 80.

15 Sources of Supply

Some of the sources of supply for specific materials have already been noticed. Much of their material generally came from the builders' own estates and from the most conveniently accessible quarries and forests, but sometimes it was necessary to supplement these sources from further afield. The interest which many builders displayed in the architecture of their friends and peers, and the freedom with which they exchanged ideas and even skilled craftsmen, often extended to the provision of quantities of materials which individual builders lacked. Sir Thomas Gresham and his agents in Antwerp were busy in the 1560s supplying building materials from the Netherlands for Sir William Cecil and the Earl of Ormond,[1] and in a more local context Sir John Strode noted that 'much stone [and] many Timber trees . . . were freely given me by my neighbours' for Chantmarle House, Dorset.[2] In 1589 Sir Edward Pytts gave two thousand boards which were surplus to his requirements at Kyre Park to Ralph Sheldon 'toward the bourding of his newe house at Weston in Warwickshire'.[3] Sir John Thynne was given a number of trees for Longleat at various dates,[4] as was Sir William More at Loseley in the 1560s.[5] Although most of the recorded gifts of materials were of timber, a few builders were given quantities of stone. Lord Burghley sent stone to the Earl of Leicester in 1575 'toward the making a lytle banquett house' in his garden,[6] and in 1601 Sir Robert Cecil was given some stone from Penshurst by Lady Sydney.[7]

The workmen engaged upon the building sometimes provided another source of supply. Masons and quarrymen acting as stone-suppliers have already been noticed, and many of the other crafts occasionally furnished some of their own materials. It was common practice for joiners to supply wainscot and even the glue and nails to fix it. Tilers frequently provided their own laths and tile-pins, and plumbers sometimes used their own lead. Many craftsmen must have accumulated limited quantities of the materials that pertained to their craft and which they were capable of supplying as the need arose. Some of the workmen employed on building the Guildhall at Plymouth in the early 17th century bought up the surplus material remaining at the completion of the work, presumably with the intention of using it on a subsequent job.[8] Similarly, at the sale of materials from the dissolved college at Fotheringhay, Northamptonshire, in 1573, William Grumbold, of the family of masons, bought most of the stone from the foundations.[9] A few craftsmen were also able to supply materials for other crafts, although the amounts involved were generally insignificant, such as the 'greate peece of timber' bought from a mason working on the market house at Aylesbury in 1645, or the five hundred and ten bricks supplied by the plumber employed on the same work.[10] Some crafts-men undoubtedly acted as dealers in building material but their overall effect on country house building was small because such large quantities of materials were required that it was necessary for the builder to establish regular links with the primary sources himself to ensure the constant availability of his supplies. In addition, although limited credit was available to workmen buying materials, it was only the builder who had sufficient reserves of capital to buy in bulk.

Small items of ready-made smiths' work such as nails and locks, and miscellaneous equip-ment like buckets and sieves, were occasionally bought at local markets and fairs. Sir Roger Townshend patronised more than a dozen fairs within a radius of forty miles of Raynham Hall, Norfolk, between 1619 and 1622,[11] but most builders only made an occasional purchase from this source. Sir John Petre of Thorndon Hall, Essex, for example, bought some pails for his mortar makers and a finishing saw at Brentwood fair in 1581 and a small quantity of lath nails at Ingatestone fair in 1589,[12] while Thomas Lucas bought lath nails, lead, and coal at the famous Sturbridge fair in 1507 and 1508 for Little Saxham Hall.[13]

When the glazier and building contractor, Bernard Dinninghof, wrote to Thomas Lumsden in October 1618, offering to rebuild Sheriff Hutton Castle, Yorkshire, he observed,

> 'You are aminded to take down the Castell, wherein will be found much timbre for that purpose, also iron for window bars and bands for doors and casements and such like necessarys, and also lead for the gutters and wankes and cant windows.'   [14]

Many other builders re-used old materials to similar effect. Sir Nicholas Bacon used materials from the existing building on the site when he built Gorhambury House in 1561,[15] and Sir Charles Cavendish employed stone from his abandoned house at Kirkby-in-Ashfield and from the ruined castle on the site when he commenced work at Bolsover Castle in 1613.[16] Even builders of the very highest status took the opportunity when it arose of incorporating old material in their new works. The old royal palace at Hatfield provided Robert Cecil with bricks which he used for some garden walls and for rubble filling to level the courtyards of his new house,[17] and when James Needham, shortly to become Surveyor of the Royal Works, contracted to make a new gallery and summer house at Exeter House, London, in 1530, he took

> 'to his owen use all the olde gallary as it now stondith holie and all the olde brik and stones as well in the fundacion as elles where towarde the newe makynge of the other gallary'.   [18]

The dissolution of the monasteries made available a vast quantity of material which was capable of re-use by domestic builders, and many of the recipients of monastic property were quick to take advantage of this opportunity to realise an immediate return on their investment. Dunkeswell Abbey, Devon, which was dissolved on 14 February 1539, was granted to Lord John Russell who, by 27 November in the same year, had sold 'all manner of glass, iron, timber, stones, tomb-stones, tile stones, and paving tile, and all other stuff' to John Haydon who was about to start work on his new house at Cadhay.[19] Bells and lead were usually expressly excluded from the sale of monastic property into lay hands, but all the other easily portable materials, such as iron and glass, were probably soon removed and sold. Few builders could have lived very far away from a monastic site, and many of them must have acquired materials after the dissolution. Amongst the various purchasers of materials from the dissolved college at Fotheringhay, Northamptonshire, in 1573, were aristocratic builders such as Lord Burghley, craftsmen like William Grumbold, and a number of smaller buyers like the inhabitants of the neighbouring village of Woodnewton who paid 10s for battlement stone 'for their church'.[20]

Former monastic stone continued to be available long after the dissolution. In the 1560s Sir William More obtained fourteen loads of stone from 'the friars in Guildford', and ninety-one loads from Waverley Abbey for his house at Loseley, Surrey.[21] Sir Nicholas Bacon's Gorhambury House, built between 1563 and 1568, incorporated stone from St. Albans Abbey,[22] and in the 17th century, the Earl of Salisbury used stone from the former monastery of St. Augustine at Canterbury for both Hatfield House and his New Exchange.[23] Fountains Hall in Yorkshire, built early in the century by Sir Stephen Proctor contained 'stone gott at hand out of the abbey walls',[24] and as late as 1621 Sir Roger Townshend was making the foundations of his first house at Raynham out of stone taken from Coxford Abbey.[25] Generally it was only possible to re-use stone for foundations and rubble walling and the supply of monastic stone for this purpose seems to have exceeded the immediate demand in the years after the dissolution. In addition, some of the owners of former monastic property chose to reserve the materials for their own possible future use, as Nathaniel Bacon discovered in 1575 when he attempted to buy stone from Edward Paston whose family had acquired Binham Priory, Norfolk, over thirty years earlier, in 1541.[26] Moral scruples, too, probably inhibited some of the new owners from fully exploiting their monastic possessions, and although they were prepared to farm the lands it was left to later generations to demolish the buildings and utilise the materials that they contained. In a number of cases, of course, the buildings were never systematically dismantled and their substantial remains are still visible in many parts of the country.

15 Notes

1   J. W. Burgon, *The Life and Times of Sir Thomas Gresham* (London 1831) ii, 117
2   Dorset County Record Office: MW/M4, f. 24v
3   Mrs Baldwyn-Childe, 'The Building of the Manor-House of Kyre Park, Worcestershire' *The Antiquary* xxii (1890) 25
4   For example from the Earl of Hertford in 1567. Longleat Archives: R.O.B., ii, f. 263
5   J. Evans, 'Extracts from the Private Account Book of Sir William More of Loseley . . .' *Archaeologia* xxxvi (1855) 294
6   J. Nichols, *The Progresses and Public Processions of Queen Elizabeth* (London 1823) i, 524
7   Historical Manuscripts Commission, *Hatfield*, xi, 358
8   *Plymouth Building Accounts* ed. E. Welch (Devon and Cornwall Record Society, new series xii, 1967) p. 60
9   Public Record Office: E101/463/23
10 Public Record Office: SP28/207, ff. 51, 34, & 38. I am grateful to Dr John Broad for drawing my attention to this document

11 H. L. Bradfer-Lawrence, 'The Building of Raynham Hall' *Norfolk Archaeology* xxiii (1927) 93–146

12 Essex County Record Office: D /DP A19 and D /DP A21

13 British Museum: Additional MSS 7097, ff. 183v, 185, 189v

14 S. D. Kitson, 'The Heraldic Glass of Gilling Castle, Yorkshire, and Bernard Dinninghof' *Journal of the British Society of Master Glass Painters,* iii (1929) 55–8

15 J. C. Rogers, 'The Manor and Houses of Gorhambury' *Transactions of the St. Albans and Hertfordshire Architectural and Archaeological Society* new series iv (1933) 35–112

16 D. Knoop & G. P. Jones, 'The Bolsover Castle Building Account for 1613' *Ars Quatuor Coronatorum* xlix (1939) 24–79

17 L. Stone, 'The Building of Hatfield House' *Archaeological Journal* cxii (1955) 107

18 Salzman, p. 577

19 Devon County Record Office: L1258 M /vol. 1, Devon G5 No. 4

20 Public Record Office: E101 /463 /13

21 J. Evans, 'Extracts from the Private Account Book of Sir William More of Loseley . . .' *Archaeologia* xxxvi (1855) 296–308

22 J. C. Rogers, 'The Manor and Houses of Gorhambury' *Transactions of the St. Albans and Hertfordshire Architectural and Archaeological Society* new series iv (1933) 41

23 Stone, *op cit* 108; L. Stone, 'Inigo Jones and the New Exchange' *Archaeological Journal* cxiv (1957) 115

24 British Museum: Harleian MSS 6853, f. 450

25 H. L. Bradfer-Lawrence, 'The Building of Raynham Hall' *Norfolk Archaeology* xxiii (1927) 101

26 Sandeen, p. 188; T. H. Swales, 'The Redistribution of the Monastic Lands in Norfolk at the Dissolution' *Norfolk Archaeology* xxxiv (1966) 27

16 Transport

The transport of building materials to the site of a country house was both expensive and difficult. For example, six chalders of coal which cost Thomas Lucas 1s 8d to purchase at King's Lynn in 1505, cost a further 6s 8d to carry to Little Saxham,[1] and Sir William More paid only 2s a load for stone ready dug and dressed at Gatton quarry in the 1560s, but the carriage to the site at Loseley cost him more than six times that amount.[2] The state of the roads and the weather added to the problems of land carriage. During the winter the average loads carried by the carters from London to Hatfield for Salisbury's new house were little more than half those carried in the summer,[3] and even in the month of June, Sir John Thynne's steward complained to him from Longleat that

> 'the wether is and hathe bene Rayne every daye of a longe tyme here insomoche that there wilbe no caryinge hadd withoute double charges'.   [4]

The transportation of materials could be further disrupted by a temporary shortage of carts during the major events of the farming calendar. The delivery of stone to Longleat was again held up in March 1562 when Thynne's tenants at Upton Scudamore refused to provide him with carriage 'before they have mayd an end of Sowynge',[5] and in August 1601 Lady Sydney was pessimistic about her ability to find carriage for the stone that she was providing for Salisbury from Penshurst, for 'in this country at harvest time [carriage] is somewhat scarce to come by'.[6]

Wherever possible, water transport was used for the bulky materials, and the effects of this on the distribution of building stone has already been noted. The rivers of East Anglia, particularly the Ouse and the Nene, were of prime importance in moving materials to the documented houses of the area, such as Little Saxham Hall and Hengrave Hall in Suffolk, and Redgrave Hall in Suffolk. They made it possible for the builders of those houses to use the limestone from the Midland quarries, and to benefit from the wide range of goods available at King's Lynn. When Sir Robert Sheffield of Butterwick in Lincolnshire made a gift of thirty-two tons of plaster in 1507 to Thomas Lucas for Little Saxham Hall, the journey of some eighty miles was largely accomplished by water, using the Wash from Boston to Lynn and then the River Ouse to Brandon.[7] Although the detailed cost is not recorded, it would probably have been prohibitive to have attempted the carriage by land for it cost 20s to carry only part of the plaster overland to Boston. Imported materials, especially the softwoods of the Baltic, penetrated deep into the country via the rivers, so that even a builder of modest means, such as Francis Farrar of Harrold House, Bedfordshire, was able to buy deal boards at Lynn and bring them by water to the site.[8] On the western side of the country, the proximity of the River Severn to Kyre Park enabled Sir Edward Pytts to get much of his stone from the quarries at Madeley in Shropshire, 36 miles away, and even to use small quantities from Bath and from Painswick in Gloucestershire,[9] while Lawrence Shuttleworth was able to buy lead at Stockport and Manchester and to bring it to the site at Gawthorpe, Lancashire, by means of the River Calder.[10]

No matter how well placed a house was in relation to water transport some land carriage was necessary, if only to bring the materials from the waterside to the building site, and for those houses, like Longleat, which were situated far from any navigable waterways, the accumulation of the required materials was wholly dependent on a system of overland transport. The organisation of transport varied from site to site. Some builders relied on local carriers, hiring them and their carts on a day-to-day basis when there were specific loads to be shifted. Although it was a policy followed by many builders, including Sir Thomas Kytson at Hengrave, the conflicting demands of the local community for the services of the carriers were capable of producing temporary shortages of carts which could disrupt the building programme. Most builders turned to local carriers for occasional help when building activity was at its height, but in general they relied on a more permanent organisation for the transportation of their materials.

On most building sites there was usually sufficient need for a certain amount of carrying throughout the building season, and a number of builders employed one or two carters on an annual basis. Lawrence Shuttleworth, who was engaged on building Gawthorpe Hall, Lancashire, in the first decade of the 17th century, paid one carter £2 a year in quarterly instalments, and in July 1601, at the height of the building season, he hired another carter 'untell mychilmes for xvd in the wicke, broken worke and holle', a phrase which implies that he was to be paid whether there was sufficient work for him to do or not.[11] Additional carts were hired for short periods when necessary, but the bulk of the work was executed by the permanent carters. Similarly, Sir Thomas Tresham employed the same carter for every week that he was building at Rushton, Northamptonshire, between 1593 and 1597, paying him by the week rather than at a daily rate as was his practice with the other workmen on the site, and finding him alternative work in the gardens when there was no carrying for him to do.[12]

Where substantial quantities of materials were being provided from the same source away from the neighbourhood of the building, some builders preferred to arrange for the necessary transportation by independent contractors. Much of the stone for Kyre Park, Worcestershire, for example, was quarried at Madeley in Shropshire. The quarryman as part of his contract arranged for its carriage down the River Severn to Bewdley, and separate contracts were made with Richard Bishop of Stottesdon, Shropshire, and Robert Tyrry of Mornall, Worcestershire, to transport it overland from there to the building site.[13] The stone from Thorney Abbey, Cambridgeshire, used to build the chapel at Corpus Christi College, Cambridge, in 1579, was similarly carried in stages by three separate contracts, being first carried from the abbey to Guyhirn by the River Nene, then to Jesus Green by the River Cam, and finally overland to the site.[14]

Sometimes a builder was able to call upon additional sources of carriage which, although by their nature only available at irregular intervals, could be of considerable assistance to his permanent labour force. Many builders for example, still retained the obligation of boon-work from their tenants, and this was usually partly fulfilled while building work was in progress by the provision of carriage. Where the builder owned a large number of manors he was able to get a substantial part of his local carrying done in this way. At Longleat, Sir John Thynne regularly used boon-labour for carriage from his tenants of Frome, Woodlands, Deverill, Marston, Longbridge Deverill, Crockerton, Cheddar, and Haselbury, and occasionally from some of his other manors. The tenants provided their own carts and generally only worked for one day. They were not paid, but were always given food and drink while they were working.[15] It appears that the tenants had a certain amount of choice as to when they would provide their labour, and that their own needs took precedence over their lord's demands for their carts.[16]

The conditions of employment of boon-labour were similar on other building sites, but few builders were able to use it on such a large scale as Sir John Thynne, who in a short period in 1568 had as many as forty tenants carrying for him.[17] Most builders appear to have been in a similar position to Sir Thomas Tresham who was able to call upon a few carts each year from his tenants in the manors of Rothwell, Orton and Rushton.[18] Although most builders only employed their tenants for a few days in the immediate vicinity of the work, there were occasions when they were sent further afield, as in 1587 when timber for Sir Francis Willoughby's house at Wollaton was brought almost forty miles from his newly acquired manor at Kingsbury in Warwickshire, a journey that necessitated several nights away from home for the carters.[19] Basically a relic of feudalism, the obligation to provide boon-labour survived on some manors well into the 17th century and as late as 1634 Sir Richard Leveson's tenants were undertaking some of the carriage during the building of Trentham Hall, Staffordshire.[20]

Some builders were also helped to transport their materials by their friends. So much carriage was given free to Sir William More while he was building Loseley House that he only had to hire a full-time team of his own for thirty-seven days in 1562,[21] and as previously noted, John Strode's costs in building Chantmarle House in Dorset between 1612 and 1623 had been considerably reduced because of the

'very great number of carraiges of stones both from Hambden & Whatley quarrs freely given me by my neighbours, especially of Beauminster & Netherbury'.   [22]

Sir John Thynne must have sorely strained many of his friendships with his frequent requests for assistance in carrying materials to Longleat. In July 1547 he wrote to his steward telling him to call upon the Earl of Hertford, Vincent Mompesson, 'and other my friends' to get as much stone as possible to Longleat for the following year's work, adding 'in any wise hire nether cariage of timber nor stoone but when you must neds'.[23] When in October of the same year the weather turned unseasonably fine he again solicited his friends' help in getting stone home,[24] and in November he turned to them for the carriage of a load of timber from Bristol.[25]

It is probable that the carriage provided by these friends of the builder was frequently undertaken by their tenants as boon-service. Thus Cecil was informed in June 1556 that 'mr barteleyes tenentes bryng to Burghley all yor plaster yt is at Sesterne [Sewstern, Leicester-shire]',[26] and Thynne's steward wrote to him in 1567 that

> 'Mr Bamfild hath pmysed to John Ryder that he will cause his tennants to helpe you with as mych carriage as ys possible from Mr Colthere'.   [27]

The equipment used by individual builders for land transport varied considerably. The stone for the final version of Longleat was carried from the quarries near Bath on wheel-less drags pulled by oxen,[28] a method also used by Sir Thomas Tresham in Northamptonshire[29] and Sir Edward Pytts in Worcestershire.[30] The Countess of Shrewsbury transported most of the materials for Hardwick Hall by pack-horse.[31] However, the most common form of transport to the building site was by carts drawn by horses or oxen. Most builders possessed some carts of their own and often these sufficed for nearly all their building requirements. Apart from four days in July 1633 when he hired a carter and his team, and some assistance from his tenants in the spring of the following year, Sir Richard Leveson used only his own carts and workmen during the nine years that he was building Trentham Hall, Staffordshire.[32] Frequently, however, extra carts were necessary. Most builders, like Sir Thomas Kytson at Hengrave Hall, preferred to hire them as the occasion demanded, paying an inclusive daily or weekly sum for the carter and his cart. Other builders bought new carts and employed labour soley to operate them. Sir Roger Townshend, for example, who began work on Raynham Hall, Norfolk, in 1619, bought a cart at Newmarket in May for £7, and then in June spent a further £12 at Newmarket on another cart, some cart wheels and an axle-tree.[33]

Oxen as well as horses were extensively used for carrying purposes. Thomas Lucas bought 'a kyne' in December 1505 to carry earth for the levelling of the site of Little Saxham Hall, Suffolk,[34] and Sir John Thynne instructed his steward in June 1547 to purchase six or eight oxen for the carriage of materials.[35] The timber brought from Kingsbury to Wollaton Hall in 1587 was carried by 'cattle',[36] and the building account for Beaudesert Hall, Staffordshire, for Lord Paget in 1575 includes 3s 'payed to the Smythe for showinge the oxen'.[37] Even as late as 1631, Sir Arthur Ingram was using oxen during the rebuilding of Temple Newsam in the West Riding of Yorkshire.[38] The animals were tended by the regular carters, who were also responsible for the routine maintenance of the carts and associated equipment. Local wheelwrights were employed on a casual basis for more specialised repair work.

Materials which were brought from a long distance away from the site, or which were carried in separate stages by different carriers, sometimes had to be stored in transit. 1s 6d was spent on 'howse rome' in Bolton for sixty-nine loads of lead being brought from Stockport to Gawthorpe Hall, Lancashire, in November 1602, and wainscot from Ireland for the same house was deposited in the tithe barn at Much Hoole near the coast in the summer of 1607 before being carried inland.[39] The iron railings for the tombs to the 3rd and 4th Earls of Rutland were stored in 'her ladyship's brewhouse at Newark' on their way from Gainsborough to Bottesford in Leicestershire in 1592.[40]

Sir Robert Cecil hired a yard and warehouse in Redcross Street, London, to store the materials coming into the capital before they were transported to the site at Hatfield,[41] but there were few other builders who required permanent storage accommodation on this scale. Sir John Petre, who made occasional purchases in London, was generally able to find sufficient space for his materials in the inns of Whitechapel and Aldgate. In March 1590, for example, he bought wainscot at an inn called The White Lion in Thames Street which he carried to The Swan in Whitechapel where he paid 4d for a week's storage before carrying it down to Thorndon in Essex.[42]

Goods in transit were particularly vulnerable to pilfering and despite the precautions taken for their storage, loads of materials did not always arrive intact at the site. Sir Edward Pytts of Kyre Park, Worcestershire, bought a ton of lead in Bristol in 1614, and he very indignantly noted that one of the eighteen pigs in the load was 'by the way stollen', and although 'contrary to promise', he nevertheless had to pay for it.[43] Once on the site, stringent arrangements were made for the security of the building materials. At Kyre Park, timber was stored in the 'masons work-house',[44] and the scaffolding being used at Dublin Cathedral in 1564 and 1565 was kept in 'safety in the Mary chapel under lock'.[45] During the building of Whitehall Palace in 1531, stakes, thorns, and bushes were bought to surround some of the materials and to safeguard them.[46] However, the more conventional form of protection on most domestic building sites was to keep the materials under lock and key wherever possible. Thus at Raynham Hall a stock lock was bought in 1621 for 'ye Closett Dore on ye gardinge Chambr, to shett upp ther instrumts & necessaries'[47] and another lock was purchased in 1622 for the door where the 'wrought fresestone lyeth & An other stocke locke for ye Dore of ye Smithes fforge'.[48]

The last step in the transportation of materials came when they were placed in their final position on the building itself. The more portable materials, of course, could be carried by the craftsmen and their labourers, but heavier materials such as stone and timber required specialised lifting gear. This could be provided by a simple system of ropes and pulleys, and in 1568 Sir John Thynne bought two brass pulleys in London for Longleat.[49] However, most country house building sites seem to have been equipped with more sophisticated machinery. Wooden cranes were in use at Redgrave Hall in the 1540s,[50] and Rushton Hall in the 1590s.[51] At Raynham Hall in 1621 the carpenter and the smith made 'a crane to drive downe pylles'.[52] These cranes were almost certainly operated by hand, but an iron crane used in the construction of the New Haven at Chester in 1567 was powered by a form of treadmill worked by female labourers who were also employed in other tasks about the site.[53]

16　Notes

1　British Museum: Additional MSS 7097, f. 174v
2　J. Evans, 'Extracts from the Private Account Book of Sir William More of Loseley...' *Archaeologia* xxxvi (1855) 303
3　L. Stone, 'The Building of Hatfield House' *Archaeological Journal* cxii (1955) 108
4　Longleat Archives: R.O.B., i, f. 371. Dodd to Thynne, 20 June 1549
5　*Ibid* R.O.B., ii, f. 147. George Walker to Thynne, 15 March 1562
6　Historical Manuscripts Commission, *Hatfield* xi, 358

7   British Museum: Additional MSS 7097, f. 182

8   Bedfordshire County Record Office: TW 818

9   Mrs Baldwyn-Childe, 'The Building of the Manor-House of Kyre Park, Worcestershire, 1588–1618' *The Antiquary* xxi (1890) 205

10   *The House and Farm Accounts of the Shuttleworths* ed. J. Harland (Chetham Society xxxv 1856) 147–8

11   *The House and Farm Accounts of the Shuttleworths* ed. J. Harland (Chetham Society xxxv 1856) 137

12   British Museum: Additional MSS 39832

13   Mrs Baldwyn-Childe, *op cit* 205

14   E. R. Sandeen, 'The Building of the Sixteenth Century Corpus Christi College Chapel' *Proceedings of the Cambridge Antiquarian Society* lv (1961) 23–35

15   Longleat Archives: R.O.B., iii, f. 14

16   *Ibid* ii, f. 147, where Thynne's tenants at Upton Scudamore refused him carriage until they had completed sowing

17   *Ibid* iii, f. 14

18   British Museum: Additional MSS 39832, ff. 59, 60, 63, *et passim*

19   Nottingham University Library: Mi A 60 /6, f. 4v

20   Staffordshire County Record Office: D593 R /1 /2. 29 March and 5 April 1634

21   J. Evans, 'Extracts from the Private Account Book of Sir William More of Loseley. . .' *Archaeologia* xxxvi (1855) 284–310

22   Dorset County Record Office: MW /M4, f. 24v

23   Longleat Archives: R.O.B., i, ff. 165 –6. Thynne to Dodd, 4 July 1547

24   *Ibid* f. 287. Thynne to Dodd, 2 October 1547

25   *Ibid* f. 299. Thynne to Dodd, 8 November 1547

26   J. A. Gotch, 'The Renaissance in Northamptonshire' *Transactions of the Royal Institute of British Architects* new series vi (1890) 104

27   Longleat Archives: R.O.B., ii, f. 257. Thomas Vyttery to Thynne, 22 May 1567

28   Girouard, *Smythson* p. 59

29   British Museum: Additional MSS 39832, f. 81

30   Mrs Baldwyn-Childe, *op cit* xxii, 53

31   B. Stallybrass, 'Bess of Hardwick's Buildings and Building Accounts' *Archaeologia* lxiv (1913) 186

32   Staffordshire County Record Office: D593 R /1 /2

33   H. L. Bradfer-Lawrence, 'The Building of Raynham Hall' *Norfolk Archaeology* xxiii (1927) 111 & 114

34   British Museum: Additional MSS 7097, f. 176v

35   Longleat Archives: R.O.B., i, f. 136. Thynne to Dodd, 21 June 1547

36   Nottingham University Library: Mi A 60 /6, f. 4v

37   William Salt Library, Stafford: D1734 /3 /4 /101

38   Leeds City Library: TN /EA /13 /39

39   *The House and Farm Accounts of the Shuttleworths* ed. J. Harland (Chetham Society xxxv 1856) 147 & 165

40   Historical Manuscripts Commission *Rutland* iv 405

41   L. Stone, 'The Building of Hatfield House' *Archaeological Journal* cxii (1955) 108

42   Essex County Record Office: D /DP A21

43   Mrs Baldwyn-Childe, 'The Building of the Manor-House of Kyre Park, Worcestershire' *The Antiquary* xxii (1890) 52

44   *Ibid* 25

45   J. Mills, 'Peter Lewys: His Work and Workmen' *Journal of the Royal Society of Antiquaries of Ireland* xxxi (1901) 101

46   Public Record Office: E36 /251 f. 233

47   H. L. Bradfer-Lawrence, 'The Building of Raynham Hall' *Norfolk Archaeology* xxiii (1927) 129

48 *Ibid* 131
49 Longleat Archives: T. P., Box lxviii, Bk. 59, f. 12
50 Sandeen, p. 82
51 British Museum: Additional MSS 39832, f. 92
52 Bradfer-Lawrence, *op cit*
53 E. Ridout, 'The Account Book of the New Haven, Chester, 1567–8' *Transactions of the Historical Society of Lancashire and Cheshire* lxxx (1928) 86–128

Part IV: The Workmen

17 Craftsmen

The requirements of the country house building industry meant that many of the craftsmen employed in it were both wage-earners and itinerant, and that consequently their way of life differed radically from that of artisans in other occupations in the 16th and early 17th centuries. There were, of course, exceptions to this general pattern. A number of building artificers were small masters who hired out their own labour and who undertook works by contract, and in some urban areas there was sufficient building and maintenance work to support a permanently settled labour force. However an analysis of the building accounts that survive for country houses makes it clear that many of the craftsmen engaged in this branch of the industry were undoubtedly itinerant wage-earners.

Insufficient accounts remain to give anything more than an outline picture of the mobility of most craftsmen. It is known, for instance, that William Cotes, mason, came from Gloucester in February 1615 to work for Sir Edward Pytts at Kyre Park, Worcestershire, but nothing is known about his subsequent movements after the completion of the house.[1] Other masons and bricklayers working on the same house came from Bromsgrove, twenty-five miles away, and Alvechurch, thirty miles away. Some of the chimney-pieces were executed on the site by Gerard Holleman, the Dutch carver resident in London, who moved on to make the monument to Richard Barneby and his wife at nearby Bockleton after he had finished at Kyre.[2] Six of the eleven masons known to have worked at the house definitely came from over twenty miles away, and of the remaining five, one probably came from outside the district. The carpenters were probably all local men, but this only reflects the less specialised nature of their craft which provided them with sufficient employment opportunities in the neighbourhood.

Carpenters were in an advantageous position because they were not tied to the fluctuating demands of the local building industry, but other craftsmen were more restricted in their choice of work. Sometimes there was enough building activity within a fairly short radius to keep them occupied for much of their working life without having to move out of the district. Richard Wright, a glazier of Bury St. Edmunds, worked at Little Saxham Hall, four miles away, in 1509 and 1510.[3] He was still living in Bury three years later when he undertook a contract to glaze the hall, chapel, and Master's Lodgings at St. John's College, Cambridge, a distance of twenty-five miles.[4] In the 1520s he was back in the neighbourhood of Bury working for Sir Thomas Kytson at Hengrave Hall, and he continued to be employed there at intervals until at least 1536.[5] Although little else is known about him, it is clear that there was sufficient work in the area to enable him to live and practise close to Bury for over twenty-five years.

The proximity of the university of Cambridge, where a considerable amount of building activity took place thoughout the period, acted as a stabilising influence on the neighbouring building industry, providing alternative employment to supplement the irregular opportunities available locally. There is no evidence that the demands of the university caused a shortage of skilled building labour in the surrounding countryside. On the contrary, by encouraging craftsmen to remain in the area, it seems to have had the reverse effect. The case of Richard Wright has already been noted, and some of the other craftsmen who worked with him at Little Saxham Hall similarly found employment in Cambridge. William Burden and Thomas Butler, who originally came from Ely, were the principal freemasons at the house between 1505 and 1509. They then departed to Cambridge, but in 1511, when the contractor employed by Sir Thomas Lucas had left with some of his work unfinished, they returned to the site.[6] Burden, at least, went back to Cambridge, for in 1513 he was working on the church of St. Mary the Great.[7] The most important carpenter employed at Little Saxham was Thomas Loveday, who came from Sudbury in 1505. He finished working at the house in 1510, and six years later he undertook a contract for fittings in the chapel, hall, and library, of St. John's College, Cambridge, where Richard Wright had been employed a few years previously.[8] Loveday continued to find employment in Cambridge, working on the gateway of Trinity College between 1528 and 1535.[9]

By any strict definition, these craftsmen were, of course, itinerant. Loveday for example, had to travel almost twenty miles from Sudbury to work at Little Saxham, and if, as seems likely, he came from Sudbury to Cambridge in 1516 that entailed another journey of over thirty-five miles. But, as far as can be traced, during the thirty years of his known working career he never had to leave an area more than two or three days away from his home town in search of work.

The movements of many other building craftsmen were similarly restricted. Conditions in the neighbourhood of Oxford and large urban centres, particularly London, were similar to those near Cambridge, and in certain areas enough country house building was being undertaken to provide almost continuous employment for a nucleus of craftsmen. In Suffolk, John Lynge, a mason and bricklayer, worked at Little Saxham Hall from 1507 to 1514 and at Hengrave Hall from 1525 to 1537.[10] Richard Wright, as noted above, glazed both houses. William Ponyard worked as a mason at Hengrave from 1536 to 1540, where he seems to have been responsible for the remarkably sophisticated oriel window over the main entry.[11] His subsequent movements are unknown until 1553, but he presumably remained in the area, for in that year he was employed in a well-paid advisory capacity by Sir Nicholas Bacon at Redgrave Hall.[12] Of the other craftsmen working at Redgrave, the Brenning family of tilers from Bury and Simon Field, a plumber from Diss, are known subsequently to have been working in 1564 for Sir Thomas Cornwallis at Brome Hall in the same county.[13] These accounts only document a small number of the country houses that were built in the area in the first half of the 16th century, and clearly the employment prospects for skilled craftsmen in Suffolk were good.

Similar patterns of employment can be seen elsewhere. In the north Midlands the houses built by the related families of the Talbots and the Cavendishes kept large numbers of building craftsmen employed for over three generations. Chatsworth House, Derbyshire, was begun in 1552 and continued into the 1570s. Worksop Manor, Nottinghamshire, dated from the 1580s, as did the remodelling of Old Hardwick Hall, Derbyshire. In the 1590s Hardwick Hall and Oldcotes, Derbyshire, Kirkby-in-Ashfield, Nottinghamshire, and Pontefract Hall, Yorkshire, were built, and in the 17th century the building activity of the Cavendishes included Welbeck Abbey, Nottinghamshire, Bolsover Castle, Derbyshire, and Slingsby Castle in Yorkshire. The names of the craftsmen who worked on most of these buildings are unrecorded, but in many cases they must have been the same. This can be suggested on stylistic grounds, and partly confirmed by the records that survive for Chatsworth and Hardwick.[14] At least sixteen of the craftsmen who were employed at Chatsworth also worked at Hardwick, and some of them seem to have exceeded twenty years' service on the two houses. John Hibard and John Rowarth, carpenters who were working at Chatsworth in 1560 were still working for Bess of Hardwick at Hardwick Old Hall in 1587, and George Hicket, another carpenter, was working at Chatsworth in 1576 and at Hardwick in 1597, while a mason, Thomas Outram, worked at Chatsworth from 1560 and at Hardwick from 1587. Other craftsmen who were employed at these houses are known to have also found work elsewhere in the area. Thomas Beighton, a carpenter employed at Chatsworth from 1580 and Hardwick from 1588, had been working in 1575 for William Dickenson in Sheffield.[15] Dickenson was bailiff to the Earl of Shrewsbury and possibly Beighton was already in the employ of the Talbots at that date. Other important houses going up in the north Midlands at the same time provided further employment opportunities for craftsmen, and Thomas Accres, a highly skilled marble mason who had worked at Chatsworth in 1576, travelled to Wollaton to work for Sir Francis Willoughby between 1584 and 1588, before returning into the service of the Talbots at Hardwick in 1594.[16] Robert Smythson, 'Architector and Surveyor unto yee most worthy house of Wollaton', was paid for unspecified work at Hardwick in 1597, possibly relating to the design of the house,[17] and other craftsmen from Wollaton who later worked at Hardwick included the masons, John and Christopher Rodes, and possibly Christopher Lovell.[18]

Fragmentary evidence for similar mobility within a restricted area is available for other parts of the country. In the south west the sketch books of the Abbott family of plasterers show them to have found continuous employment in Devon over a period in excess of one hundred and fifty years.[19] The earliest designs date from about 1575 and were compiled by John Abbot (born 1556). They were continued by his son, Richard (born 1612), and the final designs were made by his son, John (born 1640). As far as can be determined, none of the family were ever employed outside the south-west.[20] In Staffordshire, John Greaves was the principal carpenter employed in the alterations to Lord Paget's Beaudesert Hall in 1575 and 1576,[21] and when in 1591, part of the roof of the newly-built Shire Hall at Stafford, twelve miles away, collapsed, Greaves was called in to make the necessary repairs.[22] As fifteen years separate the two dates it is probable that Greaves had not had to move far out of the county in search of employment during the intervening period. Henry Hobbes, alias Hunt, a freemason of Arundel, Sussex, seems to have been similarly occupied by the work available in his own county. In 1586 he undertook a contract for Giles Garton to build a kitchen wing for his house at East Lavington, about ten mile from Arundel,[23] and nine years later he was employed by the ninth Earl of Northumberland on 'the new building near the wine-cellar' at Petworth, fifteen miles from Arundel.[24]

Nearly all the craftsmen in the building accounts for the additions to Holland House in 1638-40 can be associated with other work in the London area.[25] William Dodson, the bricklayer, had probably been employed earlier in the century in the building of Ashley Park, near Kingston-upon-Thames.[26] William Mason, the principal mason, had been the main contractor for St. Paul's Church, Covent Garden in 1631, and in 1635 had taken a number of building leases on houses in the Piazza.[27] Amongst the other craftsmen who had also been invlved in the Earl of Bedford's development in Covent Garden were the carpenter, Richard Vesey, Thomas Stephens, mason, Thomas Bagley, a glazier who had also worked on Whitehall Palace in 1614,[28] Erasmus Marsh, smith, and Thomas Charley, plumber.[29] Hugh Justice, another of the Holland House plumbers, had previously worked for the Earl of Middlesex both on his London House in St. Bartholomews and at Copthall, his country seat in Essex.[30] Undoubtedly, the most esteemed craftsman employed at Holland House was the painter, Matthew Goodrich, who had also worked for the Earl of Middlesex[31] and on St. Paul's Church, Covent Garden,[32] as well as painting some of the mouldings at the Queen's House, Greenwich,[33] and the woodwork of the stairs at Ham House, Surrey.[34]

These craftsmen, whose movements were largely confined within an area of twenty or thirty miles, probably formed the nucleus of the labour force on most building sites. The reputation of the most skilled of them would be well known in the area, and consequently they would be employed when work was available. However, although the mobility of most craftsmen was of limited extent, others undoubtedly travelled long distances during their working career. The limitations of the evidence make it almost impossible to trace all the movements of individual craftsmen, but enough is known about some of them to demonstrate the remarkable range of their itinerancy. Research into the career and work of Robert Smythson has shown that before 1568 he was working for Sir Francis Knollys, presumably on his principal house at Caversham near Reading. In that year he travelled the seventy-five miles to Longleat, Wiltshire, to work for Sir John Thynne. He remained at Longleat until the building was halted by Thynne's death in 1580, and then moved to Wollaton in Nottinghamshire, some one hundred and seventy miles away. Work on Sir Francis Willoughby's Wollaton Hall was completed in 1588, but Smythson remained in the village until his death in 1614, his subsequent architectural career being in an advisory capacity which did not require his continuous attendance at the site. By the age of forty-three Smythson had moved home three times and had travelled almost two hundred and fifty miles to practise his craft.[35]

Similar distances were travelled by other craftsmen. A group of Yorkshire building craftsmen, including the masons John and Martin Akroyd, and John Bentley, and the carpenter Thomas Holt, came south to Oxford in 1609 to work at Merton College. They were subsequently employed on the Schools Quadrangle of the Bodleian Library, and in 1611 Bentley travelled briefly into Worcestershire to draw plans for Sir Edward Pytts at Kyre Park.[36] Pytts also brought a mason called Sergianson fifty miles from Coventry for the same purpose. Ralph Symons, one of the leading masons working in Cambridge in the late 16th and early 17th centuries, had originally come from Berkhamstead in Hertfordshire.[37] He is first noted in Cambridge in 1585, but early in the 1590s he seems to have been working in London. He was back in Cambridge by 1596 where he continued to work until 1605. In that year he was described as 'late of Cambridge', and presumably he had moved in to find employment elsewhere.

One of the reasons for Symons' departure from Cambridge was a dispute over his workmanship for King's College, and a similar motive in 1563 led the Somerset mason William Spicer to leave Longleat, where he had been employed since 1554. Nunney, his home village, was only a few miles away from Longleat, but by 1571 he was working for the Earl of Leicester at Kenilworth Castle, one hundred and twenty miles away. In 1584 he was made Surveyor of the Queen's Works at Berwick, and in 1596 he was appointed Surveyor of the Royal Works in London.[38] John Hills, another of Thynne's masons at Longleat, originally came from Kent. In 1550 he seems to have been working for the Duke of Somerset at Brentford, and in 1568 he moved to Longleat. Twelve years later he accompanied Robert Smythson to Wollaton, were he worked until the house was completed in 1588. At the time of his death in 1592 he was living in Worksop, where it is possible that he had been employed in the building of the Manor Lodge for the Earl of Shrewsbury.[39]

It was not only masons who were prepared to travel great distances in order to practise their craft. John Scampion, a carpenter, was born in 1580 in the Hertfordshire parish of Great Hormead. At the time of his second marriage in March 1622 he was living in London, but shortly afterwards he had moved to Montgomery in Wales where, together with his brother Samuel, he played a prominent role in the erection of a substantial new building for Lord Herbert at Montgomery Castle. The evidence from the parish registers suggests that the Scampions remained in Montgomery until some time after 1625, and then moved on elsewhere.[40]

There were many different reasons why some craftsmen spent most of their working lives in the same area, whilst others followed their employment across the country. When work on a particular house came to an end it is very unlikely that there were ever enough building jobs available in the neighbourhood for all the craftsmen to obtain immediate alternative employment. Some, no doubt, did find building or maintenance work, while others probably temporarily left the building industry altogether until such a time as another house was commenced in the area. But some at least of the more adventuresome craftsmen must have gone in search of work, and the rumour of secure employment on a major country house probably spurred some of them to travel considerable distances, such as the two masons noted in the Kyre Park Building accounts 'that came to seek work' from Weston in Warwickshire,[41] or the blacksmith at Raynham Hall, Norfolk, in

1619 'whoe cam from Blicklinge', where he had been working on Sir Henry Hobart's house.[42]

However, apart from those craftsmen who moved to the largest towns or university cities where a certain amount of building was almost continually in progress, it is unlikely that many craftsmen undertook to travel without the certain knowledge that building was in progress at their destination. It is difficult to conceive of groups of craftsmen vaguely wandering the countryside in search of work. As knowledge of new building projects probably only travelled a limited distance to reach the ears of interested craftsmen, it remains to explain such extraordinary journeys as that made by the Scampions from London to Montgomery. One possible reason is that the reputation of some craftsmen was so exceptional that they were eagerly sought by prospective builders, and in this respect it is possibly significant that John Scampion was described in the parish register at Montgomery as 'artificiossimi jam architecti novi operis in Castello de Montgomeri'. Other craftsmen were certainly recruited on account of their reputation. Sir Edward Hext, referring to William Arnold, the Somerset mason who had contracted to supervise the erection of Wadham College, Oxford, wrote in 1610

> 'If I had not tyed him fast to this businesse we shold hardly keepe him; he ys so wonderfully sought being in deede the absolutest & honestest workeman in Ingland'. [43]

The subject of patronage and its part in the recruitment of labour has already been dealt with in some detail. It was obviously an important factor in the encouragement of itinerancy amongst skilled craftsmen. The point can, perhaps, be further emphasised by considering the Yorkshire craftsmen working in Oxford in the early 17th century. Sir Henry Saville, Warden of Merton College, who originally brought them down to work at the College, was himself a native of Yorkshire. He had previously employed John and Abraham Akroyd on a number of enterprises in his own county, notably at Bradley Hall and Methley Hall,[44] and it was clearly as a result of his personal knowledge of their skill that he recruited them to work in Oxford. Similarly, when Sir Edward Pytts returned to Worcestershire with John Bentley, another of the Yorkshire craftsmen, it was largely because Bentley had 'wrought the newe addition to Sir Thomas Bodleigh his famous library'.[45]

It is difficult to assess the extent to which craftsmen's lives were disrupted by the insecurity of their peripatetic existence. Some, no doubt, were acutely conscious of it; such as the painter from London who found only two days' work at Trentham Hall, Staffordshire, in 1633, and who left such a small impression on the accountant that he was recorded simply as 'London John'.[46] But the effects on many craftsmen must have been largely mitigated by the considerable length of time often taken to build a country house. This meant that the more skilled craftsmen frequently enjoyed long periods of employment on one house. When Robert Smythson appeared at Longleat in 1568, work had already been in progress for over twenty years, yet he stayed for twelve years before moving on to Wollaton, where Sir Francis Willoughby's building provided him with a further eight years' employment. At least ten other masons at Longleat were employed for periods of twelve years or more and Allan Maynard, the principal mason from 1563, was connected with the house for over twenty years. Some of the other craftsmen working at Longleat enjoyed a similar security of employment. William Palmer, a glazier, was employed for sixteen years, and the carpenters John Lewis and William Brown worked respectively for twenty-four and twenty-six years on the house. In addition, a number of craftsmen accompanied Smythson to Wollaton, so that John Hills, a mason who had arrived at Longleat with Smythson, was employed by Sir John Thynne for twelve years and then by Sir Francis Willoughby for eight years, and Richard Crispin, the head carpenter at Wollaton, had previously worked at Longleat between 1568 and 1580. Christopher Lovell, a mason who worked for nine years at Longleat and seven years at Wollaton, seems to have found a further period of employment at Hardwick, another house with Smythson connections.[47]

Longleat, with its continual revisions and remodellings spanning a period in excess of thirty years, was something of an exception even in an age when most country houses were necessarily built at a leisurely pace. Nevertheless, a number of other houses provided a similar length of employment for some of the craftsmen working on them. At Hengrave Hall in Suffolk, several masons and bricklayers were employed for periods of nine to twelve years,[48] and one of them, John Lyng, had previously worked at Little Saxham Hall for seven years.[49] Thomas Lem, a mason and bricklayer, worked for Sir Edward Pytts during both his periods of building activity at Kyre Park, Worcestershire, totalling over seventeen years' employment between 1586 and 1617, while John Chaunce of Bromsgrove, the 'Cheiff mason . . . and Survey'r of the work', saw almost twenty years' service at the site.[50] Those craftsmen who had achieved positions of responsibility, like Chaunce, were inevitably employed for the duration of the work and they consequently enjoyed a greater continuity of employment than the ordinary craftsmen. Walter Madison, the carpenter who directed part of the labour force for Sir John Petre's Old Thorndon Hall, Essex, was present on the site from about 1577 to at least 1594,[51] and Robert Liming, another carpenter by trade, acted successively as surveyor at Hatfield House for five years and at Blickling Hall, Norfolk, for eleven or twelve years.[52]

Such lengthy periods of employment encouraged many of the itinerant craftsmen to bring their families with them, and to set up home close to the building site, sometimes in a house provided by their employer. Two pairs of sawyers who travelled from London in 1576 to work at Stiffkey Hall, Norfolk, were accompanied by their wives,[53] as was Thomas Accres when he came to Hardwick at the end of 1594.[54] John Scampion took his bride of a few months with him when he went to work for Lord Herbert at Montgomery, where she died in childbirth and was buried in the parish church.[55] At Longleat, Smythson lived with his wife at the parsonage of Monkton Deverill, which he rented from Sir John Thynne,[56] and Allen Maynard lived in another house rented from Thynne at Woodlands, on the edge of the park.[57] William Arnold and his wife were provided with a house, apparently rent-free, actually on the site of Wadham College, Oxford, in 1610, 'that he may contynually attend the worke',[58] but it was more usual for the craftsmen to pay rent for their accommodation, even if at times it was on favourable terms, such as the tenement in Cambridge leased to Ralph Symons by Emmanuel College in 1586.[59]

The effects of the itinerancy that was inevitably the common experience of the building craftsmen can be exaggerated. Many, perhaps most, never moved outside the county of their birth, whilst for those who did, the upheaval that this implies was often greatly diminished by the length of employment that they could expect at the average country house site, with the opportunity that this provided of setting up a stable home in the neighbourhood. Far greater problems for many building craftsmen must have arisen from their position as wage-earners in a society where such a dependence was unusual. Apart from a few contractors working for a fixed sum, the majority of those employed in the building trades were paid either a daily wage or a piece rate dependent upon the actual amount of work that they had executed. The workmen employed by the contractors were paid on a similar basis. Whether paid by the day or by the measure their economic well-being depended on the number of days on which they were offered work. As they were paid only for the days that they had actually worked, the number of years that they were employed on a particular house is an uncertain guide to their economic security. This can be properly assessed only by considering the number of days that they worked in each year that they were employed at the site.

Due to the limitations of the various methods of accounting and the incompleteness of the documentation, few building accounts are capable of sustaining the close analysis necessary to establish the daily work record of all the craftsmen. This is especially true of the accounts that survive for the early part of the 16th century, but by the latter half of the century the methods of book-keeping employed on a number of building sites are sufficiently full and lucid to enable the attempt to be made.

Although some of the accounts for Wollaton Hall, Nottinghamshire, are missing, and parts of those that remain are illegible, there is a complete record of the workmen employed at day-rates extending from the last week in October 1584 to the week ending on 15 November 1585.[60] The period covered comprises fifty-six weeks, or three hundred and thirty-six working days based on a six-day week. As there was a complete break of three days in the first week of August 1585 during which no work was done, the maximum number of working days possible for any workman was three hundred and thirty-three. Fifty-three masons and stone-layers, and twenty-four carpenters and joiners were employed during the period, but a number of these did not start work until the spring of 1585 when the labour force was considerably enlarged, and consequently only the work-records of the craftsmen employed in the last week of October 1584 have been set out in *Figure 1* as the inclusion of those starting later would distort the general picture. Of the twenty-eight workers in stone, five left the site shortly after the beginning of the period, and have also been excluded. The attendance record of the remaining twenty-three men is remarkably high. Over half of them were present on the site for more than fifty weeks, and three of these found some employment in every single week of the period.

Laurence, the most consistently employed of all the masons, missed only twenty-four possible working days, some of which can be accounted for by holidays, such as Christmas and Easter, which were not specifically mentioned in the account. In fifty-one of the fifty-six weeks he worked for five days or more. The records of several of his colleagues were only slightly inferior to this. Fifteen masons found employment on two-thirds or

Figure 1: Craftsmen employed by the day at Wollaton Hall, October 1584–November 1585

MASONS	Weeks present	Weeks absent	Days	6-day weeks	5-day weeks	Comments
Laurence	56	—	309	36	15	
Tobyas	56	—	293	29	16	
Wichenden Jnr.	56	—	307	35	15	
Otes	55	1	293	32	13	
C. Rodes	55	1	291½	31	13	
C. Wichenden	54	2	279½	22	23	
Berington	54	2	288	32	14	
Symson	53	3	295½	35	14	
Stone	53	3	275	27	16	
Hills	52	4	295½	34	15	
W. Evenden	52	4	292½	33	27	
Coles	51	5	281	33	15	
G. Evenden	45	11	244	26	14	
Vinsent	44	12	239	25	14	
Atkynson	41	15	211½	22	12	
Collyar	27	29	129½	10	7	Absent January–June 1585
Styles	13	43	70½	6	6	Absent December 1584, October 1585
More	8	48	40½	3	2	Leaves December 1584
Warde	6	50	33	4	1	Leaves November 1584
Henlay	2	54	11	1	1	Leaves November 1584
Butler	2	54	11	1	1	Leaves November 1584
Myller	2	54	10	1	—	Leaves November 1584

LAYERS (No work available 7 December 1584–8 February 1585)						
Wodnett	41	15	206½	18	13	
Raphell	38	18	203	20	13	
Whitworth	37	19	200	22	12	
Mason	37	19	199½	19	14	
Jacke	35	21	182½	18	11	
Marshall	28	28	149½	14	12	

JOINERS						
Hargrave	56	—	310½	37	15	
Chester	56	—	310½	37	15	
Thicke	37	19	205	24	10	Leaves July 1585
Chadson	36	20	201	23	11	Leaves July 1585

CARPENTERS						
Sherwin	56	—	302	34	16	
Smallwood	46	10	254	27	15	Absent November and December 1584
R. Crispin	40	16	219	25	13	Absent July–October 1585
Chester	35	21	195	22	11	Absent November 1584, March 1585
Crispin Jnr.	32	24	177	21	9	Absent February–March and August–September 1585
Marshall	8	48	39	4	2	Leaves December 1584

more of the possible working days and only Collyar and Styles were absent for long periods. The layers were in a less advantageous position than the more highly skilled masons. During the bad weather of the winter months there was little work for them to do, and none were employed at all between the weeks of 1 December 1584 and 8 February 1585. By the end of February they had all returned and they were employed regularly until the beginning of July, when their employment became more erratic, presumably as a result of the approaching completion of the walls of the fabric. Nevertheless, four of the six layers worked for approximately 200 days, and they all found employment in over half of the weeks of the period.

One of the carpenters left the site after eight weeks, but the employment opportunities for the remaining ten wood-workers were almost as good as those for the workers in stone. All of them worked for over half the possible number of weeks, and, if the joiners who disappeared in July 1585 are included, seven of them were employed for more than two-thirds of the working days. As with the stone workers, it was the more skilled craftsmen who found the greatest continuity of employment. Two of the four joiners were absent for only twenty-two-and-a-half days throughout the whole period, and the other two joiners only missed a few days before they departed in July. One of the joiners who replaced them worked for all but five of the remaining days in the period. The carpenters were more susceptible to periods of unemployment, but even so, Sherwin was employed for the full fifty-six weeks, during fifty of which he managed to work for five or more days.

The prospects of regular employment were clearly very good for craftsmen at Wollaton in 1584 and 1585. Building activity was at its height, and this undoubtedly had a beneficial effect on the amount of work available for the workmen at the site. Possibly in the years for which full documentation is lacking the craftsmen suffered longer periods of unemployment or worked for fewer days in the week, but this seems unlikely for the labour force was considerably smaller in those years. The total number of craftsmen working by the day at the end of June 1585 was fifty, whereas in 1582 it was twenty-eight, in 1586, twenty-one, and in 1587 twenty-two, which suggests that extra workmen were hired in the years of greater activity and that the regular work force were fully employed in the other years. Thus craftsmen, such as the mason John Hills, who were employed for the full period of the enterprise, probably enjoyed a high degree of job security.

The accounts for Trentham Hall, Staffordshire,[61] provide the opportunity to study the employment pattern for craftsmen employed by the day over a longer period than those for Wollaton. The work began in June 1630 and a full series of accounts exists from the week ending 23 March 1633 to the completion of the house in February 1639. The masonry work was organised in two separate ways, with the decorative carving being paid for at piece-rates, and the construction of the fabric by the day. Many of the masons were employed at times by both methods, but those masons who were predominantly paid piece-rates and who only occasionally worked by the day have not been tabulated in *Figure 2*. Casual masons, who only worked for a few days, have also been excluded. The general pattern, although complicated by occasional piece-payments, is similar to that discernible at Wollaton. In 1633, five out of the six masons who worked solely by the day found employment in more than half the possible weeks, as did three of the masons who also reeived piece-payments. Butler, the one mason working by the day who worked less than half the weeks in the year, did not arrive at the site until late in July, and Vaughan, who only worked for ten weeks at day wages, received almost ten times as much money for his piece-work during the period and was almost certainly working at the site by one method or the other throughout the whole year. Only Chester, who by reason of his general availability seems to have been a local mason, had a noticeably poor employment record. He worked for one day in March, received a small payment for piece-work at the end of June, and was then regularly employed for eight weeks from the beginning of September.

Figure 2: Masons employed predominantly by the day at Trentham Hall, 1633–35

1633: 40 weeks	Weeks present	Weeks absent	Days	6-day weeks	5-day weeks
T. Griswell	38	2	206	30	2
Mr H. Bellamie	35	5	200	26	3
W. Bellamie	32*	8	135	13	1
Holt	32*	8	138½	12	4
M. Griswell	27	13	140	18	2
Vaughan	10*	30	34	2	1
N. Bellamie	24	16	123	14	4
Clayton	21*	19	95	10	2
Bond	22	18	128	18	3
Butler	12	28	58½	6	2
Chester	10*	30	40½	3	1
1634: 50 weeks					
T. Griswell	44	6	248	37	2
Mr H. Bellamie	44	6	231½	32	2
W. Bellamie	30*	20	120	12	1
Holt	28*	22	113	12	5
M. Griswell	27	23	155	23	1
Vaughan	19*	31	67½	3	3
N. Bellamie	2*	48	9	—	—
Clayton	3*	47	14½	1	1
Butler	16*	34	53	4	—
Wright	33	17	199	29	2
1635: 48 weeks					
T. Griswell	31	17	159½	20	3
Mr H. Bellamie	28*	20	136½	9	11
W. Bellamie	29	19	148	19	2
Holt	11*	37	31	1	1
M. Griswell	13	35	73½	10	1
Vaughan	24*	24	79	4	3
Wright	24	24	112	13	1

* Also worked at piece rates in this year

In 1634, all four masons working by the day were employed in over half the weeks that any building activity took place. Two of the masons who also did piece-work were employed by the day for more than half the possible weeks, whereas most of the remainder derived a greater proportion of their income from their piece-work payments. Nicholas Bellamie and Clayton, the two masons with the worst record, had both left the site by the summer, and it is possible that they had moved on to find employment elsewhere. The fabric of the house was largely completed by the end of August 1635, and consequently the amount of work available for masons after that date was drastically reduced. Nevertheless, five of the masons were employed for more than half the weeks in the year, and if we exclude the eighteen weeks from 22 August, when only occasional masons' work was required, their employment was comparable to previous years. They must have been aware that their work at Trentham was coming to a close, and it is possible that some of them had made arrangements for alternative employment after the end of August, although Henry Bellamie, Thomas Griswell, Wright and Vaughan continued to find occasional work at the site until the end of the year.

Those masons who worked for the full three years generally enjoyed a consistently high level of employment. Some, such as Thomas Griswell and Henry Bellamie, were only absent for a few weeks each year and when they were present were predominantly employed for six days in the week. Others, such as Holt and Vaughan, were probably employed with an equal regularity but spent a significant part of their time working at piece-rates. Michael Griswell and Wright, who regularly worked for fewer weeks in each year than the other masons employed by the day, were apprentices learning the craft and consequently were always amongst the first masons to be laid off when there was insufficient work available.

The organisation of the carpenters and joiners at Trentham falls into two distant phases. Up until the summer of 1635 most of the work was carried out at piece-rates with only a few small tasks being executed by the day. All the principal craftsmen worked during those three years, some of them being paid very substantial sums, but there is no way of effectively establishing whether any of them were unemployed for long periods during this time. The evidence from their annual incomes suggests that, on the contrary, they enjoyed a very high continuity of employment. By 1635, much of the carpentry on the building had been completed and most of the skilled carpenters and joiners left the site. The remaining woodwork was executed by a small group of carpenters who were employed exclusively by the day, and their work record between 1636 and the conclusion of the work in 1639 has been set out in *Figure 3*. Their security of employment was truly remarkable. Bradwall, who was probably the estate carpenter and a permanent member of Sir Richard Leveson's establishment, had been paid an annual salary in the early years of the work. He commenced working by the day in June 1635 and in the remainder of that year was absent for only three weeks. He was consistently employed for the full duration of the building accounts. Walker was initially hired in January 1636 to assist Bradwall. During the following two years he was absent for only one week when work was in progress, but early in 1638 he left the site. Thomas, the other carpenter assisting

Bradwall, was almost as consistent. He began work at the end of March 1636 and, apart from one week in September that year, he was employed in every week until 23 September 1637. Although he was occasionally absent during the winter of 1637–38, from 7 April 1638 to 23 February 1639, when the carpenters' work was finished, he was again ever-present. Porter, who was of equal status with Bradwall, similarly missed only five weeks' work from his arrival in June 1637 to his departure in March 1638. Clearly the small number of carpenters working during the final years of the construction of Trentham Hall enjoyed a level of security in their employment fully comparable to that of any modern building craftsman, who is equally likely to be temporarily laid off during periods of bad weather or when there is insufficient work available.

Figure 3: Carpenters employed by the day at Trentham Hall, 1636–38

1636: 49 weeks	Weeks present	Weeks absent	Days	6-day weeks	5-day weeks
Bradwall	47	2	227	13	14
Walker	48	1	$242\frac{1}{2}$	20	15
Thomas	39	10	$198\frac{1}{2}$	14	15
1637: 50 weeks					
Bradwall	48	2	$212\frac{1}{2}$	13	14
Walker	50	—	$247\frac{1}{2}$	21	12
Thomas	45	5	$219\frac{1}{2}$	23	8
Porter	23	27	104	8	5
1638: 50 weeks					
Bradwall	43	7	169	8	12
Walker	2	48	$1\frac{1}{2}$	—	—
Thomas	42	8	204	17	12
Porter	6	44	29	3	1

Confirmation of the validity of the results obtained from an analysis of the accounts for Wollaton Hall and Trentham Hall is provided by those for the building of Sir Thomas Tresham's Triangular Lodge at Rushton, Northamptonshire.[62] The attendance records for the craftsmen in 1595 have been set out in *Figure 4* and will only be discussed briefly here. Among the stone-workers, it was again the more skilled freemasons who had the most regular employment pattern. William Tirroll was absent for the whole of July, and his brother, Thomas, did not begin work until the second week in March. Hence appeared on the site only at the beginning of July, and then worked continuously until the end of November. Employment for the roughmasons commenced with the more temperate weather in the spring, and extra labour was taken on during the summer months when the work was at its height. The carpenters suffered from a lack of work between March and July, but were then fully occupied until the end of December.

There were, of course, other craftsmen apart from masons and carpenters who were employed on every country house building site. The small numbers of painters, glaziers, plumbers and smiths working at any one time, together with the nature of their work, meant that it was not necessary to direct their tasks closely and they were generally paid at piece-rates. This makes it difficult to establish in any detail the pattern of their employment. As far as continuity of employment is concerned, however, some of them worked for more years on one house than many of the carpenters and masons. At Trentham Hall, for example, Thomas Leversage, who worked as both a painter and a glazier, was

Figure 4: Craftsmen employed by the day at Rushton, 1595

1595: 50 weeks

FREEMASONS	Weeks present	Weeks absent	Days	6-day weeks	5-day weeks	Comments
Old Tirroll	45	5	$233\frac{1}{2}$	25	9	
J. Tirroll	45	5	230	24	10	
T. Tirroll	41	9	209	21	11	
W. Tirroll	39	11	$201\frac{1}{2}$	22	7	
Hence	21	29	117	16	2	begins 3 July
ROUGHMASONS						
Hitchcock Snr.	36	14	182	16	10	begins 5 April
J. Hitchcock	36	14	184	17	10	begins 5 April
Longe	28	22	126	10	6	begins 10 May
Weston	30	20	$153\frac{1}{2}$	13	10	begins 10 May
Kirke Snr.	18	32	93	7	8	begins 26 July
S. Kirke	18	32	94	8	7	begins 26 July
C. Hitchcock	7	43	39	5	1	works 17 August–27 September
T. Hitchcock	7	43	38	4	2	works 17 August–27 September
CARPENTERS (no work available between March and July)						
Watts	28	22	$138\frac{1}{2}$	12	9	
his man	27	23	$134\frac{1}{2}$	10	10	
Ellyott	17	33	$78\frac{1}{2}$	6	4	
his man	27	23	$126\frac{1}{2}$	11	7	

employed in every year from 1633 to 1638, earning quite substantial sums in the first four years, and Zachery Kirkes, another painter, who subsequently decorated the nave ceiling at Staunton Harold Church, Leicestershire, worked from 1633 to 1636. Similarly, the slater found employment in every year, and of the two smiths, one worked for the full period and the other until March 1636. Other craftsmen were employed for shorter periods. The plumbers worked only in 1633 and 1635, and the tiler in 1638. At Wollaton Hall, where the documentation is less complete, the principal painter seems to have worked from the end of 1585 until 1588, and the two smiths were employed in 1585 and 1586, but the glazier and the plasterers were regularly employed for less than a year. On the whole there appears to have been less work available on any particular building for these craftsmen, but, on the other hand, their specialised skills and the smaller numbers engaged in their crafts probably meant that they were more in demand than all but the most skilled masons and carpenters, and consequently it was easier to find alternative employment.

Despite the fairly secure picture of employment that has been presented for some craftsmen whilst engaged on particular buildings, not every building workman was so fortunate. There are examples in every building account of craftsmen working only for a few weeks, and even those craftsmen who were more regularly employed experienced periods without work. Once the house that they were building was completed, there was always the problem of finding work on another site. Some craftsmen, such as Robert Smythson, were of sufficiently high reputation to be immediately offered alternative employment, and some of the other craftsmen undoubtedly moved with them, but many craftsmen must have remained unemployed for an unpredictable length of time, especially if they were reluctant to move out of the area. It must have been a very common experience, and there is evidence of measures taken by some building craftsmen to alleviate its effects.

Many of them had small agricultural holdings at which they could work during times of slack, and which could be maintained by their wives and young children when they were fully engaged on their craft. Sometimes these holdings were rented from the country house builders for whom they were working, and these tenancies were no doubt partly granted to ensure the continued services of particularly desirable craftsmen in a period when skilled men were at a premium. However, the combination of agriculture and building seems to have been general throughout the industry. In about 1670, Sir William Coventry wrote that few building craftsmen

> 'rely entirely on their Trade as not to have a small Farm, the Rent of which they are the more able to pay by the gains of their Trade. . .', [63]

and there is evidence that this was a well-established practice. Such by-employments were, of course, a necessary prerequisite for those itinerant craftsmen who were not accompanied by their families to distant sites, for it was only in this way that their families could be supported during the period of their absence; but it is equally probable that they also served as an insurance against unemployment for the families of most building craftsmen. Indeed, some of them seem to have farmed on a fairly large scale. William Thomas, an Oxford plumber who died in 1552, had 50 sheep, 9 beasts, and a nag,[64] and John King, a carpenter of Ravensden in Bedfordshire, had 9 beasts, 6 bullocks, 5 pigs, 2 sheep, and a quantity of poultry as well as eight-and-a-half acres under cultivation.[65] But most craftsmen possessed only a few animals or a small amount of land which they worked on a subsistence basis, like the mason Thomas Hill of Wardington in Oxfordshire, who had a cow and 'the crope of a quarterne Lande',[66] or the Halifax mason, Martin Akroyd, who grew some corn and kept a few beasts to maintain his family while he was working in Oxford.[67] The expansion of the woollen industry enabled the wives of some craftsmen to undertake spinning and carding, and the inventory of a mason, Richard Rothwell, taken in 1565, included four stones of wool.[68] Another mason, William Ardon of Pavenham in Bedfordshire, kept an ale-house in addition to a small farm,[69] and other craftsmen bought and sold building materials. The income from these activities was probably less important than the security that they provided. Even those craftsmen working on a large country house must have been constantly in fear of unemployment, whether temporary, due to unpredictable factors such as bad weather or a lack of materials, or permanent, due to the completion of the work, and the knowledge that they could always supply their families with the basic necessities must have had a profoundly stabilising effect on their lives.

Despite a decline in their economic position during the period, and despite their itinerant existence and their basic dependence on a money wage, there was a very strong family tradition in the building trades that resulted in several generations following the same craft. At least eleven members of the Grumbold family from Weldon in Northamptonshire are known to have been working as masons in the late 16th and 17th centuries, and two generations of the Frisbey family from the same area were masons at the turn of the century, while the presence of a mason called William Frysby at Hengrave in 1537 suggsts an even longer family involvement in the craft.[70] Elizabeth Frisbey was the first wife of the King's Cliffe mason, Thomas Thorpe, whose father had also been a mason, and whose two sons by his second marriage were also to enter the building world.[71] One, Thomas, also became a mason, and the other was the highly successful surveyor, John Thorpe.[72] Almost every building account contains several examples of related craftsmen working alongside each other, and amongst the more well-known families we can cite the Smythsons and the Akroyds already mentioned.

Many sons must have followed their father's craft as a matter of course, out of family tradition or as a result of a lack of local opportunity to do anything else, but for many others there must have been a conscious choice to become building craftsmen. The possibilities of advancement probably attracted some of them and certainly the most successful craftsmen achieved a social status beyond their humble origins. The mason William Arnold was called 'gentleman' in chancery proceedings of 1617,[73] and the Smythsons had achieved gentry status by 1600.[74] John Symonds, the mason extensively patronised by Lord Burghley in the latter part of the 16th century, was granted arms in 1591,[75] and the son of Thomas Bertie, another mason, married the widowed Duchess of Suffolk.[76] Other, lesser, craftsmen, were styled 'Mr' on several building sites, apparently with the social meaning of 'mister' rather than the craft meaning of 'master'.[77] However, few could have realistically hoped to rise out of their social class, and most of them remained simply wage-earning craftsmen as their fathers had been before them. Nevertheless, the incidence of family continuity in the building crafts suggests that successive generations found the working conditions sufficiently rewarding despite the unpredictability of employment and remuneration. Indeed, by the 1650s if not earlier, the members of the London Carpenters' Company were even able to recruit a number of apprentices from amongst the sons of the minor gentry.[78] Wage-earners and artisans they might be, but clearly building craftsmen were following a trade which was not without a degree of estimation.

17 Notes

1. Mrs Baldwyn-Childe, 'The Building of the Manor-House of Kyre Park, Worcestershire' *The Antiquary* xxii (1890) 51
2. *Ibid* xxi (1890) 262
3. British Museum: Additional MSS 7097, ff. 174–200
4. Willis and Clark, ii, 347–8
5. Cambridge University Library: Hengrave Hall Deposit 80
6. British Museum: Additional MSS 7097, f. 199
7. *Churchwardens' Accounts of St. Mary the Great, Cambridge* ed. J. E. Foster (Cambridge Antiquarian Society xxxv 1905) p. 14
8. Willis and Clark, ii, 243–5
9. *Ibid* 453–4
10. British Museum: Additional MSS 7097, ff. 174–200; Cambridge University Library: Hengrave Hall Deposit 80
11. Cambridge University Library: Hengrave Hall Deposit 80
12. Sandeen, p. 57
13. *Ibid* pp. 50 & 52
14. B. Stallybrass, 'Bess of Hardwick's Buildings and Building Accounts' *Archaelogia* lxiv (1913) Appendix iii, 393–8
15. J. R. Wigfull, 'House Building in Queen Elizabeth's Days' *Transactions of the Hunter Archaeological Society* iii (1925) 68–75
16. Nottingham University Library: Mi A60 /3–7; Stallybrass, *op cit* 293
17. Girouard, *Smythson* pp. 122–3
18. See the payment at Hardwick in May 1596 to 'Lovells wyffe' for polishing stone: Stallybrass, *op cit* 379
19. Devon County Record Office: 404 M /B1–3
20. K. & C. French, 'Devonshire Plasterwork' *Transactions of the Devonshire Association* lxxxix (1957) 124–44
21. William Salt Library, Stafford: D1734 /3 /4 /143–4; *Ibid* 101
22. *Ibid* D1721 /1 /4
23. W. H. Godfrey, 'An Elizabethan Builder's Contract' *Sussex Archaeological Collections* lxv (1924) 211–23
24. G. R. Batho, 'The Percies at Petworth, 1574–1632' *Sussex Archaeological Collections* xcv (1957) 12
25. Leeds City Library: TB /EA /13 /74
26. Surrey County Record Office: Acc. 1030, f. 114
27. Survey of London, xxxvi, *The Parish of St. Paul, Covent Garden* (1970) pp. 274, 282
28. British Museum: Harleian MSS 1653
29. Survey of London, *passim*
30. Kent County Record Office: U269 A505 /1 & A508 /3
31. *Idem* U269 A462 /5
32. Survey of London, *op cit* p. 279
33. *Idem* 14th monograph, *The Queen's House, Greenwich* (1937) p. 104
34. R. Edwards & P. Ward-Jackson, *Ham House* (4th edition London 1959) p. 36
35. Girouard, *Smythson* p. 50 *et seq*
36. T. W. Hanson, 'Halifax Builders in Oxford' *Transactions of the Halifax Antiquarian Society* (1928) 253–317; Mrs Baldwyn-Childe, 'The Building of the Manor-House of Kyre Park, Worcestershire' *The Antiquary* xxi (1890) 202
37. Willis and Clark, ii, 693n *et passim*
38. Girouard, *Smythson* p. 54
39. *Ibid* p. 57, and information kindly communicated by David N. Durant
40. J. D. K. Lloyd, 'The New Building at Montgomery Castle' *Archaeologia Cambrensis* cxiv (1965) 60–8
41. Mrs Baldwyn-Childe *op cit* 204

42 H. L. Bradfer-Lawrence, 'The Building of Raynham Hall' *Norfolk Archaeology* xxiii (1927) 116

43 N. Briggs, 'The Foundation of Wadham College, Oxford' *Oxoniensia* xxi (1956) 67—8

44 T. W. Hanson, 'Halifax Builders in Oxford' *Transactions of the Halifax Antiquarian Society* (1928) 253—317

45 Mrs Baldwyn-Childe *op cit* 202

46 Staffordshire County Record Office: D593 R /1 /2

47 Longleat Archives: *passim*

48 Cambridge University Library: Hengrave Hall Deposit 80

49 British Museum: Additional MSS 7097

50 Mrs Baldwyn-Childe, 'The Building of the Manor-House of Kyre Park, Worcestershire' *The Antiquary* xxi—ii (1890)

51 Essex County Record Office: D /DP A18—22

52 L. Stone, 'The Building of Hatfield House' *Archaeological Journal* cxii (1955) 103—4

53 Sandeen, p. 186

54 B. Stallybrass, 'Bess of Hardwick's Buildings and Building Accounts' *Archaeologia* lxiv (1913) 379

55 J. D. K. Lloyd, 'The New Building at Montgomery Castle' *Archaeologia Cambrensis* cxiv (1965) 67

56 Girouard, *Smythson* p. 58

57 M. Girouard, 'New Light on Longleat: Allen Maynard, a French Sculptor in England in the 16th Century' *Country Life* cxx (1956) 594—7

58 N. Briggs, 'The Foundation of Wadham College, Oxford' *Oxoniensia* xxi (1956) 69

59 Willis and Clark, ii, 693

60 Nottingham University Library: Mi A60 /3

61 Staffordshire County Record Office: D593 R /1 /2

62 British Museum: Additional MSS 39832

63 'An Essay Concerning the Decay of Rents and their Remedies', British Museum: Sloane MSS 3828, f. 208. I am most grateful to Dr John Broad for drawing my attention to this document

64 *Household and Farm Inventories in Oxfordshire, 1550—1590* ed. M. A. Havinden (Oxfordshire Record Society xliv, 1965) pp. 42—3

65 *Jacobean Household Inventories* ed. F. G. Emmison (Bedfordshire Historical Record Society xx, 1938) p. 59

66 Havinden, *op cit* p. 258. A Land was usually a strip in the open field of approximately half an acre

67 T. W. Hanson, 'Halifax Builders in Oxford' *Transactions of the Halifax Antiquarian Society* (1928) 316

68 W. J. Williams, 'Wills of Freemasons and Masons' *The Masonic Record* xvi (1936) 224

69 Emmison, *op cit* p. 60

70 Cambridge University Library: Hengrave Hall Deposit 80

71 H. M. Colvin, 'Haunt Hill House, Weldon' in *Studies in Building History* ed. E. M. Jope (London 1961) p. 224

72 *The Book of Architecture of John Thorpe* ed. J. Summerson (Walpole Society xl, 1966) p. 4

73 A. Oswald, *Country Houses of Dorset* (2nd edition London 1959) p. 28

74 Girouard, *Smythson* p. 133

75 J. Summerson, 'Three Elizabethan Architects' *Bulletin of the John Rylands Library*, xl (1957) 213

76 J. Harvey, *English Medieval Architects* (London 1954) p. 32

77 See, for example, Christopher Lovell at Wollaton: Nottingham University Library: Mi A60 /4, f. 9

78 *Records of the Worshipful Company of Carpenters* ed. B. March (i, 1913) pp. 3, 23, 27, 34, 36

18 Labourers

The number of labourers required on the building site varied considerably according to the stage which the work had reached. Initially large numbers were needed to clear the site, dig the foundations, and help with the preparation of materials, but once the construction of the building had commenced far fewer labourers sufficed to serve the craftsmen and prepare the materials. From time to time, as the building progressed, additional labour was temporarily taken on for the erection of scaffolding, and other jobs such as the raising of the roof and the digging of trenches for the connection of the water supply. When the building was nearing completion the number of labourers again increased to deal with the landscaping of the site and the preparations necessary to make the house ready for occupation.

Consequently the labouring force usually consisted of a nucleus of consistently employed workmen who performed a wide variety of tasks, and a large number of more casual workers who were engaged at irregular intervals for short periods working on specific jobs. Thus at Trentham Hall one hundred and four different labourers were employed between 1633 and 1638, but only three of them worked in all six years and a further four worked for five years. Sixty-three of the labourers were employed only for a brief period in a single year.[1] Between 1594 and 1597, sixty-three labourers worked for Sir Thomas Tresham at Rushton, of whom twenty-nine were employed only in one year, four were employed for the whole period, and two worked for three years.[2] The regular labourers at Trentham were consistently employed in the early years of the work, but after the completion of the shell of the building in 1635, their prospects of employment became more erratic and they were all subject to fairly long spells of unemployment (See Figure 5). The Triangular Lodge, which was a much smaller building, provided a more stable pattern of employment for the regular labourers, one of them, Watson, missing only two weeks work during the three years that he was employed at the site (See Figure 6). The number of casual labourers required each year was comparatively high, but it was probably easier on a small enterprise to plan the work so that the regular labourers were almost fully employed.

There is little evidence for itinerant building labourers and the majority of them were probably either drawn from the immediate neighbourhood of the site or already employed on other duties on the estate. Many of the casual labourers were employed for short periods at widely spaced intervals and were clearly local men. The tasks that they carried out required little specialised skill, and only a few of them seem to have been given the opportunity to learn any of the building crafts. Some of the sons of craftsmen, including John Smythson at Wollaton in April 1585, worked as labourers, but generally only for a few weeks as an introduction to the building site before starting to learn their fathers' craft. Conversely, some craftsmen, such as John Drake, a bricklayer who worked at Old Thorndon Hall, were the sons of labourers.[3] But the only documented example of a man

Figure 5: Labourers regularly employed at Trentham Hall, 1633–38

| | 1633: 40 weeks | | 1634: 50 weeks | | 1635: 51 weeks | | 1636: 49 weeks | |
	weeks	days	weeks	days	weeks	days	weeks	days
Greatbatch	35	151	43	$163\frac{1}{2}$	38	$147\frac{1}{2}$	29	$128\frac{1}{2}$
Hassall	24	$91\frac{1}{2}$	34	146	34	157	30	$157\frac{1}{2}$
Moreton	35	160	47	191	39	$165\frac{1}{2}$	31	146
Rushton	38	$215\frac{1}{2}$	46	$236\frac{1}{2}$	27	124	20	97
Gervace			10	42	27	$119\frac{1}{2}$	17	67
Chere			24	88	6	18	16	76
Plymley	11	51			17	82	18	77
Total number employed	31		45		51		27	

| | 1637: 50 weeks | | 1638: 50 weeks | |
	weeks	days	weeks	days
Greatbatch	17	$78\frac{1}{2}$	45	$222\frac{1}{2}$
Hassall	20	83	8	$14\frac{1}{2}$
Moreton	3	14		
Rushton	1	6	7	23
Gervace	20	78	8	19
Chere	25	137	17	$71\frac{1}{2}$
Plymley	15	$48\frac{1}{2}$	4	14
Total number employed	29		17	

Figure 6: Labourers regularly employed at Rushton, 1594–97

| | 1594: 22 weeks | | 1595: 50 weeks | | 1596: 51 weeks | | 1597: 49 weeks | |
	weeks	days	weeks	days	weeks	days	weeks	days
Horner	11	$59\frac{1}{2}$	33	$160\frac{1}{2}$	50	234	49	259
Benton	12	66	16	$86\frac{1}{2}$	35	$181\frac{1}{2}$	49	$256\frac{1}{2}$
Watson			48	237	51	$246\frac{1}{2}$	49	252
Hueson	4	14	14	78	25	122	47	$212\frac{1}{2}$
Bartle	9	$49\frac{1}{2}$	42	$213\frac{1}{2}$	25	108	5	22
Rice	1	4	49	$243\frac{1}{2}$	25	$112\frac{1}{2}$		
Total number employed	18		35		32		21	

who began his working life as a labourer and later became a craftsman was that of someone called Brykleton who was labouring at Loseley House in 1561, and in 1563 was 'entred to lere' as a mason on the same house.[4] However, for most labourers the building of a country house was no more than an interlude when there were increased opportunities for employment in the neighbourhood, and after the completion of the work even those who were most regularly employed no doubt returned to working on the land.

On most sites the labourers were generally employed by the day, even where the craftsmen were working at piece-rates or by contract. This method of working was probably more convenient for many of the tasks that they carried out which required close direction, but some of the basic jobs needed less supervision and were occasionally paid for by contract. These jobs invariably involved simple digging which could be easily measured and required few instructions. At Little Saxham Hall and Hengrave Hall, Suffolk, Ingatestone Hall, Essex, and Trentham Hall, Staffordshire, ditching was executed in this way, as was the digging of the foundations at Trentham and Bolsover Castle, Derbyshire, and the trenching for the water supply at Redgrave Hall, Suffolk. Generally the labourers formed temporary associations in gangs to carry out contract work, payment being made to them collectively rather than individually, But sometimes even the minimal organisation that this required was beyond them. The four labourers who were working on the foundations at Trentham in 1634 so miscalculated their contract that

'being not able to pforme theire bargaine desire to leave it & take day wage'.   [5]

Women were occasionally employed as labourers for short periods on a number of sites. Their duties were usually light, as at Hengrave Hall where they gathered rushes for thatching, cleaned and swept the rooms as the craftsmen finished work on them and watched the kilns during firing.[6] At Bolsover Castle, where unusually high numbers of women were employed, their jobs were mainly similar, although some of them also served the craftsmen with materials,[7] as did a woman employed on William Dickenson's house in Sheffield in 1576.[8] However, on a small number of sites, no allowance appears to have been made on account of their sex. In June 1587 women helped the labourers unload slate from barges at Grays Thurrock for Old Thorndon Hall, Essex.[9] At Wollaton Hall, Nottinghamshire, they carried limestone and plaster,[10] and at Chester they worked a treadmill that operated a crane.[11] The numbers employed were generally small, rarely exceeding two or three women at one time, but at Bolsover as many as ten were employed in some weeks. Apparently there was a shortage of labour in the area, for boys and girls were also regularly employed. In almost every case the women were related to labourers already working on the site, and their wages must have been a welcome if irregular supplement to the family budget. Most women worked for only a few days or weeks in any year, but at Trentham Hall, Staffordshire, where they were mainly engaged on weeding in the garden in the spring and summer, a small number were regularly employed for the last three years of the building. A total of five women worked during this period, but the most consistently employed were the wife and daughter of the labourer, Gervace, and indeed between 1636 and 1638 he worked in fewer weeks in the year than his wife.[12] However, in general, women were a very insignificant element in the labour force on most building sites.

18   Notes

1   Staffordshire County Record Office: D593 R /1 /2
2   British Museum: Additional MSS 39832
3   Essex County Record Office: D /DP A 18−20
4   J. Evans, 'Extracts from the Private Account Book of Sir William More of Loseley . . .' *Archaeologia* xxxvi (1855) 284−310
5   Staffordshire County Record Office: D593 R /1 /2
6   Cambridge University Library: Hengrave Hall Deposit 80
7   Knoop & Jones, *op cit* 36−7
8   J. R. Wigfull, 'House Building in Queen Elizabeth's Days' *Transactions of the Hunter Archaeological Society* iii (1925) 72−3
9   Essex County Record Office: D /DP A20
10   Nottingham University Library: Mi A60 /5, f. 11
11   E. Ridout, 'The Account Book of the New Haven, Chester, 1567−8' *Transactions of the Historical Society of Lancashire and Cheshire* lxxx (1928) 86−128
12   Staffordshire County Record Office: D593 R /1 /2

19 Working Conditions

There is little direct evidence for the number of hours worked each day on country house sites. A shorter day was undoubtedly worked during the winter when there was less daylight, and in the 16th century this was generally reflected in a lower wage rate paid during those months, but the actual hours are nowhere specified. The ideal for the 16th century was clearly laid down by the Statute of Artificers of 1563,[1] which repeated the terms of earlier statutes of 1495[2] and 1514[3] concerned specifically with masons, in which workmen hired by the day or week were to start work in summer (mid-March to mid-September) at or before 5 o'clock in the morning and to finish between 7 and 8 o'clock in the evening with breaks of no more than two and a half hours during the course of the day. In the winter they were to work 'from the springe of the daye in the mornynge untill the nyght of the same day'. However, the length of the statutory working day is an uncertain guide to the actual practice on private building sites, and Sir Roger Pratt seems to imply that by the latter part of the 17th century, at least, shorter hours were being worked when he posed the rhetorical question, 'How many bricks will an able workman lay ordinarily in one day, from 6 of ye clock to 6'.[4] Many country houses were built on isolated sites some miles from the nearest village, which must have meant a long walk for most of the craftsmen, and this possibly had an effect on the time that they started work. Robert Smythson, for example, lived five miles away from Longleat, and even though he was provided with a horse at his employer's expense, the daily journey must have been quite time-consuming.[5]

In the absence of any clear documentary evidence, it is probably correct to suggest that the normal working day on a country house building site was effectively from dawn to dusk during the winter months and varied in the summer between the extremes of the Statute of Artificers and the shorter day mentioned by Pratt.

The day was punctuated by a number of breaks for eating and drinking, but, again, their exact length and the times of their occurrence are not divulged by any of the private building accounts that have survived. The Statute of Artificers specified

'at every drynkyng one halfe howre, for his Dynner one hower, and for his Slepe when he is allowed to slepe, the which is from the middest of May to the mydest of August, halfe an houre at the most, and at every Breakefast one halfe hower;. . .',

but it is impossible to know how closely this practice was followed on individual country house sites.

In most accounts the working week ran from Monday to Saturday, when those on daily and weekly wage rates were paid. Sundays were occasionally worked, generally by labourers tending the kilns, which, once lit, had to be attended throughout the night, and there are frequent references to labourers on 'night watche', when they were paid their normal day wage. When the lime kiln was being burnt for the Hawkefield Lodge at Rushton, in October 1597, Sir Thomas Tresham provided beds for the two labourers engaged 'on watching their kill'.[6] Apart from these extra duties associated with the manufacture of brick and lime, overtime was rare on the majority of country house sites, in contrast with the growing practice in the Royal Works.[7] Speed of construction was not a prime consideration for most private builders, and the occurrence of overtime was usually the result of unusual circumstances, as when a number of masons and joiners engaged on interior decoration at Chatsworth worked through the night and on a Sunday prior to the arrival of the Queen in 1579.[8] Sir John Thynne, who, at least in the early years at Longleat, was more concerned than most builders with rapid progress, instructed his steward in 1547 that the workmen were to work part of their meal breaks, but the principal motive for this was his determination to reduce the size of the labour force in the autumn.[9] Despite Thynne's continual exhortations of haste to his steward at this period, there is no other record of overtime being worked at Longleat.

Holidays tend to be mentioned in the various building accounts only on the few occasions when individual workmen worked during them. Thus at Bolsover Castle in 1613 eight labourers demolished part of the castle wall that was possibly dangerous 'in the three Christmas holidays',[10] and Sir Thomas Tresham's boon tenants from Rothwell were paid 3s 6d in 1595 'in respect of servinge their daies work on good fryday'.[11] Christmas and Easter were observed on all building sites, but it is difficult to ascertain how many other holidays the workmen were allowed in each year. An Act of 1552 named twenty-seven days apart from Sundays that were to be observed as holidays, provided always

'that it shall be lawful. . . [for every person] upon the holy-days aforesaid, in harvest, or at any time in the year when necessity shall require, to labour. . .or work any kind of work, at their free wills and pleasure',   [12]

but it was repealed in the following year,[13] and it is unlikely that it was ever enforced. No doubt the actual practice varied on individual sites. At Kyre Park, Worcestershire, St. Luke's Day was specifically mentioned as a holiday in 1611 and St. Matthew's Day in 1612.[14] The workmen were not paid for these days, and, as far as it can be determined, this was the common practice on most country house sites during the period, although in 1550 only, the masons working at Redgrave Hall were apparently paid for one day's holiday out of every two that they took.[15]

The lack of payment for holidays meant that in some weeks the workman's income was greatly reduced, and to these days must be added those that were lost through bad weather when no work was possible. In September 1612 the labourers digging stone at Kyre Park were paid for only five days in the week 'for one daye they wrought not for Raine',[16] and longer rainy periods must have resulted in considerable financial hardship.

Craftsmen were less vulnerable than labourers to redundancy caused by wet weather, because they could often work inside the house or in their workshops when it was not possible to venture outside. During the wet October of 1561 Sir William Cecil's steward was able to report from Burghley, 'there is some store of aslar hewen these Rayne days',[17] and masons at Longleat in 1547 were saving work on the interior of the hall to 'do yt in foule wether and nar wynter when they can not worke abrode'.[18]

However, on many houses building stopped completely during the winter months, and even on those sites where work continued, it was generally with a greatly reduced labour force. In 1594, the first year of the construction of Sir Thomas Tresham's Triangular Lodge, the partially built walls were covered with furze as protection against the frost during the week ending 2 November and the labourers were dismissed. The carpenters continued to work at day rates preparing the framework of the roof in their workshop, and six of the freemasons remained on the site carving decorative stonework at piece rates. All the roughmasons and the other six freemasons who had been working in October were made redundant. Work ceased completely in the first week of January 1595, and the only workmen employed during the rest of the month were a number of labourers searching for building-stone. The freemasons and the carpenters returned in the middle of February, but the roughmasons remained unemployed until the milder weather of May enabled the construction of the walls to be restarted. The roof had been erected and tiled by November, and consequently there was sufficient work available to occupy most of the labour force until the middle of December. In January 1596 the labourers who were digging stone were again the only workmen employed on the site. Three freemasons returned at the end of February to work on the interior decoration of the lodge at piece rates, but it was the second week of April before there was any work for the roughmasons. Most of the work on the lodge was finished by October of that year, although it was September 1597 before the painter had completed the decoration.[19]

The possibility of frost meant that work on the fabric of the building was generally confined to the period between March and October or November, and consequently the craftsmen who were most vulnerable to seasonal redundancy were the less skilled men engaged on laying and other tasks which could only be carried on out of doors. Sometimes other work was found for them, such as the stonelayers at Bolsover Castle who spent the winter of 1613 dressing stone,[20] but most of them were usually laid off for the duration of the winter. The craftsmen who remained tended to be more skilled and capable of decorative work which could be prepared in their workshops or executed in the interior of the house if the construction was sufficiently advanced. Thus during the remodelling of Old Thorndon Hall, Essex, the bricklayers worked only between March and October, but the glaziers, plasterers and joiners continued to be employed throughout the winter,[21] and at Redgrave Hall, Suffolk, most of the work stopped shortly after Michaelmas in each year but a few skilled workmen always remained throughout the winter months.[22] At Longleat in 1547, Sir John Thynne determined not to 'kepe oon workman that shall work day work after Michaelmas',[23] but his joiners spent the winter wainscoting the parlour and a chamber,[24] and the principal mason was engaged on squaring stone at the quarry at piece rates.[25] Some of the masons at Hatfield worked through the winter of 1610—11 on the sculpture so that it was ready to be set up in the following spring,[26] and a mason at Gawthorpe Hall, Lancashire, made the moulded 'windowe stuffe' during the winters of 1600—01 and 1601—2. The hall at Gawthorpe was roofed in June 1602, and in subsequent winters a glazier, a plasterer, and several joiners were also employed.[27]

Besides the skilled craftsmen, a number of labourers were also generally retained throughout the winter. When necessary they were able to serve the craftsmen, but they were principally engaged in replenishing the supply of materials against the re-commencement of construction work in the following spring.

Temporary redundancy caused by the weather or the irregular demands for their particular skills must have formed a predictable part of the craftsmen's lives, but the unexpected occurrence of sickness or injury must have severely strained their resources. When an accident occurred on the site the builder sometimes paid for the necessary medical treatment, as when Sir Richard Leveson paid 5s 'to hemings the plaisterer towards the cure of his wounds received by a fall in the Kitchin' at Trentham Hall in 1635,[28] or when Sir Roger Townshend gave 11s in 1619 to the father of one of his workmen who broke a leg during the demolition of Coxford Abbey, from which stone was being provided for Raynham Hall, Norfolk,[29] but compensation was not provided for the wages that the victim lost during the period that he was absent from work. Corporate organisations were more benevolent towards their workmen. The trustees of London Bridge spent the large sum of 58s 4d in 1547 on two surgeons 'for healing of a great wound in the head of John Alerton, carpenter, hurt at the bridge by default of the old gin', and amongst other sickness gratuities they made an allowance of 6s 8d in 1494

'To oon John Isaac, late servaunt and laborer unto the said bridge, in consideracion of his good and true service doon unto the same bridge by meny yeris past and nowe is fallen blynde and impotent'. [30]

The fellows of Trinity College, Cambridge, made several payments in 1601 to a stone carver 'in ye time of his sickness for his releif',[31] but private builders seem to have felt no such obligation, and the mason at Rushton who fell sick after three days' work in October 1596 but had five days 'allowed him by yor. wo. appointment because of his sickness' was exceptionally fortunate and he was left to his own devices in the following week when he continued to be absent from work.[32]

The extra two days' wages for his sick mason were given by Sir Thomas Tresham as compensation for his misfortune, rather than as a regular sickness payment. Similar philanthropic actions were occasionally taken by other builders. Sir Richard Leveson gave 3s to a mason working at piece rates in June 1634 'for working a stone yt was broken, wherin he lost 3s'[33] and Sir William Petre paid a carpenter the large sum of £5 after he had completed the framework of the gallery at Thorndon, Essex, in 1550 'in way of rewarde in recnpance of an harde bargeiyne yt he hadde before at Thorndon'.[34] John Tusle, the carpenter who made the roof of the Shire Hall at Stafford in 1590 for £30, was subsequently given a further £1 'in respect of his hard bargaine'.[35]

Although, as these examples show, some builders were prepared to compensate for the difficulties in accurately estimating for contract work, they were under no obligation to do so, and even when the craftsman had carried out extra work that was not specifically part of his contract it appears that any additional payment was largely at the discretion of the builder. Thus in April 1575 when John Greaves submitted his bill to Lord Paget for carpentry work executed 'over and besydes my bargaynes' at Beaudesert Hall, Staffordshire, he simply stated what he had done

> 'not valuinge any porcion thereof but leavinge that and referringe my self therin to yor Lordshippes goodnes and gentlenes. . .'

Greaves received £8 'wch his lordshippe off his goodnes paieth'.[36] The wording used by the accountants to record similar payments at other building sites implies that it was general practice for the builder to fix an arbitrary price for extra work. The payment of £1 to a mason at Little Saxham Hall, Suffolk, in August 1507 was

> 'in ful paiement of his task of xix *li*. for my first house wt vj*s*. viij*d*. rewarded hym for making there of a window of ij lights', [37]

and Richard Rogers, the Southwark stonecarver who made a chimneypiece at Old Thorndon Hall, Essex, in 1590, was paid an additional £2 in 'consideracon of doynge more than bargayne & for well doynge of the worke'.[38]

The occasional payment of a bonus or reward to individual craftsmen for well-executed work was fairly common. Usually only small sums were involved, such as the 15*s* divided amongst four labourers at Trentham Hall in December 1634 'over & above theire wage' for finishing the trenching ready for laying the water supply to the house,[39] or the 4*s* 4*d* given to four roughmasons at their completion of a bridge at Rushton in 1595.[40] However, rewards equivalent to several weeks' wages were not uncommon. In the week after the labourers had received their bonus at Trentham, the smith was given £1 'by yor appoyntment after I had paid him for all his locks', and a freemason was also given £1 in January 1509 at Little Saxham Hall 'by way of reward'.[41] When the house was ready for occupation substantial *ex gratia* payments were sometimes made to those craftsmen who had been prominent in the supervision of the work. John Kniveton was given a reward of £10 by Bess of Hardwick in October 1597, immediately after she had moved in to Hardwick Hall,[42] and the Earl of Salisbury gave Robert Liming the enormous sum of £100 in 1612 at the completion of Hatfield House.[43]

In addition to their workmanship, craftsmen were also rewarded for ideas that increased efficiency or saved the builder money. The churchwardens of St. Mary-the-Great, Cambridge, gave 3*s* 4*d* in 1593 to a mason 'for his great pains in saving much scaffolding',[44] and Bess of Hardwick paid £2 in 1596 to the wife of Thomas Accres 'in respect of her husbands devise of sawing blackstone to buy her a gowne withal'.[45] A benevolent concern for the families of her principal craftsmen was characteristic of the later years of Bess of Hardwick's life. In 1592 she had given £2 to Abraham Smith, a mason, 'against his weddinge', and when Accres' daughter got married in December 1595, Bess gave her £1 and her mother £5. She also contributed £1 to John Kniveton's wife in February 1597 'when she was robbed'.

Indirect bonuses were sometimes found for workmen in the form of tools or clothing. Usually it was the craftsman's responsibility to provide the specialised tools for his particular trade, and the only tools supplied by the builder were of a more general nature, such as pick-axes, shovels, and pails. This is sometimes made explicit in contracts of employment, such as that between the Earl of Shrewsbury and two masons in 1576, by which the latter were to find 'themselves all maner of toyles to worke with pertayning to their scyence of their owne Costs & chardgs',[46] and is implied by the arrangements made at various sites for the carriage of the tools of those craftsmen who came from a distance. At Trentham Hall, for example, the plumber's son was paid his expenses in June 1635 for going to Bridgnorth to collect the plumbers' tools and at the completion of their work in September a labourer returned their tools to the same place.[47] However, on a few occasions individual craftsmen were given an allowance for their tools by the builder. Two London joiners employed at Old Thorndon Hall in 1587 received 6d each for their tools,[48] and the three masons hired by the year at Loseley House, Surrey, between 1563 and 1566 were provided with all their tools by Sir William More.[49] At Longleat, a saw was bought for the masons in 1572,[50] and stone axes and chisels were provided at Kyre Park, Worcestershire, in 1611,[51] although on both these sites the majority of their tools were supplied by the workmen themselves.

Protective clothing was sometimes provided for those workmen engaged on tasks which placed them at risk of minor injury. The most frequent references are to gloves for carpenters, who were vulnerable to splinters from the great baulks of framing timber that they handled, and to blisters from the ropes used to manoeuvre the timbers into position on the building. Some examples have already been given, and to these may be added gloves bought for the carpenters at Hengrave Hall in 1532 and 1535,[52] and the 2s 'gyven to the carpenters for gloves at the raysinge of the Rofe of the chappell' at Trinity College, Cambridge, in July 1564.[53] Brickmakers were also given gloves to protect their hands when they were firing the kilns at Hengrave Hall and Redgrave Hall, Suffolk.[54]

However, the gloves presented by Lawrence Shuttleworth to six masons, ten labourers, the housekeeper, two maids, and eight estate servants including the cow-boy, on 26 August 1600 were a symbolic gesture occasioned by the laying of the first stone of Gawthorpe Hall, Lancashire.[55] Such a gift was similar to the practice on some building sites of providing some of the craftsmen in the most responsible positions with a livery, in common with other servants in permanent employment. At Kyre Park in 1611 the gesture was unusually elaborate, the 'cheiff mason' being given boots, slippers, a coat, 'cognizance hat band, feather & cognizance of silver'.[56] Another mason at Kyre Park received annually 'a livery to make him a coat'. Generally it was only those craftsmen who were employed on an annual basis, and therefore formed part of the builder's permanent establishment who were given a livery. The two masons who agreed to serve the Earl of Shrewsbury for a year in January 1575 were to have a 'Coate' in addition to their wages, and the contract with two bricklayers at Thorndon Hall, Essex, in 1550 specified a livery coat for each of them.[57] At Loseley House, Surrey, the three permanent masons were given two liveries a year, costing 10s each.[58] Presumably these were equivalent to the winter and summer liveries mentioned at Old Thorndon Hall, Essex.[59] It is possible that the practice of giving a livery to permanent employees was dying out by the end of the period for, while examples from the 16th-century are common, that from Kyre Park is the only established example from the following century.

19   Notes

1   5 Eliz. I.c.4
2   11 Henry VII, c. 22
3   6 Henry VIII, c. 3
4   *The Architecture of Sir Roger Pratt* ed. R. T. Gunther (Oxford 1928) p. 229
5   Girouard, *Smythson* p. 58
6   British Museum: Additional MSS 39832, f. 119
7   D. Knoop & G. P. Jones, 'Overtime in the Age of Henry VIII' *Economic History* iv (1938) 13–20
8   B. Stallybrass, 'Bess of Hardwick's Buildings and Building Accounts' *Archaeologia* lxiv (1913) 356
9   Longleat Archives: R.O.B., i, f. 141. Thynne to Dodd, 22 June 1547
10   D. Knoop & G. P. Jones, 'The Bolsover Castle Building Account for 1613' *Ars Quatuor Coronatorum* xlix (1939) 34
11   British Museum: Additional MSS 39832, f. 42
12   5 & 6 Edward VI, c. 3
13   I Mary Sess. 2, c. 2
14   Mrs Baldwyn-Childe, 'The Building of the Manor-House of Kyre Park, Worcestershire, *The Antiquary* xxii (1890) 50
15   Sandeen, p. 47
16   Mrs Baldwyn-Childe, *op cit* 52
17   J. A. Gotch, 'The Renaissance in Northamptonshire' *Transactions of the Royal Institute of British Architects* new series vi (1890) 105
18   Longleat Archives: R.O.B., i, f. 206. Dodd to Thynne, undated but probably 1547
19   British Museum: Additional MSS 39832
20   Knoop & Jones, *op cit*
21   Essex County Record Office: D /DP A19–22
22   Sandeen, p. 46
23   Longleat Archives: R.O.B., i, f. 237. Thynne to Dodd, 3 August 1547
24   *Ibid* f. 299
25   *Ibid* f. 228
26   L. Stone, 'The Building of Hatfield House' *Archaeological Journal* cxii (1955) 120
27   *The House and Farm Accounts of the Shuttleworths* ed. J. Harland (Chetham Society xxxv 1856) 133 & 141
28   Staffordshire County Record Office: D593 R /1 /2
29   H. L. Bradfer-Lawrence, 'The Building of Raynham Hall' *Norfolk Archaeology* xxiii (1927) 102
30   C. Welch, *History of the Tower Bridge* (London 1894) p. 53
31   Willis and Clark, ii, 482n & 487n
32   British Museum: Additional MSS 39832, f. 93
33   Staffordshire County Record Office: D593 R /1 /2
34   Essex County Record Office: D /DP A10, f. 80

35 William Salt Library, Stafford: D1721 /1 /4
36 *Ibid* D1734 /3 /4 /101
37 British Museum: Additional MSS 7097, f. 182v
38 Essex County Record Office: D /DP A21
39 Staffordshire County Record Office: D593 R /1 /2
40 British Museum: Additional MSS 39832, f. 63
41 British Museum: Additional MSS 7097, f. 192
42 B. Stallybrass, 'Bess of Hardwick's Building and Building Accounts' *Archaeologia* lxiv (1913) 383
43 L. Stone, 'The Building of Hatfield House' *Archaeological Journal* cxii (1955) 104
44 D. Knoop & G. P. Jones, 'The Sixteenth Century Mason' *Ars Quatuor Coronatorum* l (1937) 209
45 Stallybrass, *op cit* 379. A contemporary 'sawe for Blacke stone' is illustrated in R.I.B.A. Drawings Collection, Smythson Collection, II /26
46 J. A. Wigfull, 'Extracts from the Note-Book of William Dickenson' *Transactions of the Hunter Archaeological Society* ii (1921) 192
47 Staffordshire County Record Office: D593 R /1 /2
48 Essex County Record Office: D /DP A20
49 J. Evans, 'Extracts from the Private Account Book of Sir William More of Loseley . . .' *Archaeologia* xxxvi (1855) 303
50 Longleat Archives: T.P. Box lxviii, Bk. 60, f. 30
51 Mrs Baldwyn-Childe, 'The Building of the Manor-House Kyre Park, Worcestershire' *The Antiquary* xxii (1890) 26
52 Cambridge University Library: Hengrave Hall Deposit 80
53 Willis and Clark, ii, 569
54 Sandeen, *op cit* p. 48
55 *The House and Farm Accounts of the Shuttleworths* ed. J. Harland (Chetham Society xxxv 1856) p. 130
56 Mrs Baldwyn-Childe, *op cit* 51
57 Essex County Record Office: D /DP A10, f. 85
58 Evans, *op cit* 303
59 Essex County Record Office: D /DP A19 and A22

20 Accommodation and Food

The workmen who came to the site from outside the neighbourhood must often have incurred considerable expenses on their journey, but they were not always re-imbursed by their new employer. Such payments seem to have been largely a matter for individual negotiation with no specific obligation on the part of the builder. Indeed, Sir Roger Pratt, in his advice on the best terms for drawing up contracts with workmen, wrote in 1665 'Nothing to be expected for carriage of tools, or journeys',[1] and the 6s 8d divided amongst thirteen masons who came to Redgrave Hall, Suffolk in March 1551, 'in rewardes for parte of there charges from London' seems to have been thought of as a considerate gesture on the part of Sir Nicholas Bacon and could hardly have covered their costs.[2] However, some craftsmen were sufficiently in demand to insist upon recompense for the time that they spent in travelling to the site, and they were generally paid a day's wage for each day taken. The only workman who received any travelling expenses at Loseley House, Surrey, was a mason who was specially summoned from Oxford in 1562 and given 2s 4d 'for his costes in comyng from thens'.[3] The plumber from Bridgnorth employed at 2s a day at Trentham Hall, Staffordshire, was paid 4s in July 1635 'for 2 dayes coming & going',[4] and at Raynham Hall, Norfolk, in 1620, a limeburner who came from Thetford received 3s 'for ij daies cominge & returninge as . . . was my Mrs comand to give him'.[5] In some cases the craftsman was in a strong enough position to demand the repayment of travelling expenses as a necessary condition of his employment. A clause in William Arnold's contract with Sir George Luttrell for additions to Dunster Castle in 1617 included the payment of travelling expenses as part of his remuneration,[6] and one of the conditions laid down by Humphrey Lovell when he sent Robert Smythson and his assistants to Longleat in 1568 was that they were 'to have dayes wages for theare travel whiles they are in cominge'.[7]

On arrival at the site, the itinerant workmen were faced with problems of finding accommodation. Those craftsmen who could reasonably expect a long period of employment often brought their families with them and set up house in the neighbourhood, but there were others who travelled alone or who were employed to execute specific tasks which were unlikely to last for longer than a few months and who required little more than somewhere to eat and sleep when they were not working. The builder, with his local influence and knowledge, was clearly better placed than the men themselves to provide them with lodgings, and generally he made all the arrangements. Thus at Hengrave Hall, Suffolk, in 1526 a joiner and his servant who came from London to work for sixteen days were boarded for three weeks by Sir Thomas Kytson at a cost of 6*s*, and six men were accommodated for a week by one of the local workmen in 1529.[8] The labour employed on the house during these years was mainly drawn from the locality and consequently only the occasional craftsman required accommodation, but in 1530 the increase in the size of the enterprise and the arrival of a large number of workmen from elsewhere made it necessary to make regular arrangements. Thomas Shethe, the former overseer of the work, was now made solely responsible for boarding and carriage. Although a contract with a mason specified that he

> 'and all his company yt he setts a worcke for ye said house shall be bordyd at Thomas Shethes for xvj*d*. a week'   [9]

Shethe did not actually provide the accommodation, his role being to make the necessary arrangements. Shethe's accounts survive for the period 1536–8, and at times he was finding accommodation for well over twenty workmen. The cost for each man was 16*d* for every seven days as set out in the contract, mentioned above, but there is no indication where they were lodged. The unvarying uniformity of the rates and the large numbers of men involved, suggest that they were probably accommodated in the completed part of the house itself, and that the 16*d* represented the allowance made to Shethe for providing the necessary facilities. The wording of the contract would seem to indicate that it was the contractor's responsibility to pay the 16*d*, but in the building account all the payments to Shethe 'ffor bordyng' were made by the accountant on Sir Thomas Kytson's behalf and, although it is possible that appropriate deductions were made in settling the contractor's bill, there is no evidence for this. Certainly, at Beaudesert Hall, Staffordshire, in 1576, it was the builder who paid the boarding expenses of the craftsmen,[10] and this seems to have been the practice on a number of other sites. At Rushton, for example, five masons came twelve miles from Lyveden to work at the cornice of the Triangular Lodge in August 1595. For the first three days they were boarded and paid 16*d* a day each, but on the fourth day when they had finished their work and had returned home, they were paid only 10*d*.[11] The extra 6*d* a day allowed for their accommodation corresponds with a similar sum paid by Tresham to two limeburners in August of the following year.

Where accommodation was required for only a short period for a few workmen as at Rushton, it was usually possible to make arrangements with a local innkeeper or with the wife of one of the local craftsmen. Thus at Haddon Hall, Derbyshire, in November 1549, 2*s* 8*d* was paid

> 'unto Wyllm bowryngs wyff for ye borde of henrye wagstafe, Ryc wyght, Tomas noytte, and Robarte handerton for iiij dayes workynge at Elkar for great Tymbre for ye howsse',   [12]

and the craftsmen employed during the first five years at Redgrave Hall, Suffolk, appear to have lodged at the village inn.[13] As work on the house progressed, the workmen were often provided with sleeping accommodation in those parts which had already been roofed.

From 1550 the Redgrave craftsmen were boarded in the house, and Trentham Hall, which was begun in 1630, was ready to accommodate the workmen in March 1634.[14] A joiner employed at Old Thorndon Hall was noted to be 'lodging in the house' in 1587[15] and mention was made at Hardwick Hall in June 1597 of 'the turret where Accres lyeth'.[16] No doubt on those sites where there was already an existing house it was frequently used to provide accommodation for the workmen engaged on building the new house.

Although accommodation, when necessary, was usually arranged by the builder, this was not always the case. When Stephen Chappell, a carpenter, contracted to execute all the woodwork for the stables at Stiffkey Hall, Norfolk, in 1582, he agreed to find board for himself and his men.[17] Chappell and his men had previously worked on the house from at least 1579, during which period they had generally been boarded by Sir Nathaniel Bacon,[18] and it is probable that the change in policy was brought about by the virtual completion of the internal decoration of the house towards the end of 1581, which meant that it was no longer desirable to use it as temporary lodgings for the workmen. Having worked in the area for at least three years, Chappell was presumably perfectly capable of making his own arrangements for accommodation, as was no doubt the painter, Thomas Selby, who had worked on several occasions at Bramshill in Hampshire before he petitioned Lord Zouche in 1619 for payment for

> 'the last peece of worke [which] held you peticioner on worke 16 weekes, duringe which tyme your Peticioner borded himself'.   [19]

However, in the contract made by the mason Roger Palmer of North Buckland, Devon, with Sir Richard Edgecumbe for the building of Mount Edgecumbe, Cornwall, in 1547, the former bound himself to find 'loddgyng' for himself and his men for the duration of the work.[20] It is difficult to understand the motive for the inclusion of the clause, unless, perhaps, Palmer had already made a preliminary journey to view the site during which he had secured satisfactory lodgings in the neighbourhood for the number of men that he intended to employ. Palmer certainly appears to have been a very shrewd negotiator, and the covenants of his contract were unusually precise. In addition to providing lodging for his men, he was also to find them 'mete and dryngke', but he ensured that they were to have adequate facilities for this by getting Edgecumbe to agree to the unique condition that he would 'bylde make and Cover a Convenyent & Syfficient house or leyney [linhay] for dressyng of their mete'.

The provision of food and drink for workmen varied considerably from site to site. Sir Richard Edgecumbe was not alone in leaving the responsibility for feeding arrangements to his contractor, although he was unusual in providing him with the necessary facilities. None of the workmen employed at Little Saxham Hall, Suffolk, were fed by Thomas Lucas,[21] and neither were those at a number of other country house building sites. During the additions to Syon House, Middlesex, in the early 17th century, the only workmen who were fed were a few craftsmen who had been specially brought in to execute specific tasks,[22] and at Trentham Hall, Staffordshire, only the small number of workmen employed on an annual basis were provided with their 'dyett'.[23] In contrast, most of the day workers at Gawthorpe Hall, Lancashire, were either fed or given an allowance for their 'table' when they were working away from the site, while those working by contract made their own arrangements.[24] Sir John Petre provided food for most of his craftsmen at Old Thorndon Hall, Essex, with the exception of his bricklayers who were mainly local men. However, as the house was predominantly built of brick, the number of craftsmen requiring to be fed at any one time was fairly small. Up until the 1580s he also supplied the food and drink of his labourers, but for some unrecorded reason he had largely discontinued the practice by 1587, although he continued to feed the craftsmen.[25] Similarly, John Talbot fed most of the men working on Grafton Manor, Worcestershire, in 1568, but by 1576 they had to feed themselves.[26] All the small labour force employed to build William Dickenson's house at Sheffield in 1575 were fed by the builder's wife,[27] and Sir William More managed to feed the much larger number of men working on the site of Loseley House, Surrey; his stone-diggers, who were necessarily employed away from the site, being the only workmen who were left to fend for themselves.[28]

As with so many aspects of the administration of the work at Hengrave Hall, Suffolk, the expansion of Sir Thomas Kytson's plans in 1530 resulted in a corresponding change in his attitude towards the feeding of his workmen. From 1525 when the work commenced with a predominantly local labour force, the workmen provided their own food and drink, but in 1530 when large numbers of workmen were imported from outside the district, Kytson reversed the practice and began to feed all his men, including those who had previously been accustomed to providing for themselves.[29] Given the necessity to make arrangements for feeding the new workmen, he no doubt found that it was more efficient to extend the facilities to his established labour force.

A number of factors must have influenced the decision of individual builders as to whether to feed their workmen or not. Breakfast and dinner, which were the main meals of the workman's day, were both consumed during normal working hours, and consequently some facilities for the preparation of his food on the site were necessary. If the builder undertook to supply and prepare the food, the operation would undoubtedly proceed more quickly and efficiently than if each workman, or groups of workmen, made their own individual arrangements; but, on the other hand, the extra administrative burden might not have been acceptable to the builder. The composition of the labour force was probably fairly crucial. Single workmen coming to the site from other areas, living in lodgings, and ideally working six days a week, were poorly placed to supply their own food in a largely subsistence-based local economy, whereas local workmen were in a far better position. This situation seems to be reflected in the change of practice at Hengrave Hall in 1530.

Another factor of some importance was that of finance. When the builder provided his workmen with food and drink, he paid them correspondingly less. Thus at Hengrave the wages of those workmen employed before 1530 fell by 2*d* a day when Kytson began to feed them. On most sites the food was probably the produce of the builder's own estates and, although its use represented a loss of potential profit from selling it on the open market, its most immediate result was an effective reduction in the builder's expenditure on wages. As many builders seem to have had some difficulty in raising sufficient cash for their work, the payment of part of their wage-bill in kind must have seemed an attractive proposition.

20 Notes

1 *The Architecture of Sir Roger Pratt* ed. R. T. Gunther (Oxford 1928) p. 88
2 Sandeen, p. 62
3 J. Evans, 'Extracts from the Private Account Book of Sir William More of Loseley . . .' *Archaeologia* xxxvi (1855) 296
4 Staffordshire County Record Office: D593 R /1 /2
5 H. L. Bradfer-Lawrence, 'The Building of Raynham Hall' *Norfolk Archaeology* xxiii (1927) 122
6 A. Oswald, *Country Houses of Dorset* (2nd edition, London 1959) p. 28
7 Longleat Archives: R.O.B., iii, f. 61
8 Cambridge University Library: Hengrave Hall Deposit 80
9 *Ibid* Hengrave Hall Deposit 81
10 William Salt Library, Stafford: D1734 /3 /4 /143
11 British Museum: Additional MSS 39832, f. 54
12 F. H. Cheetham, *Haddon Hall* (London 1904) p. 32
13 Sandeen, p. 43
14 Staffordshire County Record Office: D593 R /1 /2
15 Essex County Record Office: D /DP A20
16 B. Stallybrass, 'Bess of Hardwick's Building and Building Accounts' *Archaeologia* lxiv (1913) 379
17 *Camden Miscellany* xvi (Camden Society 3rd Series lii, 1936) p. 50
18 Sandeen, pp. 202–3
19 W. H. Cope, *Bramshill* (London 1883) p. 121
20 Cornwall County Record Office: MTD /48 /10
21 British Museum: Additional MSS 7097, ff. 174–200
22 G. R. Batho, 'Henry Earl of Northumberland and Syon House, Middlesex, 1594–1632' *Transactions of the Ancient Monuments Society* new series iv (1956) 104
23 Staffordshire County Record Office: D593 R /1 /2
24 *The House and Farm Accounts of the Shuttleworths* ed. J. Harland (Chetham Society xxxv 1856) 125–174
25 Essex County Record Office: D /DP A18–22
26 J. Humphreys, 'The Elizabethan Estate Book of Grafton Manor' *Transactions of the Birmingham Archaeological Society* xliv (1918), 1–24. British Museum: Additional MSS 46461
27 J. R. Wigfull, 'House Building in Queen Elizabeth's Days' *Transactions of the Hunter Archaeological Society* iii (1925) 66–73
28 J. Evans, 'Extracts from the Private Account Book of Sir William More of Loseley . . .' *Archaeologia* xxxvi (1855) 284–310
29 Cambridge University Library: Hengrave Hall Deposit 80

21 Working Accommodation

The standards of working accommodation for workmen engaged on country-house building varied from site to site, but usually the buildings that were provided were of a fairly makeshift nature. In 1589, shortly after work had commenced at Kyre Park, the carpenter moved a house two and a half miles to the site 'for the masons to work in' and built '2 other Hovells for the masons brickmakers and a smith to work in'. In 1590 he built a 'house' for drying bricks and squaring timber, and another masons' lodge at the quarry, and two years later he moved one of the lodges to a different position on the site. The first period of building at Kyre was completed by 1595, and when work began again in 1611 it was necessary to build another two lodges for the masons, the original structures presumably having been dismantled at the end of the earlier building phase.[1]

Freemasons needed covered workshops protected from the elements in which to dress and carve their stone, but they were not the only craftsmen who were provided with specialised accommodation. At Trentham Hall, Staffordshire, in April 1633, the 'kilnhouse' was whitewashed.[2] This was possibly similar to the lodge built by the Royal Works next to the limekiln at Dartford in 1543 'for to laye chalk drye in & for the . . . brekers of chalk to wurk in',[3] a function no doubt also fulfilled by the 'morter howse' constructed at Old Thorndon Hall, Essex, in December 1589.[4] The bricklayers also had a 'howse' at Old Thorndon, and at Longleat in 1563 a workshop was built for the brickmaker.[5] At Hardwick Hall 'the old plumery', where the plumber had worked, was demolished in 1594,[6] and in John Smythson's survey plan of Worksop Manor, Nottinghamshire, one of the rooms is entitled the 'plomerye'.[7] When work commenced at Raynham Hall, Norfolk, in 1619, one of Sir Roger Townshend's first actions was to construct 'an hovell for the Sawrs',[8] and during the repairs to Aylesbury market house in 1645 a similar building, called the 'sawpitt house', was made.[9]

Most workshops were simple timber-framed structures. The 'cabin' used by the masons employed on the Shire Hall at Stafford in 1590, was constructed of birch poles and had a thatched roof.[10] A carpenter at Trentham Hall spent five days making 'a Cabbyn for ye masons to worke in' in November 1634,[11] and the 'old lodg wher the masons wrought' at Hardwick Hall was taken down by a carpenter and was presumably timber-framed.[12] Essentially, it was only necessary to have a covered-in space, and often it was possible to adapt buildings already existing on the site. When Sir Edward Hext wrote to John Lord Petre, in March 1610, about the site proposed for Wadham College, Oxford, he pointed out that it contained

'Many hangyng houses which will serve to hewe our stones in or work in tymber in all weathers', [13]

and at Raynham Hall an 'old Bearn [was] ther agayne to be builded for a Workehouse'.[14] The loft above the coachhouse at Trentham Hall was used by the painter as a workshop where he could prepare and store his materials.[15] Those craftsmen who were primarily concerned with fitting out the building were sometimes accommodated in an unoccupied room in the house itself. The glazier sent to work at the Earl of Shrewsbury's house at Chelsea in 1578 was to have 'good glasse to worke and a room in Shrewsbury House to lye in and to worke it',[16] and at Longleat in an inventory taken in 1580 on the death of Sir John Thynne, when work was still in progress on the house, one of the rooms was noted as the glazier's chamber.[17]

21   Notes

1   Mrs Baldwyn-Childe, 'The Building of the Manor-House of Kyre Park, Worcestershire' *The Antiquary* xxii (1890) 24, 25, 51
2   Staffordshire County Record Office: D593 R /1 /2
3   Bodleian Library, Oxford: MS Rawl. D784, f. 38
4   Essex County Record Office: D /DP A21
5   Longleat Archives: R.O.B., ii, f. 156. Walker to Thynne, 14 April 1563
6   B. Stallybrass, 'Bess of Hardwick's Buildings and Building Accounts' *Archaeologia* lxiv (1913) 376
7   R.I.B.A.: Drawings Collection, Smythson Collection III /17
8   H. L. Bradfer-Lawrence, 'The Building of Raynham Hall' *Norfolk Archaeology* xxiii (1927) 107
9   Public Record Office: SP28 /207, f. 14
10   William Salt Library, Stafford: D1721 /1 /4
11   Staffordshire County Record Office: D593 R /1 /2
12   Stallybrass, *op cit* 376
13   N. Briggs, 'The Foundation of Wadham College, Oxford' *Oxoniensia* xxi (1956) 69
14   Bradfer-Lawrence, *op cit* 125
15   Staffordshire County Record Office: D593 R /1 /2
16   Stallybrass, *op cit* 355
17   Longleat Archives: R.O.B., iii, f. 237

22 Labour Relations

Most workmen were engaged on a daily basis and were instantly dismissed as soon as they were no longer required. The policy of most employers was probably similar to that at Burghley House, Northamptonshire, where the steward reported in 1578 that

> 'there be no moe in woorke then of necessities must nedes be to performe those works yor L. did appointe, and yet as the same ende I doe discharge the superflouous nombre'. [1]

As has already been suggested, the workmen must have become accustomed to insecurity in their employment, but some employers appear to have been excessively unscrupulous in their dealings with them. Sir John Thynne's instructions to his steward in August 1547 seem particularly harsh:

> 'I wol not kepe oon workmen that shall work day work after Michaelmas . . . but ye shall not nede to let the workmen themselfs know it.' [2]

Employment by the week was comparatively rare, but on the few occasions where it did occur, as at Grafton Manor, Worcestershire, the workmen seem to have been considerably better off, for the employers usually undertook to pay them their full wage irrespective of the availability of sufficient work to occupy them in any particular week. This seems to be the correct interpretation of the phrase 'broken worke and Holle',[3] or its equivalent,[4] often used to describe the conditions of employment enjoyed by the weekly workers. However, although their short-term prospects were more secure, they were still subject to summary dismissal.

Those craftsmen who undertook contracts to execute specific tasks for a negotiated sum were in a better position because their period of employment was reasonably predictable, but perhaps the most fortunate workmen were those who were hired by the year. A small number of workmen were employed on this basis on most building sites. Sometimes they were paid a small retaining fee to which were added wages at the prevailing rate for work that they actually executed, and sometimes they were paid an inclusive annual salary, usually in quarterly instalments. Sir Francis Willoughby used both methods simultaneously at Wollaton in 1585, when he paid Thomas Accres, the marble mason, and Thomas Greenway, the joiner, £30 each for the year, and Christopher Lovell, the principal mason £16, whereas two other masons, John Hills and Clement Wynchenden received

£1 in addition to their normal day wages.[5] Whichever way they were paid, they were generally employed for the duration of the work, and were treated as permanent members of the builder's household, their position often being marked by the annual gift of a livery. It is probable that some of them remained in the service of the builder after the completion of the house to carry out the necessary maintenance work. Certainly, Thomas Leversage, a glazier, was in receipt of an annual 'pencon for the repare of the windows' of Sir Richard Leveson's two houses at Trentham and Lilleshall during the building of the former,[6] and another glazier, Mark Wells, was paid £5 per annum by the Earl of Middlesex to maintain the glass at Copthall, Essex.[7]

Such workmen could reasonably expect employment throughout the year, and in some cases they were guaranteed work for longer periods. In February 1590, Sir Edward Pytts

'Bargayned with Thomas Lem to serve for 7 yeares as my covenant Servant . . . for a mason a brickmaker & bricklayer',   [8]

and in 1612 he hired another mason, John Chaunce, to be his surveyor 'till the work be finished God will'. When Pytts died in April 1618, his son negotiated a further four-year contract with Chaunce. Very few craftsmen, however, were given contracts of employment covering such a long period of time. The usual contract, such as that between the Earl of Shrewsbury and two masons in 1575,[9] was for no more than a year, which enabled the builder to make an annual review of his labour requirements. Thus Sir Richard Leveson employed a number of carpenters and labourers on an annual basis in 1633 and 1634. In 1635, as the pace of work slackened, he 'discharged' them, but many of them continued to work at the site at day wages during the following years.[10]

Annual workmen were in a privileged position, but the conditions under which most workmen were employed were generally very much in favour of the builder. The two masons who came from Bromsgrove to work for Sir Edward Pytts at Kyre Park in October 1611 at 11s a week, must have assumed that they were going to be employed for a considerable period, especially as they agreed to 'contynue winter and sommer at that rate', and yet little over a month later, following Pytts' election as Sheriff of the county, they had been dismissed. They, on their part, had bound themselves 'to contynue in the work without going out or changinge during the time I shall sett them to work'. This was a clause common to most contracts of employment, and many builders took steps to ensure that it was honoured. The threats made by Sir John Thynne when he heard that his principal mason was working for another builder 'before he have fynished my works without my license for the redres' have already been noticed, and when in 1563 a joiner at the same house quarrelled with a workmate and left the site, he got only as far as Mere in Somerset before the steward had him stopped 'and caused hyme to come back agayne'. On his return to the site, the joiner refused to continue with his work so the steward stopped 'his whole wags purposinge therby to stay him at worke'. Undeterred, he again escaped, and this time he was actually working in Dorset before the steward was able to trace him.[11] When two pairs of London sawyers left Stiffkey Hall, Norfolk, in August 1576 after only two weeks' work, Nathaniel Bacon sent his father 'ye bargaine I concluded wth them and ther markes unto it', apparently with the intention of apprehending them in London and taking action against them.[12]

There is no evidence whatsoever for any form of gild organisation amongst the crafts on country house sites, and workmen in dispute with their employer had very little redress. If they left the site, there was always the possibility that they would be caught and forced to return, and if they remained, the terms of any settlement were invariably dictated by the builder to his own advantage. Sir John Thynne exploited this situation to the full in 1574 when he cut the piece-rates that he was willing to pay for the carving of the bay windows at Longleat. From 1572 this work had been executed by Allen Maynard and Robert Smythson, but they were understandably reluctant to work at the reduced rates, and in 1574 they were superseded by three of the lesser masons. Smythson and Maynard held out for a time, but with their financial resources rapidly dwindling they were forced to capitulate and in 1575 they were back working at the windows at the lower rates.[13]

Despite the shortage of skilled labour, most builders seem to have had sufficient powers of coercion to prevent any strike action, and few workmen were independent enough to do anything more than complain about conditions that they considered to be unsatisfactory. When the accountant at Beaudesert Hall, Staffordshire, drew up the list of payments that he had made in 1575 for the boarding expenses of the workmen, he noted that the principal carpenter 'demandeth more for his men', but there is no indication that his demands were ever met.[14] The only effective form of protest that a workman could make with impunity was to announce his intention to leave when he had completed his period of service; and even this course was presumably open only to those men who had been hired for a specific length of time. When Bess of Hardwick heard that one of her craftsmen at Chatsworth 'sayth he will departe at our Ladeday next', she angrily called him a false knave and ordered her steward to 'have hym bunden in an oblygacyon to avoyde at the same day', but she was powerless to prevent him leaving.[15]

Although some builders appear to have been hard masters, there were many occasions, no doubt, when they were sorely tried by their workmen. As in any age, examples of unsatisfactory workmanship abound. At Little Saxham Hall in October 1506, a brick wall ten yards long and sixteen feet high had to be completely demolished because the bricklayer had skimped the foundations,[16] and at Longleat in 1565, two of the chimneys were crooked as a result of a mistake made by the mason, Allen Maynard, who was later to be in dispute with Thynne.[17] No action seems to have been taken against the craftsmen responsible for these errors, but at Bolsover Castle in 1613, a mason engaged on dressing stone at piece rates had an unspecified sum 'abated for bad scappling',[18] and an incompetent mason at Kyre Park in the same year was grudgingly paid 'for 15 dayes naughty work . . .& so discharged for a bungler'.[19]

Complaints about the behaviour of the workmen are even more numerous. Some of the more general accusations of dilatoriness were, no doubt, intended to placate absent builders who were making unreasonable demands for progress on their stewards, and must be treated with circumspection. However, despite the rhetoric of Bryan Teshe in writing to Sir John Thynne about the Protector Somerset's house at Wulfhall, asking him to

'pardon the rudeness of my letter because I write in haste, for if I be absent the tyme of the writing of this letter ther wyl be almost nothing done among the workmen', [20]

his complaint was probably justified. In the week that the letter was written two labourers had been dismissed for insubordination, and one of the other administrators had complained to Thynne about

'such a lewde company of Frenchmen masons as I never saw the lyke. I assure you they be the worst condicyoned people that ever I saw and the dronkenst; for they will drynke more in one day than three days wages wyll come to, and then lye lyke beasts on the floor not able to stonde'.

Drunkenness was also the subject of comment at Kyre Park, where a quarryman was paid for only half a week in 1612 'for the other 3 [days] he spent idelly at Ale', and in the following year he was dismissed for a similar offence.[21] Sir John Thynne had his own share of labour problems at Longleat, although, given his attitude towards his workmen, it is perhaps permissible to feel some sympathy for the carpenters, about whom the steward wrote in 1563

'I have more adoe wth them then wth all the rest of yowre folks for nether they will apply ther worke or be content with any reasonable allowance . . .' [22]

22 Notes

1   J. A. Gotch, 'The Renaissance in Northamptonshire' *Transactions of the Royal Institute of British Architects* new series vi (1890) 108

2   Longleat Archives: R.O.B., i, f. 237. Thynne to Dodd, 3 August 1547

3   Used with reference to a carter employed by the week at Gawthorpe Hall in July 1601, *The House and Farm Accounts of the Shuttleworths* ed. J. Harland (Chetham Society xxxv, 1856) 137

4   e.g. 'broke & hole' at Loseley in 1562, and 'broken & hole' at Old Thorndon Hall in 1590

5   Nottingham University Library: Mi A 60 /4, f. 7

6   Staffordshire County Record Office: D593 R /1 /2

7   Kent County Record Office: U269 A505 /1

8   Mrs Baldwyn-Childe, 'The Building of the Manor-House of Kyre Park, Worcestershire' *The Antiquary* xxi (1890) 264

9   J. R. Wigfull, 'Extracts from the Note-Book of William Dickenson' *Transactions of the Hunter Archaeological Society* ii (1921) 192

10   Staffordshire County Record Office: D593 R /1 /2

11   Longleat Archives: R.O.B., ii, ff. 155, 169, 179

12   Sandeen, p. 186

13   Girouard, *Smythson* pp. 60 – 1

14   William Salt Library, Stafford: D /1743 /3 /4 /143

15   B. Stallybrass, 'Bess of Hardwick's Buildings and Building Accounts' *Archaeologia* lxiv (1913) 352

16   British Museum: Additional MSS 7097, f. 179

17 Longleat Archives: R.O.B., ii, f. 209. Vyttery to Thynne, 9 December 1565
18 D. Knoop & G. P. Jones, 'The Bolsover Castle Building Account for 1613' *Ars Quatuor Coronatorum* xlix (1939), 46
19 Mrs Baldwyn-Childe, *op cit* 51
20 J. E. Jackson, 'Wulfhall and the Seymours' *Wiltshire Archaeological Magazine* xv (1875) 184
21 Mrs Baldwyn-Childe, *op cit* 51–2
22 Longleat Archives: R.O.B., ii, f. 147. Walker to Thynne 15 March 1562–63

23 Social Conditions

Building accounts and contracts, by their nature, disclose little about the social conditions of the workmen involved in the construction of country houses. The information to be gained from wills and inventories is valuable, if often incomplete, but the majority of building craftsmen did not need to make such a record in settling their affairs. All that is known about many of them is their mere existence, and in some cases, the wage-rate that they were paid while working on a particular building site. This is especially true of the lower ranks of craftsmen. Their more successful fellow workmen sometimes achieved sufficient wealth or local importance to have left a more substantial record of their life. The evidence that has been accumulated refers largely to these men and it provides a necessarily imperfect picture of their life away from the building site.

The houses lived in by building craftsmen were probably indistinguishable from those of agricultural labourers and husbandmen. There is not much information about those craftsmen at the lower end of the social scale, but Thomas Hill, a mason of Wardington in Oxfordshire who died in 1588, inhabited a simple two-roomed building,[1] and Christopher Gold, a glazier who died in Banbury in the following year, lived in a larger town house containing a shop and hall on the ground floor, a chamber over, and a cockloft in the roof.[2] Both these men were worth well under £5 when they died, and the more moderately successful craftsmen seemed to have lived in more spacious accommodation. Giles Haell, a carpenter living at the same time in Oxford, had a hall, shop, and buttery, with a great chamber, a little chamber, and another chamber over the shop.[3] In the early 17th century, a mason of Writtle in Essex worth just over £6, lived in a house containing a hall, shop and buttery, with chambers over the hall and shop,[4] and another mason, worth over three times as much, lived in a similar house in Bedford.[5] In the north Midlands in 1647, the house of Isaac Smith, a mason of Lichfield, with its hall, parlour, and kitchen, and two chambers over, provided him with the same kind of accommodation.[6]

In a few cases existing houses can be identified with particular craftsmen, and the evidence that they provide helps to substantiate the information to be derived from the probate inventories of the comparatively well-off craftsmen. The house of Arthur Grumbold (1603–70) of the well-known family of Northamptonshire masons, still stands in the village of Weldon. It is dated 1654, and is built of stone with a thatched roof. There are three rooms on both ground and upper storeys, and two rooms in the roof space. It is heated by chimneystacks at both gable ends, and conforms to a house-type common in the

House of the mason Arthur Grumbold in Great Weldon, Northamptonshire

House of the mason Humphrey Frisbey in Great Weldon, Northamptonshire

Midlands from the seventeenth century onwards. An equally common equivalent contained the same number of rooms on the principal floors, but was heated by a massive axial stack. Such a house, perhaps was the one lived in by Henry Rogers, a carpenter of Southill, Bedfordshire, which had in 1613 a hall, lower chamber, buttery, and kitchen, with three chambers over.[7] A smaller house in Weldon was built by another mason, Humphrey Frisbey, in 1643.[8] It consists of two rooms on both floors, on either side of a centrally placed axial chimneystack, with further accommodation in the attic. It was a logical variation on the larger type noted above, and examples are to be found throughout the Midlands and the south-east. Frisbey's house is distinguished from that of a prosperous husbandman merely by virtue of the richness of the architectural decoration, which was no doubt inspired by pride in his own skill, and partly intended as an advertisement for his craftsmanship.

Some of the more prosperous craftsmen lived in a much grander style. William Thomas, an Oxford plumber who died in 1553, had accommodation in his house for both male and female servants, as well as a hall, parlour, buttery, kitchen, and three other chambers.[9] Thomas Holt, the carpenter who was in charge of the work on the Schools Quadrangle at the Bodleian Library, Oxford, in 1618 and 1619, lived in a house in Holywell Street similar to some that still survive there. It was three storeys in height, with a hall, kitchen, and entry passage on the ground floor, three chambers above, and two cocklofts in the top storey.[10] The most successful men, the surveyors and the craftsmen with more than local reputations, were probably housed in conditions similar to those of the smaller gentry, to whose ranks some of them aspired. The house of John Smythson at Bolsover, for example, included amongst its principal rooms the hall, parlour, kitchen, chamber over the parlour, middle chamber, and closet,[11] and John Hills was living in a house with the descriptive name of Chilwell Hall at the time of his death in 1592.[12]

The furnishings and possessions to be found in their houses predictably reflected the wealth of the individual craftsmen. Apart from the animals and crops owned by those who were farming as a by-occupation, the most important possessions were invariably their furniture and utensils. Thomas Burger, a Bedfordshire carpenter whose total estate in 1620 was only worth £3 19s 2d, had a bed, three chests, and a little old cupboard,[13] and Luke Baggat, another carpenter from Oxfordshire, whose most valuable possession was a cow worth £1 6s 8d, had a bed, a table, and a form, when he died in 1584.[14] Further up the social scale, Giles Haell had six beds and a truckle bed,[15] and one of the four beds owned by Leonard Dalton, a Witney carpenter, was proudly noted as being joined.[16] Most craftsmen, including some of the very poorest, seem to have had a few pieces of pewter or brass. Thomas Hill, the Oxfordshire mason who was worth £4 5s 0d in 1588, had two brass pots and seven pieces of pewter,[17] and Christopher Gold, a glazier who died in Banbury in 1589, had two pewter dishes amongst his assets of £3 2s 2d.[18] The pewter and brass of John King, a Bedfordshire carpenter was worth £3 10s 0d in 1620, out of a total estate of £78 10s 8d,[19] and William Thomas, the prosperous Oxford plumber who died in 1553 worth £78 3s 4d, had £8 in plate.[20]

A surprising number of craftsmen had decorative furnishings in some of the rooms of their houses. Thomas Hill might have lived in only two rooms, but they must have been considerably brightened by the painted cloth that hung in one of them.[21] Christopher Gold had three painted cloths in his house,[22] and Giles Haell had an unspecified number of cloths and some panelling in the hall of his Oxford home.[23] Leonard Dalton had a panelled hall and painted cloths in some of his other rooms,[24] and in Worcester the joiner Anthony Ould had no doubt panelled the walls of his hall himself.[25]

There is little information about the food eaten by building workmen. A tantalising document in the Longleat Archives refers to the diet of six men at the house in May 1567. It mentions cheese and butter, wheat and malt, and arrangements made 'wth Hogetts wif to bak[e and] brewe', but unfortunately it has been badly mutilated and is incomplete.[26] At Hardwick in 1590, 'oats and dredge' and peas were used to make bread for the workmen;[27] an inferior mixture which accords with Harrison's comment on the gentility providing sufficient wheat for their own table while their household were

'inforced to content themselves with rie, or barlei, yea, and in time of dearth, manie with bread made either of beans, peason, or otes'.   [28]

Carters, who were often tenants fulfilling their obligations of boon work, were invariably given a simple meal on arrival at the site. The carriers of stone and tile to Condover Hall in 1587 were refreshed with bread, 'three owlde cheeses . . . fower softe cheeses & butter'.[29] Similarly, the carters bringing timber to the site at Wollaton in the same year were provided with 'a cheise for their breakefaste',[30] and the carters working at the Shire Hall, Stafford, in 1590, were also given bread and cheese,[31] but few of the other building accounts specify the nature of any of the food that was provided for the working craftsmen. The most complete record of the diet of a group of building workmen in the 16th century is provided by the diary of Peter Lewys, Proctor of Dublin Cathedral. The masons engaged on the work there in 1564 and 1565 were given two meals a day, which usually consisted of bread, beef, and ale, with fish on Fridays, and sometimes cheese, butter, and eggs as a substitute for beef at breakfast.[32] Corporate organisations were often able to provide better conditions for their workmen, and it is not necessarily possible to draw any conclusion about the diet of English country house craftsmen from the evidence of an Irish cathedral, but, nevertheless, in the absence of any other evidence, it is possible that conditions were not dissimilar.

It is difficult to be precise about the extent to which building craftsmen were literate. Certainly the bills and contracts to which many of them laboriously appended their mark are testimony to a high degree of illiteracy, and the comment of Thomas Stirrup that 'but few of them can write',[33] is indicative of the prevailing situation as late as 1651. Generally, the bills that they submitted were written out by clerks or by the builder's accountant, and if a craftsman managed to sign his name it is probable that those were often the only words that he could write. Some craftsmen of course, were capable of reading and writing, and drew up their own bills themselves, but they appear to have been in a minority. Often they were craftsmen, such as smiths and glaziers, who worked independently of the main labour force, and provided their own materials, and who were therefore obliged to document in some way the purchases that they had made, and the details of the work that they had executed. Craftsmen who undertook limited supervisory duties were another group for whom it was an advantage to be able to write. If they were working away from the main site, quarrying stone or felling timber, they were invariably responsible for recording the hours and wages of the workmen under their charge. Thus William Grumbold kept the accounts for the work carried out at the stone pits for Sir Thomas Tresham during his building at Lyveden in the early 17th century. These were then submitted to the accountant who entered them into the main accounts.[34] Most of the craftsmen who graduated to more responsible administrative positions were almost certainly literate, and the ability of some, such as John Thorpe and Robert Stickles, went beyond the mere facility of being able to read and write. However, the majority of artisans were incapable of leaving any written evidence in their own hands, and the only documentation of their very existence is in the writing of the professional scribes of the age, the clerks and accountants.

23   Notes

1   *Household and Farm Inventories in Oxfordshire, 1550–1590* ed. M. A. Havinden (Oxfordshire Record Society xliv, 1965) p. 258
2   *Ibid* p. 282
3   *Ibid* p. 261
4   F. W. Steer, *Farm and Cottage Inventories of Mid-Essex* (Chelmsford 1950) p. 71
5   *Jacobean Household Inventories* ed. F. G. Emmison (Bedfordshire Historical Record Society xx, 1938) p. 86
6   *Probate Inventories of Lichfield and District, 1568–1680* ed. D. G. Vaisey (Staffordshire Record Society, Collections for a History of Staffs., 4th series v, 1969) pp. 72–3
7   Emmison, *op cit* p. 132
8   H. M. Colvin, 'Haunt Hill House, Weldon' *Studies in Building History* ed. E. M. Jope (London 1961) pp. 223–8
9   Havinden, *op cit* pp. 42–3
10   T. W. Hanson, 'Halifax Builders in Oxford' *Transactions of the Halifax Antiquarian Society* (1928) 314
11   Girouard, *Smythson* p. 200
12   Nottinghamshire County Record Office: PRNW. A transcript of his will was kindly supplied to me by David N. Durant
13   Emmison, *op cit* p. 55
14   Havinden, *op cit* p. 169
15   *Ibid* p. 262
16   *Ibid* p. 129
17   *Ibid* p. 258
18   *Ibid* p. 282
19   Emmison, *op cit* p. 59
20   Havinden, *op cit* pp. 42–3
21   *Ibid* p. 258
22   *Ibid* p. 282
23   *Ibid* pp. 261–2
24   *Ibid* p. 129

25 *Probate Inventories of Worcester Tradesmen 1545–1614* ed. A. D. Dyer (Worcester Historical Society, new series v 1967) pp. 43–5
26 Longleat Archives: R.O.B., ii, f. 258. Vyttery to Thynne 22 May 1567
27 B. Stallybrass, 'Bess of Hardwick's Buildings and Building Accounts' *Archaeologia* lxiv (1913) 389
28 *Harrison's Description of England* ed. F. J. Furnivall (New Shakspere Society, series vi, 1877) p. 153
29 Shrewsbury Public Library: Deeds 6883 f. 22
30 Nottingham University Library: Mi A60 /6, f. 4v
31 William Salt Library, Stafford: D1721 /1 /4
32 J. Mills, 'Peter Lewys: His Work and Workmen' *Journal of the Royal Society of Antiquaries of Ireland* xxxi (1901) 105
33 T. Stirrup, *The Artificers Plain Scale* . . . (London 1651) p. 2
34 British Museum: Additional MSS 39836, ff. 288–96

24 Wages

The basis from which any consideration of wages paid to artisans working on the construction of country houses must commence is the pioneering study of masons' wages made by D. Knoop and G. P. Jones,[1] and the more recent research into building wages and prices by E. H. Phelps Brown and S. V. Hopkins.[2] Both studies used the figures collected in the late 19th century by J. E. Thorold Rogers,[3] and show a remarkable decline in the real wages of building workers beginning in the early years of the 16th century and continuing throughout the period, caused by wage increases lagging behind rapidly rising food prices.[4] This general picture of economic decline is unlikely to be altered. However, an analysis restricted to the wage rates in the country house sector of the building trade suggest a number of criticisms of the detailed validity of their findings.

By extrapolating a predominant wage rate from the various annual statistics collected by Thorold Rogers, both Phelps Brown and Hopkins and Knoop and Jones were able to present a simple graph of the progress of wages over a given period of time. Although acceptable as an indication of the general trend of wages, this method tends to disguise the variety and complexity of the actual situation at any particular point,[5] and, based as it is on comparatively few figures largely drawn from one or two areas in Southern England, it suggests a general application that is more apparent than real.[6] The country house building accounts that have survived are characterised by a marked regional variation in wage rates. For example, in 1576 the carpenters working on William Dickenson's house in Sheffield were paid the equivalent of 8d a day,[7] while those working for Lord Paget at Beaudesert Hall, Staffordshire, in the previous year had been paid 9d and 10d a day,[8] and the carpenters employed at Longleat House, Wiltshire, and Old Thorndon Hall, Essex, were receiving 10d a day during the same period.[9] A similar regional variety in wage rates can be discerned at other periods. Undoubtedly one of the reasons for this lay in the length of employment enjoyed by many building workers at country house sites. Wage rates generally remained at their initial level for the duration of a particular enterprise and consequently workmen at one house could be receiving a wage agreed as long as ten years before, whilst those on a newly commenced house were being engaged at a currently higher rate. During the thirty-four years that building was taking place at Longleat, the only general wage increase was in 1568 and can be partly explained by the arrival of a large number of highly skilled workmen in that year,[10] while wage rates at houses which were built in a shorter length of time, such as Wollaton Hall and Trentham Hall, remained stable for the duration of the work.[11]

However, regional differences in wage rates are not solely explicable by the variety of dates at which particular engagements commenced, and the surviving wage assessments drawn up by the local justices in response to the statute of 1563 suggest that there was a general diversity in the prevailing rate from area to area. Master craftsmen in the building trades in Hertford in 1592, for example, were not to take more than 12d a day in summer, and the 'second sort' of craftsmen were to take no more than 10d a day,[12] whilst the equivalent rates in Wiltshire eleven years later in 1603 were only 11d and 7d.[13] Labourers at York in 1563 were assessed at 5d a day,[14] and their more fortunate colleagues at Lincoln in the same year were assessed at 7d a day.[15] Although the publication of a scale of maximum wage rates does not imply its effective enforcement, the variety of scales in different areas does seem to imply a regional diversity in the rates that were actually being paid.

In addition to this regional disparity, different rates were often paid to workers in the same craft on the same site. Thus at Wollaton between 1582 and 1588, four masons were paid at 14d a day, one at 13d, thirty at 12d, four at 11d, nineteen at 10d, and one at 9d, and amongst the woodworkers, one was paid 14d, another 13d, thirteen were at 12d, seven at 10d, and five at 9d.[16] Although 12d a day was clearly the predominant rate for craftsmen on the site, to ignore the other rates being paid simultaneously to some of the other craftsmen would be a misleading simplification of the true situation. The diversity of rates seems to reflect a combination of the degree of skill attained by the individual craftsmen and possibly their method of recruitment; the inducement of higher wage rates being necessary to attract itinerant craftsmen, with the local men being content to work at a lower rate in return for a period of comparatively secure employment. Whatever the reason, the majority of country house sites from the mid-16th century onwards exhibit a variety of wage rates similar to that at Wollaton, suggesting that tables of predominant wage rates largely based on short-term engagements involving only a few local workmen must be treated with a degree of caution.

The graph of wage rates published by Phelps Brown and Hopkins is a composite figure which makes no distinction between the rates paid to the different crafts.[17] Although it tacitly assumes that all craftsmen were paid the same wage, the authors point out in their text that the carpenter 'showed more upward variants, and led the field in the Tudor rise'. As the carpenter provided their most numerous and continuous quotations, they generally followed him when there was a divergence from the rates paid to the other crafts. However, the evidence from country house accounts, in addition to showing a variety of rates between workmen in the same craft, also demonstrates that there was often a disparity between the rates paid to different crafts, and, in contrast to the assertion of Phelps Brown and his collaborator, the higher rates were generally paid to masons and bricklayers rather than to workers in wood. Thus at Longleat between 1568 and 1580, the majority of the carpenters were paid 10d a day, with 12d and 14d for a few of the more skilled men, whilst the predominant rates for the masons were 10d and 12d, with the

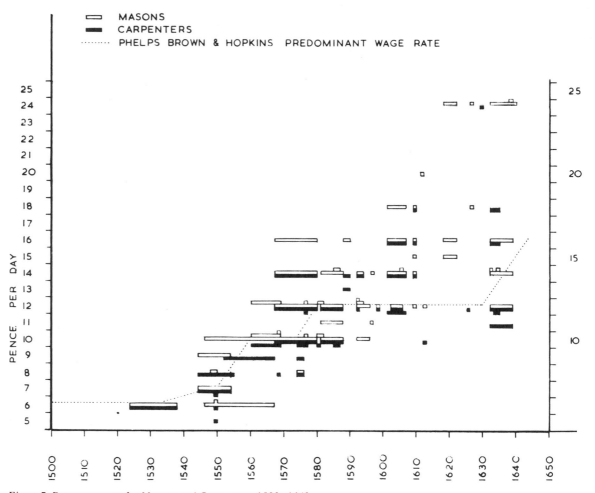

Figure 7: Day wage-rates for Masons and Carpenters, 1500–1640

skilled men getting 14*d* and 16*d*.[18] Similarly at Ashley Park, Surrey, between 1602 and 1607, the carpenters working by the day were generally paid 14*d* with occasional payments at 16*d* and 12*d*, and the masons and bricklayers were paid 16*d* and 18*d* with only a few at 14*d*.[19] The wage rates for other crafts, such as plasterers and tilers, are too fragmentary to allow of any consistent comparison, but they generally seem to have been lower than those paid to the masons and bricklayers. At Trentham Hall, Staffordshire, for example, the plasterers were paid 12*d* a day, whereas the majority of the masons were paid 16*d*,[20] and at Wollaton the plasterers received 10*d* in comparison with the predominant rate for masons of 12*d*.[21]

Another factor which detracts from the validity of predominant wage tables is similarly connected with the complexity of the wage structure on many country houses. Such tables can only be constructed from the evidence provided by those workmen who were paid by the day, for piece-rate and contract payments from different engagements can never be strictly compared due to the individual methods by which such payments were calculated and the frequent confusion as to the precise number of workmen being paid for a particular piece of work. However, from the late 16th century there was a growing trend on the part of many country house builders to pay their skilled craftsmen at piece-rates. By the 17th century this had become the predominant method of working, and on most major houses only the labouring and some of the more routine craftwork were carried out at day-rates. Consequently the daily wage rates that exist for the early 17th century often refer only to the less-skilled craftsmen and it is probable that this has a depressing influence on the general trend of wages in that period. The striking effect that the contrasting methods of working could have on the annual income of craftsmen working on the same site can be illustrated from the accounts for Trentham Hall, Staffordshire. In 1633 and 1634, Henry Smethley, a carpenter and joiner, was paid respectively £105 11s 6d and £130 10s $9\frac{1}{2}d$ for his piece-work on the house, whilst his colleague, Ralph Sutton, received £103 8s 9d and £64 17s 3d during the same period. Out of these sums both men made unspecified payments to two or three assistants, but, even so, a large proportion of the money must have remained to them as income. Between 1635 and 1638, when the more skilled woodworkers had left the site, the remaining carpentry was executed at day-rates by John Bradwell, the estate carpenter, and two assistants. Although they were consistently employed in almost every week during that period, none of them earned more than £12 in any one year. The predominant day wages for carpenters at Trentham were 12d for Bradwell and 11d for his assistants, but it is arguable that the piece-rate payments to Smethley and Sutton are of equal significance in assessing the economic position of the carpenters on the site, especially as the numbers of men receiving such payments between 1630 and 1634 probably exceeded those employed at day rates in the later years of the work. On the few occasions that Smethley worked at day rates he was paid 18d a day, and his men were paid 16d, which seems to suggest that the movement towards piece-work certainly conceals a higher general wage-level than is apparent from a consideration of only those workmen who were paid exclusively at day rates.

The wide variety of wage rates that were often paid on a single site, both to the different crafts and to different groups of men within those crafts, makes it difficult to chart the course of wages between 1500 and 1640. In *Figure 7* an attempt has been made to show the limits of the movement of wages during that period. For the reasons outlined above, and also on account of the limited number of entries obtainable from country house accounts, it seemed inadvisable to construct a predominant wage rate, but the results of Phelps Brown and Hopkins have been superimposed on the figure for the purposes of comparison. There were insufficient entries to usefully include the other crafts so the figure has been confined to the wage rates for masons and carpenters. The practice on some sites of providing food and drink for workmen, or of paying them less during the winter months, necessitated adjustments to some of the examples. Where the value of meat and drink could be firmly established, as at Hengrave Hall, the entries were adjusted accordingly, but where there was some doubt as to the exact value that the builder placed on the food that he supplied to his workmen, the entries have not been included. Thus the wage rates for Gawthorpe Hall, Lancashire, were not plotted on the figure. Most accounts were of sufficient duration to give both the summer and the winter wage rates, and where there was a divergence between the two, only the summer rate has been considered.[22]

There was an unfortunate lack of entries for the early years of the 16th century. However, wage rates for craftsmen seem to have been stable at 6d a day during this period, as they had been for much of the preceding century. The 6d a day paid to carpenters and masons at Hengrave Hall from 1525 to 1538 accords with the similar sum paid to the craftsmen at Kirby Muxloe Castle, Leicestershire, in the 1480s.[23] The evidence from Hengrave suggests that during this settled period a uniform rate was being paid both to the various crafts and to the men within those crafts. By the middle of the century, wages were beginning to rise. The increase in prices which had effectively begun some decades before, was clearly beginning to have an influence on wage rates.[24] Some craftsmen continued to be paid at the former rate, but a divergence in wages between individual workmen within the same craft was becoming apparent, creating maximum and minimum wage scales on most sites. Thus at Longleat some masons were being paid 10d a day, whilst others were only receiving 6d a day. By the third quarter of the century wages had continued to rise and the maximum and minimum rates at Longleat were now 16d and 10d. In some parts of the country, however, wage rates remained at a lower level. In 1575 and 1576, for example, the masons and carpenters in Sheffield were paid 8d a day, and the carpenters at Beaudesert Hall, Staffordshire, received 9d and 10d, but, as these are the first entries from the Midlands, and the north of England, it is impossible to know whether wages were slow to rise in these areas or whether they had risen from a comparatively lower base and thus represented an improvement similar to that noted for the southern and eastern parts of the country.

In the last quarter of the 16th century craftsmen's wages appear to have stabilised for a period at the level to which they had been moving in the previous decade. The various rates paid to the different groups of craftsmen at Longleat in the 1570s are approximately similar to those paid at Wollaton in the 1580s, and to Sir Thomas Tresham's workmen in Northamptonshire in the 1590s. Minor upward movements were certainly taking place during this period, but the general pattern was for the lowest wage scales to gradually disappear whilst the maximum scales of 14d and 16d, first discernible at Longleat in 1568, were not exceeded until the early years of the 17th century. During that century the maximum rate rose from 18d a day in the first decade to 24d by the end of the second decade, at which level it appears to have remained until the Civil War. The differential between the highest and lowest wage scale appears to have increased considerably in the early 17th century, so that of the masons consistently employed at Trentham Hall, Staffordshire, in the 1630s, some were being paid 24d a day whilst others were receiving only half that sum. However, the day-wage rates for the early 17th century are less representative than those available for the previous century, for on all the recorded accounts much of the work was carried out at piece rates and consequently the day rates generally reflect the routine work executed by the less-skilled craftsmen. Occasionally some of the piece workers were employed for a short period at day rates and they were invariably paid on a higher wage scale. It seems probable that these wage rates are indicative of a higher general level of wages than is apparent from the rates paid to those workmen who were exclusively employed by the day.

The movement of country house wages during the period broadly reflects the same trends plotted by Phelps Brown and Hopkins, with increases in the 1550s and 1570s, and a period of comparative stability in the late 16th and early 17th centuries. In general, however, wage rates seem to have been higher than their predominant rate indicates, especially in the early 17th century when the market seems to have been moving to a higher level at an earlier date than they allow. It is possible that such higher rates were peculiar to the country house sector of the building trade, where the difficulties of attracting sufficient numbers of skilled workmen might have compelled the builders to pay higher wages. But it is perhaps significant that in the Royal Works, where the prerogative of impressment enabled the crown to overcome any temporary shortages of labour, the wage rates were similar to those being paid on country house sites, and it seems likely that, in long-term engagements at least, Phelps Brown and Hopkins consistently underestimated the level of wage rates from the middle of the 16th century onwards.

The wage rates for labourers working on country houses have been set out in *Figure 8*.[25] As might be expected, these follow the same general pattern as has been outlined for masons and carpenters, with increases occurring during approximately the same periods.

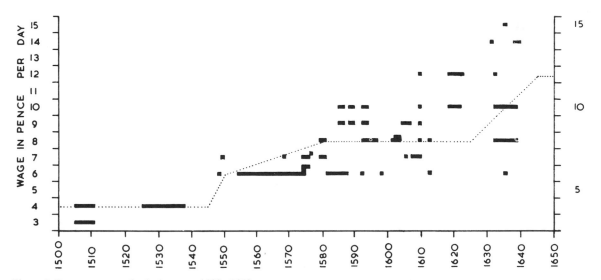

Figure 8: Day wage-rates for Labourers, 1500–1640

Although for much of the sixteenth century the wage rates agree fairly closely with those given by Phelps Brown and Hopkins, it appears that the movement towards a higher level had begun in parts of the country by 1590 and once again it is possible that they underestimated the extent of the increase in the early 17th century. In this respect, it is apposite to note that the purchasing power of the wages paid to agricultural labourers during the first four decades of the century seems to have been considerably higher than the purchasing power of the wages of building craftsmen suggested by Phelps Brown and Hopkins.[26]

The reluctance to project a predominant wage rate from the variety of figures collected from craftsmen and labourers makes it impossible to construct an index of wages for the period, and consequently no strict comparison with prices can be attempted. However, using as a guide the graph showing the price of a composite unit of consumables in southern England compiled by Phelps Brown and Hopkins,[27] it is clear that despite the improvement in wages from the mid-16th century onwards, prices had consistently risen faster and that the economic position of the wage-earner in 1640 was markedly worse than it had been in 1500. The exact extent of this decline is more difficult to assess. Little is known about the precise nature of individual expenditure during the period and the compilation of an aggregate price-index is correspondingly arbitrary. In addition, the only statistics surviving in sufficient numbers to enable such an index to be constructed are for wholesale prices, and it is not at all certain that retail prices rose quite so often or so fast. This doubt is especially pertinent to those goods which required processing and therefore contained an element of labour charge in their retail price, for wages, as has been suggested above, often remained relatively stable for a considerable period of time.

Although the graph compiled by Phelps Brown and Hopkins probably represents the most successful attempt that can be made on the available evidence to show the course of prices, it is instructive to compare it with the money equivalent of a craftsmen's food and drink over the same period. At Hengrave Hall in the 1530s it was valued at 2d a day, but by the 1550s, in Essex, Sir William Petre was assessing it at 3d, a sum which was similar to that obtaining at Longleat during the same decade. In the 1560s it had risen to 4d at Longleat, which was also the prevailing rate at Grafton Manor, Worcestershire, and at Loseley House, Surrey. Its value then seems to have remained at this level through the 1570s in Sheffield and into the 1580s at Old Thorndon Hall, Essex. In the various surviving wage assessments the value of meat and drink was calculated at 3d in Northamptonshire in 1560,[28] and in Buckinghamshire in 1562,[29] and then at 4d or 5d in all the succeeding assessments down to that of Hertford in 1631 where it had risen to 5d or 6d.[30] Such figures, of course, are only a very rough guide, as they probably represent only a theoretical value that the builder placed on produce largely derived from his own demesne, and they fail to take account of any possible lowering in the quality of the diet provided. But they do, perhaps, indicate that the rise in wholesale prices was not felt quite so strongly at a local level.

According to the evidence presented by Phelps Brown and Hopkins, by 1640 prices had risen to some five or six times their level in 1500, whilst the wage of a building craftsman had approximately doubled over the same period. This represents a catastrophic economic deterioration and even if it is assumed that building craftsmen were unusually prosperous at the beginning of the 16th century, it is difficult to accept a decline of such magnitude in their real wages without any attendant evidence of widespread starvation and distress. In the absence of such evidence, it is, perhaps, reasonable to doubt whether the impact of the price rise on wage-earners was quite as disastrous as has been generally assumed. In addition to the evidence already discussed for a higher level of wages and a slower rise in some retail food prices, it is possible that alterations in their working conditions enabled the building craftsmen to maintain a reasonable standard of living. Unfortunately there is insufficient information available about such factors as the number of holidays taken by the workmen, so that it is not possible to speculate whether a decline in the number of religious festivals and Saint's Days after the Reformation, for example, provided them with an opportunity to earn more money during the year. However, there are indications that some improvements were taking place in their earning potential, for the reduction in their wages during the winter months, which had been almost universal practice in the 16th century, occurred only rarely in the early 17th century. As the original motive for a lower wage was that fewer hours of work were possible during the shorter winter days, the abolition of the practice effectively provided the workmen with a seasonal wage increase.

In addition, many building workmen were able to supplement their wages from other sources. The evidence for by-occupations amongst the building trades has already been discussed and it is unnecessary to repeat it here, but it is relevant to point out that any agricultural surplus which they were able to sell would have benefited from the rising prices and thus helped to offset the deterioration in their real wages. However, too much emphasis must not be placed on such ameliorating factors. The building worker was primarily a wage-earner, and over a period of a century and a half he was faced by a consistent and rapid rise in prices. There is no doubt that on the whole his economic position declined, but for those workers engaged on building country houses at least, there are reasonable grounds to suggest that the extent of this decline was not as great as the wage and price statistics of Thorold Rogers would seem to indicate. It is most unlikely that the economic position of the workmen employed in other branches of the building trade was radically different, but further research into the original sources is necessary before this more general conclusion can be confirmed.

24   Notes

1   D. Knoop & G. P. Jones, *The Mediaeval Mason* (Manchester 1933)
2   E. H. Phelps Brown & Sheila V. Hopkins, 'Seven centuries of Building Wages' *Economica* new series xxii (1955) 195–206; *idem* 'Seven Centuries of the Prices of Consumables, Compared with Builders' Wage-rates' *Economica* new series xxiii (1956) 296–314
3   J. E. Thorold Rogers, *A History of Agriculture and Prices in England* 7 vols (Oxford 1866–1902)

4   Knoop & Jones, *op cit* p. 185; Phelps Brown & Hopkins, 'Seven Centuries of the Prices of Consumables . . .' *op cit* 300

5   Phelps Brown and Hopkins were well aware of this criticism, but, even so, they based their conclusions on their predominant wage graph and not on the more complex figure that they constructed for builders' wages in Oxford, 1500–1600; E. H. Phelps Brown & S. V. Hopkins, 'Seven Centuries of Building Wages' *Economica* new series xxii (1955) 203

6   Almost half of Thorold Rogers' builders' wages for the period down to 1620 came from the city of Oxford, and the remainder were predominantly derived from Cambridge and the southern counties

7   J. R. Wigfull, 'House Building in Queen Elizabeth's Days' *Transactions of the Hunter Archaeological Society* iii (1925) 68–73. They were actually paid a wage of 4*d* with an equal amount for their 'meat'

8   William Salt Library, Stafford: D/1734/3/4/143 & 144

9   Longleat Archives: T.P. Box lxviii, Bk. 60; Essex County Record Office: D/DP A18

10   Longleat Archives: *passim*

11   The workmen at Old Thorndon Hall, Essex, enjoyed periodic rises, but work was going on at this house for an even longer period of time than at Longleat

12   W. J. Hardy, *Hertford County Records: Sessions Rolls 1581–1698* (Hertford 1905) i, 10

13   Historical Manuscripts Commission, *Various* i, 162–7

14   *York Civic Records vi* ed. A. Raine (Yorkshire Archaeological Society Records Series cxii 1946) pp. 58–60

15   V.C.H. *Lincoln* ii (1906) 329

16   Nottingham University Library: Mi A60/1–7

17   E. H. Phelps Brown & S. V. Hopkins, 'Seven Centuries of Building Wages' *Economica* new series xxii (1955) 197

18   Longleat Archives: *passim*

19   Surrey County Record Office: Acc. 1030

20   Staffordshire County Record Office: D593 R/1/2

21   Nottingham University Library: *op cit*

22   The statistics for *Figure 7* have been provided by the following houses (arranged in chronological order of surviving accounts):
Little Saxham Hall, Suffolk, 1505–11
Hengrave Hall, Suffolk, 1525–38
Redgrave Hall, Norfolk, 1545–54
Longleat House, Wiltshire, 1547–81
Wolfhall, Wiltshire, 1549
East Thorndon Hall, Essex, 1550–55
Grafton Manor, Worcestershire, 1568–9, 1576
Beaudesert Hall, Staffordshire, 1575
Wm. Dickenson's house, Sheffield, 1575–6
Old Thorndon Hall, Essex, 1577, 1580–1, 1586–7, 1589–90, 1593–4
Stiffkey Hall, Norfolk, 1579–80
Wollaton House, Nottinghamshire, 1582–8
Condover Hall, Shropshire, 1592, 1598
Lyveden, Northamptonshire, 1593–7
Ashley Park, Surrey, 1601–7
West Horsley Place, Surrey, 1603–4
Brigg Milne dam, Yorkshire, 1605
Harrold House, Bedfordshire, 1608–10
Syon House, Middlesex, 1609–10
Knole, Kent, 1612
Bolsover Castle, Derbyshire, 1613

Raynham Hall, Norfolk, 1619—22
Copthall, Essex, 1623, 1627, 1630—1, 1635
Goldicote House, Worcestershire, 1626
Temple Newsam, Yorkshire, 1632
Trentham Hall, Staffordshire, 1633—9
Milcote House, Warwickshire, 1634
Sezincote House, Gloucestershire, 1635
Carreglwyd, Anglesey, 1636
Holland House, Kensington, 1638—40
Precise references to the documentation for these houses will be found in the bibliography at the end of the book

23 A. Hamilton-Thompson, 'The Building Accounts of Kirby Muxloe Castle, 1480—84' *Transactions of the Leicestershire Archaeological Society* xi (1913—14) 193—345
24 E. H. Phelps Brown & S. V. Hopkins, 'Seven Centuries of the Prices of Consumables, Compared with Builders' Wage-rates' *Economica* new series xxiii (1956) 299
25 Compiled from the same houses as *Figure 7*
26 J. Thirsk, ed. *The Agrarian History of England and Wales iv, 1500—1640* (Cambridge 1967) Table xvi p. 865
27 E. H. Phelps Brown & S. V. Hopkins, 'Seven Centuries of the Prices of Consumables, Compared with Builders' Wage-rates' *Economica* new series xxiii (1956) 299
28 B. H. Putnam, 'Northamptonshire Wage Assessments of 1560 and 1667' *Economic History Review* i (1927) 131—2
29 W. A. S. Hewins 'Regulation of Wages by the Justices of the Peace' *Economic Journal* viii (1898) 131—2
30 H. Bentley, 'A Rate for Servants' Wages Made at Easter Sessions, 7 Charles I' *Transactions of the East Hertfordshire Archaeological Society* xiii, part 2 (1952—4) 167—71. For a list of other assessments in print, see C. Read *Bibliography of British History; Tudor Period, 1485—1603* (2nd edition Oxford 1959) pp. 242—3

Part V: Conclusion

25 A Period of Transition

The important changes that took place in the way that country houses were designed and erected during the period of almost one hundred and fifty years with which this study is concerned have already been documented and discussed. The common themes which characterise the period are a growing awareness of architecture as an art form capable of intellectual analysis and appreciation, and an increased specialisation in the practical processes of construction. To a certain extent, both these themes reflect the gradual acceptance by the men who were building the more important country houses of Renaissance and Humanist ideas. They spring from the Renaissance conception of architecture as a liberal art, to be ranked with the traditional arts of grammar, dialectic, rhetoric, geometry, arithmetic, astrology, and music, and as such worthy of the educated attention of someone of gentle birth. But it was only by emphasising its intellectual and theoretical basis that architecture was able to aspire to this position. From the middle of the 16th century onwards there is growing evidence from the correspondence of the builders themselves and from the publication of authors such as Shute, Wotton, and Bacon that such an emphasis was taking place. By the 17th century the liberal status of architecture had been accepted in some quarters of educated society, especially by those close to the court, but the majority of builders, although they were fully aware of the fashionable aspects of architectural style, were still incapable of appreciating its philosophical content. However, although it was often imperfectly understood, the concept of the liberal architect whose primary role was confined to the design of a building based on his knowledge of architectural theory was sufficiently established by 1640 for it to exercise a growing influence on the remainder of the century.

In common with the changes that were taking place in the processes of design, there was a similar trend towards a more clearly defined method of administering a building enterprise. Although architecture might aspire to become a liberal art, building, the transformation of architectural ideas into a three-dimensional form, was indisputably a mechanical pursuit. However, efficiency, and the growing adoption of piece-work as the best method of working, demanded that the everyday supervision of the work should be conducted by someone who was versed in the specialised techniques of building administration. The emergent status of the architect prevented him from combining his designing role with that of surveyor of the work, although his occasional attendance at the site was often necessary to ensure the successful execution of his design. The more literate craftsmen, however, were familiar with all the practical aspects of building including the supervision of other workmen and the mathematical competence necessary to calculate piece-work. The same social barrier between architecture and building, which denied them the opportunity to become architects in any acceptable sense of the word, meant that the only opening for their talents was in the field of supervision, and consequently the construction of many of the more important country houses of the late sixteenth and early seventeenth centuries was directed by specialised building surveyors who had risen from a training in one of the crafts.

The functional and social distinction between architects and surveyors was still in a very tentative state by the beginning of the Civil War, but the intellectual and practical conditions which were to crystallise the distinction were intensifying. In essence, they were symptomatic of a growing professionalism in building, whereby the more specialised requirements of architectural design and methods of working prompted the employment of acknowledged experts to create and administer a building as well as to execute it. Something of the stage that this process had reached by the early 17th century can be seen from the arrangements that Sir Edward Pytts made in 1611 for the construction of additions to Kyre Park, Worcestershire. The design was commissioned from John Bentley, who was known to Pytts for his work on the Schools Quadrangle at Oxford, but the administration of the work was put into the hands of John Chaunce, a Bromsgrove mason whom Pytts had previously employed as a working craftsman and who he now termed 'Surveyr of the work & workmen'.[1] Similarly, the Earl of Danby employed Nicholas Stone to design his house at Corenbury, Oxfordshire, in 1631, and, although the terms of Stone's employment included the direction of the workmen, this function was in practice fulfilled by Gabriel Stacey, who had worked for Stone in a similar capacity at the Botanic Gardens in Oxford.[2]

The administrative opportunities available to the more talented and literate craftsmen did not represent a new departure from medieval practice. Master craftsmen had always played a prominent role in the organisation of most building enterprises, but the limits of their responsibility were now being circumscribed by the emergence of the architect as a separate and socially superior agent in the building process. There were other changes at a craft level which were similarly contingent on the acceptance of Renaissance ideas. Not only were many of the motifs of architectural decoration now derived from literary sources, but new criteria of correctness were imposed upon their execution. Not every craftsman had access to these sources or was capable of adapting to new ideas that had been implanted from outside rather than developed organically within the traditions of his craft. Inevitably, such craftsmen were restricted to the more straightforward aspects of their craft, whilst their more literate and adaptable fellows increasingly specialised in decorative work. It is probable that the wide variety in wages within particular crafts which characterised most building operations from the middle of the 16th century onwards was, at least in part, a reflection of this differential in skill and knowledge.

The 16th and early 17th centuries are best viewed as a period of transition. None of the developments outlined above can be said to have been universally accepted by 1640. Many country houses continued to be designed and built by traditional methods, and few builders were aware of the theoretical implications behind the new styles that they consciously adopted. But, even so, important changes had taken place during the period which were to receive more precise definition after the Restoration. The Renaissance might not have been fully assimilated, but the Middle Ages were clearly ended.

25 Notes

1   Mrs Baldwyn-Childe, 'The Building of the Manor-House of Kyre Park, Worcestershire' *The Antiquary* xxii (1890) 51
2   *The Account Book of Nicholas Stone* ed. W. L. Spiers (Walpole Society vii 1919) p. 70

Bibliography

A   MANUSCRIPT SOURCES

BRITISH MUSEUM
Additional MSS
7097 Building accounts for Little Saxham Hall, Suffolk, 1505–14 (ff. 174–200)

15891 Letter book of Sir Christopher Hatton. Includes a letter of 10 August 1579 from Lord Burghley concerning their building (f. 32)

25302 Mason's contract of 1653/4 for Thorpe Hall, Northamptonshire (f. 153)

27278 The notebook of Sir Francis Bacon. Includes a note of 1608 of proposed work at Gorhambury, Hertfordshire (ff. 24v–25v)

39830–6 The papers of Sir Thomas Tresham of Rushton, Northamptonshire

39830 Includes an inventory of his library, *circa* 1605 (f. 191v.)

39831 Includes mason's contract of 1578 for the Market House, Rothwell, Northamptonshire (f. 1); elevation and plan by Robert Stickells for the lantern of Lyveden New Build, Northamptonshire (f. 3); plan for the north porch of the same (f. 74)

39832 Steward's accounts for building work, 1593–7

39833 The same, 1598–1600

39834 The same, 1601–2

39835 Steward's journal and accounts, 1599–1602

39836 Miscellaneous accounts including those kept at the quarries and the bills of various craftsmen

46461 Building Accounts for Grafton Manor, Worcestershire & Peperhill, 1576

54332 The memorandum book of Henry Oxinden, containing information on the building history of a number of sixteenth and seventeenth century houses in Kent

Egerton MSS
2599 Notebook of Augustine Steward. Includes accounts of 1582–90 for repairs to Glastonbury Place, London (ff. 231–3)

2815 Account roll of the paymaster of the works to the Duke of Somerset, 1548–51. Summary accounts for building at Somerset House, Syon House, Banbury, Wolfhall, Odiham and Reading

Harleian MSS
98 The papers of Paul D'Ewes. Include a carpenter's contract of 1621 for work at Stowlangtoft, Suffolk (f. 16); contract of 1623 for repairs at Lavenham, Suffolk (f. 19); contract of 1624 for a tomb at Stowlangtoft (f. 20); contract of 1625/6 for three houses in London (ff. 21–4)

6853 Includes a letter of *circa* 1622–5, referring to the building of Fountains Hall, Yorkshire (f. 450)

Lansdowne MSS
43/14 Letter from Sir John Young to Lord Burghley about importing stone for Theobalds, Hertfordshire, 1584

84/10 Two papers on architecture by Robert Stickells

5828 Includes 'An Essay Concerning the Decay of Rents and their Remedies', *circa* 1670 by Sir William Coventry, commenting on the agricultural holdings of building workers (ff. 205–10)

MSS Facsimiles

372 Two volumes of photographs of the collection of maps and architectural drawings compiled by William and Robert Cecil, and deposited at Hatfield House

PUBLIC RECORD OFFICE

E101/463/23 An account of the sale of monastic materials from Fotheringhay College, Northamptonshire in 1573

SP 14/57 Includes a letter from Simon Basil to Lord Salisbury relating to the building of Salisbury House, 1610 (f. 104); a detailed proposal for a loggia on the river front of the same, *circa* 1610 (ff. 106–8); a note of payments at Hatfield House, Hertfordshire, 1609–10 (f. 172)

SP 28/207 Includes an account for repairing the Market House at Aylesbury, Buckinghamshire, 1645–6 (ff. 12–80)

BODLEIAN LIBRARY, OXFORD

Rawlinson MSS

A. 195c. Includes the building accounts for the Court House, Barking, Essex, 1567 (ff. 369–73)

CAMBRIDGE UNIVERSITY LIBRARY

Hengrave Hall Deposit 80

The incomplete building accounts of Hengrave Hall, Suffolk, 1525–40

81 Miscellaneous documents relating to the same, including a mason's contract of *circa* 1530; a joiner's contract of 1538; some notes by the steward; an inventory of 1603

NOTTINGHAM UNIVERSITY LIBRARY

The incomplete building accounts of Wollaton Hall, Nottingham

Mi A 60/1 Weekly accounts, March 1582–March 1583

/2 Summary accounts, May–December 1583, and some payments for 1584

/3 Weekly accounts, October 1584–November 1585

/4 Summary Accounts, January–December 1585

/5 Weekly accounts, March 1586–March 1587

/6 Weekly accounts, April 1587–March 1588

/7 Weekly accounts, March–November 1588

SIR BANISTER FLETCHER LIBRARY, ROYAL INSTITUTE OF BRITISH ARCHITECTS, LONDON

Drawings Collection

Smythson Collection. Architectural surveys and designs, principally made by the mason, Robert Smythson (d. 1614) and his son, John (d. 1634).

    Arranged in four boxes:

    I   Identified subjects attributed to Robert Smythson

    II   Unidentified drawings attributed to Robert Smythson

    III Identified and unidentified drawings attributed to John Smythson

    IV Miscellaneous drawings, including three late medieval drawings, and drawings attributed to John Smythson the younger

SIR JOHN SOANE'S MUSEUM, LONDON

The Book of Architecture of John Thorpe Collection of architectural surveys and designs made by John Thorpe from *circa* 1596 to the mid–1620s, and including some earlier drawings inherited from his mason father

BEDFORDSHIRE COUNTY RECORD OFFICE, BEDFORD

TW 818 Incomplete building accounts of Harrold Hall, Bedfordshire, for Francis Farrar, 1608–10

CORNWALL COUNTY RECORD OFFICE, TRURO

Mount Edgcumbe MSS MTD/48/10 Contract between Sir Richard Edgecumbe and a mason for building Mount Edgcumbe, Cornwall, 1547

DEVON COUNTY RECORD OFFICE, EXETER

L 1258 M/vol. i, D84 no. 73 Royal commission to the abbot of Tavistock for the provision of blue slate for Hampton Court, Middlesex, 1529

L 1258 M/vol. i, Devon G5 no. 4 Indenture of sale between Lord John Russell and John Haydon of Ottery St. Mary of building materials from Dunkeswell Abbey, Devon, 1539

404 M/B 1–2 Two sketch books compiled by the Abbott family of plasterers, *circa* 1575–*circa* 1685. Contain numerous designs, recipes for colours, mathematical and alphabetical tables, and miscellaneous notes

DORSET COUNTY RECORD OFFICE, DORCHESTER

MW/M4 Eighteenth-century copy of the notebook of Sir John Strode, which includes details of the building of his house and chapel at Chantmarle, Dorset, 1612–23 (ff. 22–5)

ESSEX COUNTY RECORD OFFICE, CHELMSFORD

D/DP A10 Household accounts of Sir William Petre, 1549–50. Includes building work at Ingatestone Hall and East Thorndon

D/DP A11 The same for 1554–5

The incomplete building accounts for Old Thorndon Hall, Essex

D/DP A18 June–October 1577

A19 October 1580–September 1581

A20 October 1586–September 1587

A21 October 1589–September 1590

A22 October 1593–October 1594

D/DP Q13/3/11 Letter from Sir Edward Hext to Lord Petre, relating to the building of Wadham College, Oxford, 19 March 1609/10

/13 The same to the same, 27 March 1610

KENT COUNTY RECORD OFFICE, MAIDSTONE

Sackville of Knole MSS

U269 A516/1 Accounts and bills for work carried out at Copthall, Essex, and the house of Lord Middlesex in St. Bartholomews, London, 1621–44

A505/1 Craftsmen's bills for Copthall, 1625–39

A462/4 & 5 Receipts for work at Copthall, 1638

E199 Estimates for rebuilding loggia at Copthall, 1626 and 1630

A389/1 Accounts for work at the house of Lord Middlesex in St. Bartholomews, London, 1630

A508/3 Accounts and bills for work at the same, 1629–34

A2/2 Includes accounts for repairs at Knole, Kent, 1611–12

A41/1 Includes accounts for repairs to the same, 1629–30

A2/1 Includes accounts for building at West Horsley Place, Surrey, 1603–4

A437/1 Includes accounts for repairs at Goldicote House, Worcestershire, 1626

A418/9 Includes accounts for repairs at Milcote House, Warwickshire, 1634

A419/1–2 Includes accounts for repairs at Sezincote House, Gloucestershire 1628–9

A419/4 The same, 1635

A449/1 Includes accounts for repairs at Fulham House, Middlesex, 1636–7

STAFFORDSHIRE COUNTY RECORD OFFICE, STAFFORD

D593 R/1/2 The building accounts for Trentham Hall, Staffordshire, 1633–9

SURREY COUNTY RECORD OFFICE, KINGSTON-UPON-THAMES
Acc. 1030 The building accounts for Ashley Park, Surrey, 1602–7

LEEDS. THE CITY LIBRARY
TN/EA/12/10 Various building accounts for Temple Newsam House, Yorkshire, 1618–58
    13/3 Building accounts for Brigg Milne dam, 1605
    13/16 Accounts for repairs at York, 1632
    13/39 Building accounts, probably Temple Newsam House, 1630–3
    13/71 Building contracts for Temple Newsam House, 1628–36
    13/74 Building accounts for additions to Holland House, Kensington, 1638–40
TN/SH/A3 Ten plans for Sheriff Hutton Castle, Yorkshire (*circa* 1619) and correspondence with the glazier Bernard Dinninghof (1618)

PLYMOUTH. THE CITY LIBRARY
W. 130 Receivers' accounts, 1448–1550, 1559–60. Includes a number of entries relating to building carried out by the city during the period
W. 131 Receivers' accounts, 1560–69. Includes the building accounts for the Guildhall, 1564–5
W. 137 Receivers' accounts, 1606–7. The building accounts for the Shambles and the Guildhall

SHREWSBURY. THE PUBLIC LIBRARY
Deeds 6883–5 Some building accounts for Condover Hall, Shropshire, 1586–92
    7029   The same for 1598
    7081   Contract with John Richmond, mason, for the same, 1589

STAFFORD. THE WILLIAM SALT LIBRARY
D1721/1/4 The building accounts for the Shire Hall, Stafford, 1588–1607
D1734/3/4/143–4 Incomplete building accounts for Beaudesert Hall, Staffordshire, 1575–6
D1734/3/4/101 Carpenter's bill for work at Beaudesert Hall, Staffordshire, April 1576

LONGLEAT HOUSE, WILTSHIRE
The Records of the Building of Longleat Three volumes compiled by Canon J. E. Jackson in the nineteenth century containing original accounts, bills, and correspondence
Volume i 1547–50
Volume ii 1550–67
Volume iii 1567–80
Thynne Papers Separate account books, of which the following refer to the building:
Box lxviii Book 59 Building accounts, 1568–70
    Book 60 Building accounts, 1571–5
Box lxxxv Book 143 Building accounts, 1554–5
Box lxxxix Book 159 Summary building accounts, 1578–9
    Book 161 Building accounts, 1580
    Book 162 Summary building accounts, 1580
    Book 164 Building accounts, 1580
    Book 166 Building accounts, 1582
In addition a number of original plans and designs for the house are kept in Bishop Ken's Library in the house

B   PRINTED SOURCES

(1)   Primary Sources

Aubrey, John *'Brief Lives', Chiefly of Contemporaries, set down by John Aubrey, between the years 1669 & 1696.* Includes a life of Sir Francis Bacon with information on Verulam House, Hertfordshire

Bacon, Francis 'Of Building' in *Francis Bacon's Essays.* First published in 1623

Baldwyn-Childe, Mrs 'The Building of the Manor-House of Kyre Park, Worcestershire, 1588–1618', *The Antiquary* xxi (1890) 202–5, 261–4; xxii (1890), 24–6, 50–3. Transcript of the building accounts

Boorde, Andrew *A Compendyous Regyment or a Dyetary of Helth* (London 1549). Includes a number of chapters advising on the best situation and plan of a house

Bradfer-Lawrence, H. L. 'The Building of Raynham Hall', *Norfolk Archaeology* xxiii (1927–9) 93–146. Transcript of substantial extracts from the building accounts

Camden Miscellany, xvi (Camden Society 3rd series, liv, 1936). Transcript of the contract for the stables for Stiffkey Hall, Norfolk, 1582

Cash, M. ed. *Devon Inventories of the Sixteenth and Seventeenth Centuries* (Devon and Cornwall Record Society new series xi, 1966). Includes an inventory of 1648 for a carpenter

Chamberlain, John *The Letters of John Chamberlain* 2 vols., ed. N. E. McClure (Philadelphia 1939). The complete text of all the extant letters of John Chamberlain, written between 1597 and 1626, many of which contain information about contemporary building

Emmison, F. G. ed. *Jacobean Household Inventories* (Bedfordshire Historical Record Society xx, 1938). Includes the inventories of a number of building craftsmen

Evans, J. 'Extracts from the Private Account Book of Sir William More, of Loseley, in Surrey, in the time of Queen Mary and of Queen Elizabeth', *Archaeologia* xxxvi (1855) 284–310. Transcript of the building accounts of Loseley House, 1561–9

Gedde, Walter *A Booke of Sundry Draughtes principally serving for glasiers: and not impertinent for plasterers, and gardiners: besides sundry other professions* (London 1615). Possibly the earliest English pattern book. Contains over 100 geometrical designs based on squares and circles, with instructions on drawing squares and making glass

Gerbier, Sir Balthazar *A Brief Discourse Concerning the Three Chief Principles of Magnificient Building* (London 1662). A slim volume containing general architectural advice for prospective builders
Counsel and Advise to all Builders for the choice of their Surveyours, Clarks of their works, Bricklayers, Masons, Carpenters, and other work-men therein concerned. As also in Respect of their works, Materials and Rates thereof (London 1663). The full title provides a good indication of the contents of this practical guide for builders

Goodman, G. *The Court of James I* 2 vols., ed. J. Brewer (London 1839). Includes some observations by Bishop Goodman on contemporary building

Hamilton-Thompson, A. 'The Building Accounts of Kirby Muxloe Castle, 1480–84' *Transactions of the Leicestershire Archaeological Society* xi (1913–14) 193–345. Transcript of the accounts

Harland, J. *The House and Farm Accounts of the Shuttleworths, part I* (Chetham Society xxxv, 1856). Includes the building accounts for Gawthorpe Hall, Lancashire, 1600–7

Harrison, William *Harrison's Description of England in Shakespeare's Youth* ed. F. J. Furnivall (New Shakspere Society, series vi, part i, 1877). This edition contains the second and third books of Harrison's *Description of England* originally appended to Holinshed's *Chronicles* in 1577 and expanded in 1586–7. Many comments on contemporary building and architecture

Havinden, M. A. ed. *Household and Farm Inventories in Oxfordshire, 1550–1590* (Oxfordshire Record Society xliv,1965). Includes the inventories of a number of building craftsmen

Historical Manuscripts Commission *Cecil* xv. p. 383. Northumberland to Cecil, expressing his intention to visit a number of buildings, 1603
Hatfield xi. p. 358. Lady Sydney sending stone to Cecil from Penshurst, Kent, 1601
Portland ix. p. 152. Description of part of the architectural library of Henry Percy, ninth Earl of Northumberland, undated

Rutland iv. p. 485. Collyweston slates being supplied for Belvoir Castle, Leicestershire, with carriage supplied by boon labour, 1611

Various iii. pp. 1–155. Documents relating to Sir Thomas Tresham's building

6th Report p. 228. The purchase of a 'Book of Architecture' by Northumberland, 1603

Humphreys, J. 'The Elizabethan Estate Book of Grafton Manor', *Transactions of the Birmingham Archaeological Society* xliv (1918) 1–124. Transcript of the building accounts, 1568–9

Jackson, J. E. 'Wulfhall and the Seymours' *Wiltshire Archaeological Magazine* xv (1875) 178–86. Transcript of the surviving correspondence concerning the Duke of Somerset's new house in Wiltshire, 1548–9

Jones, G. P. 'The Repairing of Crummock Bridge, Holm Cultram, 1554' *Transactions of Cumberland and Westmoreland Antiquarian and Archaeological Society* lii, new series (1952) 85–100. Includes transcript of the building accounts

Kempe, A. J. ed. *The Loseley Manuscripts* (London 1836). Includes transcripts of documents relating to Sir William More, the builder of Loseley House, Surrey

Knoop, D. and Jones, G. P. 'The Carreglwyd Building Account, 1636' *Transactions of the Anglesey Antiquarian Society* (1934) 27–43. Includes transcript of the account

'The Bolsover Castle Building Account, 1613' *Ars Quatuor Coronatorum* xlix (1939) 24–79. Includes transcript of the building account

Lister, J. and Brown, W. 'Seventeenth Century Builders' Contracts' *Yorkshire Archaeological Journal* xvi (1902), 108–13. Includes building contract of 1648 for a house at Illingworth, Halifax, and a carpenter's contract of 1682 for a house at Scriven, near Knaresborough

Loder, Robert *Robert Loder's Farm Accounts, 1610–20* ed. G. E. Fussell (Camden Society 3rd Series liii, 1936). Includes the accounts for additions to a farmhouse at Harwell, Berkshire, 1618

Millican, P. 'The Rebuilding of Wroxham Bridge in 1576' *Norfolk Archaeology* xxvi (1936–8) 281–95. Includes transcript of the accounts

Peck, F. *Desiderata Curiosa: or a Collection of Divers Scarce and Curious Pieces Relating Chiefly to Matters of English History. . .* (2nd edition London 1770). Includes the contemporary MS life of Lord Burghley 'written by one who lived in the house with him during the last xxv years of his life'

Pratt, Sir Roger *The Architecture of Sir Roger Pratt* ed. R. T. Gunther (Oxford 1928). A collection of architectural material from the MS notebooks of Pratt. Some of the notes concern practical points arising from the particular buildings on which he was engaged; others are of a more general nature and include 'certain heads to be largely treated of concerning the undertaking of any building', written in 1660, and 'rules for the guidance of Architects', written in 1665. Part of the collection seems to have been intended for publication as a treatise on architecture

Preston, W. E. 'A Sixteenth-Century Account Roll of the Building of a House at Chevet' *Yorkshire Archaeological Journal* xxxii (1934) 326–30. Includes transcript of the building account for 1516

Pricke, Robert *The Architects Store-House* (London 1674). One of the earliest pattern books of such architectural features as doors, windows and chimneypieces

The Ornaments of Architecture (London 1674). Companion volume of decorative details

Reyce, Robert *Breviary of Suffolk* ed. Lord Francis Hervey (London 1902). Written in 1618. Includes contemporary evidence for the timber shortage, with some observations on methods of building

Ridout, E. 'The Account Book of the New Haven, Chester, 1567–8' *Transactions of the Historical Society of Lancashire and Cheshire* lxxx (1928) 86–128. Includes a transcript of the account

Roper, J. S. ed. *Dudley Probate Inventories, 1544–1603* (Dudley 1965). Includes the inventories of two blacksmiths and a roughmason

Salter, H. ed. *Registrum Annalium Collegii Mertonensis 1483–1521* (Oxford Historical Society lxxvi, 1921). Includes a contract for building a house in Holywell, Oxford, 1516

Sharpe, M. and Westlake, Minor-canon 'The Mending of the Brynt Bridge' *Transactions of the London and Middlesex Archaeological Society* new series v, part iv (1928) 449–66. Includes a transcript of the account of *circa* 1530 for repairs to the bridge over the River Brent at Hanwell, Middlesex

Shute, John *The First and Chief Groundes of Architecture* (London 1563). The first English book on architecture. Largely based on Serlio and Vitruvius, it contains engravings of the five orders. Little is known about the author—apart from his own statement that he was sent to Italy in 1550 by the Duke of Northumberland. The book was popular, and subsequent editions are recorded in 1579, 1580, 1584 and 1587

Singleton, W. A. 'Traditional House-Types in Rural Lancashire and Cheshire' *Transactions of the Historical Society of Lancashire and Cheshire* civ (1952) 75—91. Includes transcript of carpenter's contract for Kenyon Peel Hall, Little Hulton, Lancashire, 1617

Stone, Nicholas *The Account Book of Nicholas Stone* ed. W. L. Spiers (Walpole Society vii, 1919). Transcript of Stone's notebook, written from memory *circa* 1641, his account book for 1631—42, and his will of 1647

Vaisey, D. G. ed. *Probate Inventories of Lichfield and District, 1568—1680* (Staffordshire Record Society, Collections for a History of Staffordshire, 4th series v, 1969). Includes the inventories of three building craftsmen before 1661

Weaver, O. J. ed. *The Building Accounts of Harrold Hall, Bedfordshire* (Bedfordshire Historical Record Society xlix, 1970) pp. 56—80. Transcript of the accounts for 1608—10, with an introduction

Welch, E. ed. *Plymouth Building Accounts of the Sixteenth and Seventeenth Centuries* (Devon & Cornwall Record Society new series xii, 1967). Transcripts of the building accounts of the Guildhall, 1564—7, and the Orphans' Aid, 1614—20, with an introduction

Wigful, J. R. 'House Building in Queen Elizabeth's Days' *Transactions of the Hunter Archaeological Society* iii (1925) 66—73. Includes transcript of the building account for a house in Sheffield, 1575—6

Wotton, Sir Henry *The Elements of Architecture* (London 1624). Critical study based on Vitruvius, with acknowledgements to Alberti, Palladio, and Philibert de l'Orme, but with many personal observations by the author

(2)   Secondary sources

Barnard, E. A. B. *Stanton and Snowshill* (Cambridge 1927). Discusses the building accounts for the rectory at Stanton, Gloucestershire, 1625

Batho, G. R. 'The Percies at Petworth, 1574—1632' *Sussex Archaeological Collections* xcv (1957) 1—27. Includes many extracts from the original documents relating to building

'Notes and Documents on Petworth House, 1574—1632' *Sussex Archaeological Collections* xcvi (1958) 108—34. Includes transcript of 'A Booke of Computations for Buildings', modifying some of the conclusions in the earlier article

'Henry, Ninth Earl of Northumberland and Syon House, Middlesex, 1594—1632' *Transactions of the Ancient Monuments Society* new series iv (1956) 95—109

'Syon House: The First Two Hundred Years' *Transactions of the London and Middlesex Archaeological Society* xix (1958) 1—17

Briggs, N. 'The Foundation of Wadham College, Oxford' *Oxoniensia* xxi (1956) 61—81. Based on the Petre correspondence in the Essex Record Office, with transcripts of a number of letters relating to the building of the College

Burgon, J. W. *The Life and Times of Sir Thomas Gresham* 2 vols. (London 1831). Some information on the building activities of Gresham and Burghley

Clifton-Taylor, A. *The Pattern of English Building* (2nd edition London 1965). Comprehensive survey of building materials, with much useful information on their distribution and use

Clutterbuck, R. *The History and Antiquities of the County of Hertford,* i (London 1815). Includes an account of the Strong family of masons and quarry owners of Oxfordshire and Gloucestershire

Colvin, H. M. *Biographical Dictionary of English Architects, 1660—1840* (London 1954)

—**and Harris, J.** eds. *The Country Seat* (London 1970). A collection of essays on country houses, of which the following are of particular relevance: M. Biddle, 'A "Fontainebleau" chimneypiece at Broughton Castle, Oxfordshire', M. Girouard, 'Designs for a Lodge at Ampthill, Bedfordshire', J. Newman, 'Copthall, Essex', M. Girouard, 'Bachegraig, Denbighshire', H. M. Colvin, 'Peter Mills and Cobham Hall, Kent'

Cope, W. H. *Bramshill* (London 1883). An account of the house built for Lord Zouche in Hampshire which includes some original correspondence relating to the work

Crossley, D. W. 'Glass Making in Bagot's Park, Staffordshire, in the Sixteenth Century' *Post-Medieval Archaeology* i (1967) 44–83

'The Perfomance of the Glass Industry in Sixteenth-Century England' *Economic History Review* 2nd series, xxv (1972) 421

Dewar, M. *Sir Thomas Smith, a Tudor Intellectual in Office* (London 1964). A biography that considers at length the building activities of one of the more important architectural patrons of the 16th century

Eltringham, G. J. 'The Extension of the Carpenters' Company Hall, 1572' *Guildhall Miscellany* i, no. 4 (1955), 30–6. A study based on the surviving building accounts

Emmison, F. G. *Tudor Secretary, Sir William Petre at Court and Home* (London 1961). The builder of Ingatestone Hall, Essex

Finch, M. E. *The Wealth of Five Northamptonshire Families, 1540–1640* (Northamptonshire Record Society xix, 1956). Includes an analysis of the expenditure and income of Sir Thomas Tresham

Fraser, P. and Harris, J. *The Burlington-Devonshire Collection* (London 1960). A typescript catalogue of the drawings by Inigo Jones and John Webb in the Burlington-Devonshire collection at the Royal Institute of British Architects

French, K. and C. 'Devonshire Plasterwork' *Transactions of the Devon Association* lxxxix (1957) 124–44. Discussion of sixteenth and seventeenth century plasterwork in Devon in relation to the sketch books of the Abbott family of plasterers

Girouard, M. 'New Light on Longleat: Allen Maynard, a French Sculptor in England in the 16th Century' *Country Life* cxx (1956) 594–7

'The Development of Longleat House between 1546 and 1572' *Archaeological Journal* cxvi (1961) 200–22

ed. 'The Smythson Collection of the Royal Institute of British Architects' *Architectural History* v (1962). Reproduces all the drawings

'Elizabethan Architecture and the Gothic Tradition' *Architectural History* vi (1963), 23–40

Robert Smythson and the Architecture of the Elizabethan Era (London 1966). The best study of late sixteenth century country house architecture. Excellent on the intellectual and aesthetic background

Godfrey, W. H. 'An Elizabethan Builder's Contract' *Sussex Archaeological Collections* lxv (1924) 211–23. Includes transcript of contract with a mason for a new wing to East Lavington House in 1586, and the reproduction of the two surviving drawings attached to the contract

Gordon, D. J. 'Poet and Architect: the Intellectual Setting of the Quarrel Between Ben Jonson and Inigo Jones' *Courtauld and Warburg Journal* xii (1949) 152–78. An interesting discussion on the emergence of the concept of the architect in the early seventeenth century

Gotch, J. A. 'The Renaissance in Northamptonshire' *Transactions of the Royal Institute of British Architects* new series vi (1890) 87–109. Includes transcript of the surviving correspondence relating to Burghley House

Hanson, T. W. 'Halifax Builders in Oxford' *Transactions of the Halifax Antiquarian Society* (1928) 253–317. Informative study of the Yorkshire craftsmen employed in Oxford in the early seventeenth century

Hartshorne, E. S. *Memorials of Holdenby* (Newcastle 1868). Includes some of Sir Christopher Hatton's letters relating to Holdenby House

Harvey, J. H. 'Side-Lights on Kenilworth Castle' *Archaeological Journal* ci (1944) 91–107. Discusses some of the work carried out in the early sixteenth century, with extracts from the accounts

English Medieval Architects: a Biographical Dictionary Down to 1550 (London 1954)

Hodson, J. H. 'The First Wollaton Hall' *Transactions of the Thoroton Society* lxxii (1968) 59–67

Holden, E. W. 'Slate Roofing in Medieval Sussex' *Sussex Archaeological Collections* ciii (1965) 66–78

Hoskins, W. G. 'The Rebuilding of Rural England, 1570–1640' *Past and Present* iv (1953) 44–59

Isham, G. 'Sir Thomas Tresham and his Buildings' *Reports and Papers of the Northamptonshire Antiquarian Society* lxv, part ii (1966)

Jackson, T. G. *Wadham College, Oxford* (Oxford 1893). Includes an account of the building of the college with extracts from the original documents

Jenkins, F. *Architect and Patron* (London 1961)

Jope, E. M. *Studies in Building History* (London 1961). A collection of essays on various aspects of building and architecture. The following are of particular relevance: E. M. Jope, 'Cornish Houses, 1400–1700'; H. M. Colvin, 'Haunt Hill House, Weldon'; H. G. Leask, 'Early Seventeenth-Century Houses in Ireland'

—and Dunning, G. C. 'The Use of Blue Slate for Roofing in Medieval England' *The Antiquaries Journal* xxxiv (1954) 209–17. Discusses the evidence for the use of West-Country slate in south-eastern England

Kenyon, G. H. *The Glass Industry of the Weald* (Leicester 1967). The best account of English glass making in the sixteenth century, although recent excavations indicate that there were other centres of glass making in the country apart from the forests of the Weald

Kitson, S. D. 'The Heraldic Glass of Gilling Castle, Yorkshire, and Bernard Dinninghof' *Journal of the British Society of Master Glass Painters* iii (1929), 55–8. Account of the plans for rebuilding Sheriff Hutton Castle, Yorkshire in 1618, with a transcript of a letter and a design by Bernard Dinninghof who had glazed Gilling Castle in 1585

Knoop, D. and Jones, G. P. 'The Rise of the Mason Contractor' *Journal of the Royal Institute of British Architects* xliii (1936) 1061–71
'The Sixteenth Century Mason' *Ars Quatuor Coronatorum* l (1937) 191–210. Mainly based on royal accounts, and many of their conclusions about the changes in working conditions that took place in the century are not applicable to private building
'The Impressment of Masons in the Middle Ages' *Economic History Review* viii (1937) 57–67. Includes evidence for the continuation of the practice into the seventeenth century
'Overtime in the age of Henry VIII' *Economic History* iv (1938) 13–20. Little relevance to private building
'The English Medieval Quarry' *Economic History Review* ix (1938) 17–37
The Mediaeval Mason (3rd edition Manchester 1967). Although its emphasis is strongly towards those engaged on royal and public works, and consequently not all their conclusions can be applied to private building, it remains the best study of a particular branch of the building crafts

Lloyd, J. D. K. 'The New Building at Montgomery Castle' *Archaeologia Cambrensis* cxiv (1965) 60–8. Discussion of the building erected for Lord Herbert, and of the craftsmen engaged on the work
'The Architect of the Herbert Tomb at Montgomery' *The Montgomeryshire Collections* lix (1965–6) 138–40. Convincingly attributes the tomb to Walter Hancock, the Shropshire mason

Maxwell Lyte, H. C. *A History of Dunster* 2 vols. (London 1909). Information on William Arnold's work at Dunster Castle, Somerset, in the early seventeenth century

Mercer, E. 'The Houses of the Gentry' *Past and Present* v (1954) 11–32. An attempt to show that the development of sixteenth and early seventeenth century house plans was determined by the changing social relationships of their builders
English Art, 1553–1625 (Oxford 1962). The architectural chapters include an elaboration on the above theme

Mills, J. 'Peter Lewys: His Work and Workmen' *Journal of the Royal Society of Antiquaries of Ireland* xxxi (1901) 99–108. Study of the entries relating to building at Dublin Cathedral, 1564–5, in the diary of Peter Lewys

Murrey, J. W. 'The Origin of Some Medieval Roofing Slates from Sussex' *Sussex Archaeological Collections* ciii (1965), 79–82. Archaeological evidence for trade in West-Country slate to Sussex

Newman, J. 'Nicholas Stone's Goldsmiths' Hall: Design and Practice in the 1630s' *Architectural History* xiv (1971) 30–39

Nichols, J. *The Progresses and Public Processions of Queen Elizabeth* 3 vols. (London 1823). Considerable amount of incidental information about many of the houses that she visited
The Progresses, Processions, and Magnificent Festivities of King James the First 4 vols. (London 1828)

Oswald, A. *Country Houses of Dorset* (2nd edition London 1959). Summarises the available information for the life and work of William Arnold, the mason and surveyor

Outhwaite, R. B. *Inflation in Tudor and Early Stuart England* (London 1969)

Pevsner, N. B. L. *The Buildings of England* (Harmondsworth 1951–74). Indispensible for the study of country house architecture

The Planning of the Elizabethan Country House (London 1960). Traces the development of symmetry and the decline in the importance of the hall

Phelps Brown, E. H. and Hopkins, S. V. 'Seven Centuries of Building Wages' *Economica* new series xxii (1955) 195–206

'Seven Centuries of the Price of Consumables, compared with Builders' Wage-rates' *Economica* new series xxiii (1956) 296–314. For a full discussion of these two key papers on prices and wages, see the relevant chapter in the text

Philip, I. G. 'The Building of the Schools Quadrangle' *Oxoniensia* xii (1948) 39–48

'A Forgotten Gate to the Schools Quadrangle' *Oxoniensia* xvii /xviii (1952–53) 185–7

Ramsey, P. H. ed. *The Price Revolution in Sixteenth Century England* (London 1971). A collection of some of the more important papers on the subject, with an introduction by the editor

Rogers, J. C. 'The Manor and Houses of Gorhambury' *Transactions of the St. Albans and Hertfordshire Architectural and Archaeological Society* new series iv (1933) 35–112. An account of Gorhambury House and Verulam House, Hertfordshire

Rogers, J. E. T. *A History of Agriculture and Prices in England* 7 vols. (Oxford 1866–1902). The relevant volumes are iii and iv (1882) for the period 1401–1582, and v and vi (1887) for 1583–1702. Although many of the author's conclusions are no longer acceptable, his statistics still form the basis of any study on prices and wages

Salzman, L. F. *Building in England Down to 1540* (2nd edition Oxford 1967). Although originally written in 1934, it remains the most important study of medieval building. The emphasis is mainly on technical matters, but it contains copious illustrations from a wealth of documentary sources

Sandeen, E. R. 'The Building Activities of Sir Nicholas Bacon' (Chicago University Ph.D. thesis 1959). Microfilm deposited in the Bodleian Library, Oxford (1959 Chicago 9). Based on the Bacon papers now deposited in the University of Chicago

'The Building of Redgrave Hall, 1545–54' *Proceedings of the Suffolk Institute of Archaeology* xxix, part i (1961) 1–33

'The Building of the Sixteenth-century Corpus Christi College Chapel' *Proceedings of the Cambridge Antiquarian Society* lv (1961) 23–35

Simpson, A. *The Wealth of the Gentry, 1540–1660* (Cambridge 1961). Study of the finances of some gentry families. Includes such builders as Sir Nicholas Bacon and Sir Thomas Cornwallis

Stallybrass, B. 'Bess of Hardwick's Buildings and Building accounts', *Archaeologia*, lxiv (1913), 347–98. Very full paper based on the original documents.

Stone, L. 'The Building of Hatfield House' *Archaeological Journal* cxii (1955) 100–28

'Inigo Jones and the New Exchange' *Archaeological Journal* cxiv (1957) 106–21

The Crisis of the Aristocracy, 1558–1641 (Oxford 1965). Important section on aristocratic building

Strype, J. *The Life of the Learned Sir Thomas Smith* (London 1698). Biography of the builder of Hill Hall, Essex

Summerson, J. 'Three Elizabethan Architects' *Bulletin of the John Rylands Library* xl (1957) 202–28. Biographical article on Robert Adams, John Symonds, and Robert Stickells

'The Building of Theobalds, 1564–1585' *Archaeologia* xcvii (1959) 107–26

Architecture in Britain, 1530 to 1830 (4th edition Harmondsworth 1963). The best general study of the period. First published in 1953, the 4th edition was extensively revised with much additional material on Elizabethan country houses and seventeenth-century architecture. Only minor alterations were made to the 5th edition (1969)

ed. *The Book of Architecture of John Thorpe* (Walpole Society xl, 1966). Reproduction of all the drawings with an important introductory essay on his life and importance

Inigo Jones (Harmondsworth 1966). The most recent and best biography of Jones

Thirsk, J. ed. *The Agrarian History of England and Wales iv, 1500–1640* (Cambridge 1967)

Whinney, M. and Miller, O. *English Art, 1625–1714* (Oxford 1957)

Wigfull, J. R. 'Extracts from the Note-Book of William Dickenson' *Transactions of the Hunter Archaeological*

Society ii (1921) 189–200. Information on the building activities of the Earl of Shrewsbury in the 1570s

Williams, W. J. 'Wills of Freemasons and Masons' *'The Masonic Record* xvi (1936) 171–236. Includes extracts from the wills of some sixteenth-century masons

Willis, R. and Clark, J. W. *The Architectural History of the University of Cambridge and of the Colleges of Cambridge and Eton* 4 vols. (Cambridge 1886). Comprehensive study firmly based on documentary sources in the college archives. Invaluable for comparative purposes

Index